Educational Computing and Problem Solving

Educational Computing and Problem Solving

W. Michael Reed and John K. Burton
Editors

The Haworth Press
New York • London

Educational Computing and Problem Solving has also been published as *Computers in the Schools*, Volume 4, Numbers 3/4, Fall/Winter 1987/88.

The Haworth Press, Inc., 12 West 32 Street, New York, NY 10001
EUROSPAN/Haworth, 3 Henrietta Street, London WC2E 8LU England

Library of Congress Cataloging-in-Publication Data

Educational computing and problem solving.

Published also as v. 4, nos. 3/4 of Computers in the schools.
Includes bibliographies.
1. Problem solving. 2. Problem solving – Data processing. 3. Problem solving – Study and teaching. 4. Computer-assisted instruction. I. Reed, W. Michael. II. Burton, John K.
BF441.E26 1988 153.4'3'0285 88-2795
ISBN 0-86656-781-X

Educational Computing and Problem Solving

Contents

ABOUT THE EDITORS

W. Michael Reed, PhD, is Assistant Professor of Computer Education and English Education at West Virginia University in Morgantown. He is President of the West Virginia Association of Computer Education, as well as a member of the International Association of Computer Education. Dr. Reed has written articles on problem solving and computers.

John K. Burton, PhD, is Associate Professor of Educational Psychology at the Education Microcomputer Lab, Virginia Tech University in Blacksburg. He is a member of the American Psychological Association, the American Educational Research Association, and the National Reading Conference. Dr. Burton has published articles on cognitive processes.

EDITORIAL

Problem Solving as Work of the Future

As we move into the information age, where many people will earn their daily bread in the business of bartering facts and ideas, knowledge of computers is becoming ever more important. Two central questions for the discipline of educational computing are: What kind of computer knowledge do we need to give students? And, how can that knowledge best be provided?

In past years when computer access was limited and the computer was thought of as a giant mysterious machine, educators thought of its usefulness in terms of a teaching machine. We are now entering a new era. The spark for this new era is the idea that children need to begin, at an early age, to think about computers as problem-solving tools. Many problems will need to be solved as we make the shift from an industrial to an information age. I believe that problems dealing with how to organize and deal with gigantic quantities of information will be high on the list.

How much of what we teach in schools today will be obsolete by the time our nation's school children reach the work place? Will they really need to know rote math facts? Will proficiency of grammar and spelling rules be essential skills for success? Does it sound too futuristic to say that the worker of tomorrow will be primarily a problem solver? As labor and clerical jobs become more and more automated, the ingenuity and creativity of the human mind will become more and more essential.

One of the most exciting prospects of the educational computing field concerns harnessing the power of the computer to enhance the development of problem-solving abilities. We are only on the threshold of understanding the implications and potential of this prospect, but one coordinated effort of research and study is presently being conducted by a group of scholars headed by W. Michael Reed at West Virginia University and John K. Burton at Virginia Tech. A collection of articles reporting the foundations, the trends, and the results of their work in this exciting and important area comprise this issue.

I believe the contents of this issue will provide a good foundation of literature for those interested in the topic of using the computer to teach problem solving. It is my hope that it will also stimulate an abundance of ideas and research on this important topic.

D. LaMont Johnson
Editor

PREFACE

W. Michael Reed
John K. Burton

In late 1985, *Computers in the Schools* published a special, double edition entitled "Logo in the Schools." This issue, which was guest edited by Cleb Maddux and subsequently published in book form by The Haworth Press, Inc., served as the inspiration and model for this collection.

In reading (and studying) that special edition, we felt that perhaps it was time to look at some rather basic issues related to the use of computers to improve the problem-solving skills of our nation's children. Several of the articles in this edition cite pleas from various national commissions and task forces, as well as content-area associations, to alter our curricular offerings to improve higher level skills such as problem solving and critical thinking. Computers are often cited as a potential tool in meeting this need.

In enlisting the use of computers in the cause of improving problem-solving skills, however, it is perhaps apropos to ask some rather basic questions. What is problem solving and how is it learned? Is there a role for computers in the learning of general problem-solving skills? What does the research in the area tell us? What direction is research in educational computing currently heading? And, what computer applications for teaching problem solving are currently taking place in the field?

Naturally, this edition does not include all possible orientations, research, or applications. We are pleased, however, with the diversity of work represented in this issue. For example, to shed light on the question, What is problem solving? we have included authors who view it from behavioral, cognitive, and philosophical perspectives. In addition, a wide range of research from "chunking" to artificial intelligence has been included as well as classroom applications from several areas. The majority of the authors are affiliated with the education microcomputer labs at West Virginia University and Virginia Polytechnic Institute and State University. Although the articles in this issue are perhaps limited to the research, philosophical, and theoretical perspectives of these people, the frameworks they use are grounded and, thus, highly related to existing theories and viewpoints used by problem-solving/programming language researchers throughout the nation. Also, several of the coauthors are graduate students who are part of the first generation of *trained* computer educators (as opposed to most of us who more or less "locked into" the area to meet a pressing need). As such, they are on the cutting edge of our infant area.

You will probably find in each section one article that supports your own personal beliefs and one that does not. At least that is our hope. Educational computing has been pushed to the crossroads prematurely. In a little over a decade, it has gone from a novelty to an amazing collection of books, journals, and conferences; from a terminal or two in a few affluent schools to the "hula hoop" of LaMont Johnson. It is our hope that this issue sheds enough light on the "crossroads" so that we can begin the dialogue necessary to select the bases for our new area and the direction or directions for our future work. It is time to begin making the transition from the nondisciplinary nature of educational computing to the interdisciplinary basis implicit in the notion of educational cognitive science.

THEORETICAL AND PHILOSOPHICAL PERSPECTIVES TO PROBLEM SOLVING

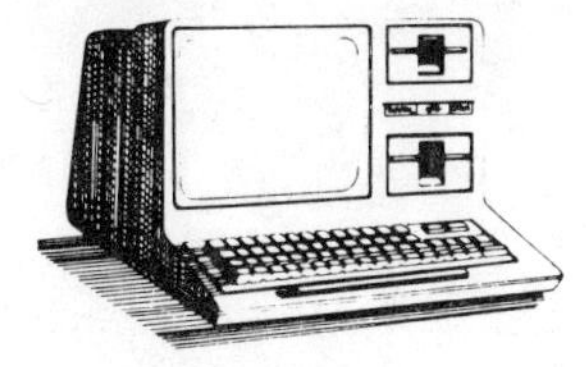

When considering computers and problem solving, it is a necessary first step to arrive at a definition for problems and problem-solving skills. In addition, as computer educators, we must think about how such skills are acquired and decide if and how such skills may be taught through the use of computers. The purpose of this introductory section is to explore answers to these questions from a variety of perspectives.

Two articles deal directly with the notion of problems and problem-solving skills and suggest how such skills may be learned: "A Brief Review of Developments in Problem Solving" by Thomas Sherman, and "Problem Solving: A Behavioral Interpretation," by David Palumbo and Ernest Vargas. Tom Sherman's position is decidedly cognitive. As such it is focused on general strategies, knowledge structures, attitudes, and metacognitive strategies. David Palumbo and Ernie Vargas, as self-professed, *radical* behaviorists, take a very different tact to how problem solving takes place and therefore how it should be taught. The two overviews provide reasonably "pure" representations of the perspectives of behavioral and cognitive psychology.

James Garrison and C.J.B. Macmillan's discussion of erotetic logic and problem solving is a personal favorite. They have done an excellent job in explaining the utility of erotetic logic in defining problems and problem-solving skills. They not only tackle the dreaded notion of "fuzzy" versus well-defined problems, but also relate their notions directly to concepts in cognitive psychology. (The careful reader will also be able to tie several of their ideas back to the Palumbo/Vargas discussion.) One caveat: Jim Garrison is an excellent philosopher and colleague, but he is, after all, a philosopher. Plan to read the Garrison/Macmillan article twice, and I think you'll find their notions as intriguing as I did. Also, *mutatis mutan-*

dis means "allowing for the appropriate changes." No sense in all of us looking it up.

Pend Armistead and John Burton's piece is an attempt to look at creativity as an aspect of problem solving and to explore the questions of computer creativity as opposed to computer problem solving. Expert systems and/or artificially intelligent systems (depending on your definition) can solve problems, but can they create new solutions? For teachers of problem solving, the question is worth considering.

The case for programming as a device to teach problem-solving skills is the topic of W. Michael Reed's contribution. Here the argument is that the computer, as an *object* of study, as opposed to an instructional tool, can be used to teach general problem-solving skills. Mike builds a case for programming as a problem-solving exercise from which skills can be learned and transferred to other settings.

The five articles in this section provide an excellent, foundational overview which includes no absolutes but a variety of perspectives that have both research and instructional implications.

Thomas M. Sherman

A Brief Review of Developments in Problem Solving

"Some form of awareness of one's own thinking is essential for efficient problem solving" (Ford, 1981, p. 364). Ford's comment appears to reflect one of several concerns that students of problem solving have pursued since Newell and Simon's classic text *Human Problem Solving* was published in 1972. The purposes of this paper are to describe the nature and importance of "awareness" as a key component of problem solving and some implications for teaching and learning problem solving based on this notion.

WHAT IS PROBLEM SOLVING?

First, there appears to be a consensus that problem solving involves pursuing a *goal*. The individual must recognize a problem (or opportunity for solving a problem) exists and understand the problem well enough to define it so that a goal can be established. Second, there is wide agreement that problem solving is a *process* which involves a sequence of activities or operations. Starting a car may be a problem but the solution is very simple: Take out your key and put it in the ignition. The process associated with problem solving is usually much more complex as could be the case if the car did not start once the ignition switch was turned. This latter problem would involve considerably more thought than the former and require a series of mental actions which could be very complex.

Third, problem solving requires *mental activity*. There are many processes we use to achieve outcomes which do not involve any significant mental activity such as walking, driving, typing, etc. To qualify as problem solving, we must actively engage in cognitive

THOMAS M. SHERMAN is Professor of Educational Psychology, College of Education, Virginia Tech, Blacksburg, VA 24061.

operations which pursue a solution. While such operations are often associated with novel situations (called creative problem solving), they may also be employed with well-known situations also (called routine problem solving). An example of the former is to derive the relationship of x to y from the following:

$R = 2^2$
$x = R + 3$
$2M = 3L + 6$
$Y = M + 1$
$R = 3L$ (Hayes, 1978)

An example of routine problem solving could be the same problem above given to a mathematician who regularly solves such equations.

Two characteristics of problem solving are worth emphasizing. First, problem solving appears to be a relatively sophisticated mental ability which is difficult to learn. Polson and Jeffries (1985), for example, noted that "many high school graduates cannot solve elementary problems involving installment purchases, simple interest or taxes. . . . Graduates from engineering programs are unable to apply theoretical knowledge . . . to actual engineering problems" (p. 417). We should expect sophisticated skills of any sort to be difficult to teach and time consuming to learn; problem solving is not an exception.

Second, problem solving is highly idiosyncratic. In addition to acquiring general problem-solving skills, if such do exist, performance is dependent upon knowledge, prior experience, motivation and many other personal attributes. Thus, what could be a problem for one person may not be for another, and a good problem solver who is effective in one situation may be inept in another.

How Are Problems Solved?

The solution to a problem results from an interaction between the task and the problem solver mainly in terms of how the individual defines or understands the problem and searches for solutions. Problem-solving research has identified a number of heuristics and algorithms through which problems can be addressed. Algorithms are rules which always lead to a correct solution, such as the algorithm for long addition. In principle, an algorithm can be constructed to solve any problem. Where specific problem solutions may not be right or wrong as in arithmetic problems, algorithms focus on generating all possible solutions and probability judging to seek an optimal solution. However, because this is a very cumbersome and time-consuming process, algorithms are generally not used with complex problems with a variety of acceptable responses. Simon (1957) has postulated that "optimal" solutions are rarely thoroughly searched for with complex problems in favor of solutions which are adequate. He coined the term *satisfice* to describe solutions which are acceptable but not necessarily optimal.

Heuristics, on the other hand, are "thinking guides" which focus mental activity on various aspects of the problem in order to capitalize on the problem solver's knowledge and to save time. Unlike algorithms, heuristics do not guarantee a correct solution. Much of the problem-solving literature has focused on these heuristics because they represent the content of the mental activity involved in identifying, defining, solving, and evaluating problems. The following are some of the common heuristics which describe how personal attributes and knowledge may interact with a problem situation to produce a solution.

Generate and test: Using this heuristic the problem solver generates solutions as they come to mind and then tests them for adequacy.

Means-End Analysis: This heuristic, which is part of the General Problem Solver of Newell and Simon (1972), involves breaking a problem into a series of substeps each with a separate goal which moves closer to the desired outcome. Working directly toward and sometimes seemingly away from a goal, the problem solver asks, "What's the difference between the current state and the state I wish to achieve?"

Simplification: Often problems can be reduced in complexity to their essential elements either by actually eliminating part of a problem or by creating analogous problems. The solution can then be applied with the real problem.

These problem-solving heuristics are examples of the processes which can facilitate problem solving. In addition, it is widely recognized that certain psychological states and actions can inhibit solving problems.

Functional Fixedness: There are a number of well-known problems (Maier, 1931; Duncker, 1945) which depend upon people using familiar objects in unusual ways (e.g., a screwdriver for a pendulum weight) to solve problems. In such situations, we tend to associate an object with its function and often cannot visualize using it in potentially different ways.

Set Effects: Luchins' (1942) famous water jar problems, in which subjects are given three jugs with various capacities (e.g., A = 14; B = 36; C = 8) and a problem to measure a quantity (e.g., 6), exemplify set effects. Those who solved a series of these problems through addition were less likely to correctly solve a subsequent problem requiring subtraction. Thus, a prior successful solution strategy can inhibit performance on subsequent problems which are similar but require different solution strategies.

To review, problem solving is generally considered a goal-oriented mental process applied to complex problems. The process of problem solving includes recognizing and understanding the problem and searching for or generating a solution. This interaction between problem solvers and tasks is dependent upon how problem solvers use their personal knowledge which can be improved with heuristics or inhibited by conditions which limit recall of relevant information. Now, consider the role of personal awareness in problem solving.

What Is Awareness and Why Is It Important?

The term *metacognition* was coined by Flavell (1979) to reference thinking about thinking. He proposed that "metacognitive knowledge is that segment of your stored world knowledge that has to do with people as cognitive creatures and with their diverse cognitive tasks, goals, actions, and experiences" (p. 906). In addition, Flavell proposed that we also learn from metacognitive experiences and use metacognitive strategies. "Metacognitive experiences are any conscious cognitive or affective experiences that accompany and pertain to any intellectual enterprise" (Flavell, 1979, p. 906). Examples of metacognitive experiences are recognizing you have not understood what you just read and an uneasy feeling that you are not as well prepared as you thought when first looking at a test. Metacognitive strategies are differentiated from cognitive strategies in that the latter are ways to operate on ideas, whereas the former monitor these operations.

Metacognitive knowledge, experiences, and strategies serve as the basis and means to regulate how and what we think. This is an important concept in cognition because there is the clear implication that thinking is a purposeful activity which may be controlled by an individual.

A study by Belmont and Butterfield (1971) with mildly retarded children illustrates this idea. They discovered that a major difference between normal and retarded children on a serial memory task was that the normal children stopped memorizing and rehearsed during the task. They subsequently taught the retarded children to rehearse and, then, discovered their performance was similar to that of normal children. Thus, by teaching these children a relatively simple skill, they markedly improved their performance.

Can Metacognition Be Taught?

It appears that metacognitive awareness is at least partially developmental. Children become more able to judge the difficulty of problems as they get older and intellectually mature. However, the intellectual maturity associated with sophisticated thinking appears to be a function of more than maturation. It is also necessary to acquire mental skills which allow the capability to think to emerge. Apparently these metacognitive skills are responsible for the differences in achievement between poor, average, and good students. The same skills also may be a key component of problem solving.

Baker and Brown (1984) described "three main metacognitive skills: awareness, monitoring, and the deployment of compensatory strategies" (p. 355). Awareness is the realization that purpose exists whether it is in terms of an author's intent in a prose passage, between variables in an experiment, or between cause and effect in a myriad of real-life experiences. One indicator of awareness may be an individual's perception of the extent to which events can be controlled. Called *locus of control* (Rotter, 1966), this perception of control can range from "life is a series of random events" to "I can control what happens to me completely." Of course, neither extreme is very realistic; but, a relatively high level of perceived personal control has been correlated with success in a variety of endeavors (Lefcourt, 1976). A reasonable assumption is that we are more likely to take action to change a situation when we believe that action will make a difference. Metacognitive awareness, then, can be considered a mind set or attitude which enables action. Awareness skills are those which allow an individual to construct some meaning from experience and generate understanding. Some examples are comparing new with prior experiences (creating metaphors or analogies), conducting memory searches, and seeking additional information.

Monitoring skills allow an individual to recognize when understanding is and is not proceeding. Anderson (1979) postulated an "automatic monitoring mechanism" which "clicks" during understanding and "clunks" during comprehension failures. It is as if we have a mental supervisor continually asking, "Do you understand this?" When the answer is "No," the mental equivalent of warning lights flash, indicating that to continue in the same way will lead to more "clunks." Monitoring skills include actions such as checking answers, summarizing, and organizing information into categories.

The final category of skills are compensatory strategies. Once a clunk has been experienced, a learner must act cognitively to remediate the deficiency. In other words, it is necessary to use some alternative cognitive actions that may also lead to understanding. Some skills that may be employed to correct learning failures are rereading, thinking from a different perspective, elaboration, and questioning.

There is considerable evidence that these metacognitive skills can be taught and that, when mastered, make an enormous difference in cognitive functioning (Pressley & Levin, 1983; Segal, Chipman, & Glaser, 1985). However, it appears that these skills are also bound to specific situations and do not generalize well (Bransford, Stein, Arbitman-Smith, & Vye, 1985). Thus, while they can be taught, metacognitive skills are similar to other forms of sophisticated performance; they probably require considerable practice, time, effort, and dedication to develop. In addition, at some point, they become idiosyncratic as personal factors interact with skill use and developmental differences.

What Does Metacognition Imply for Problem Solving?

Problem solving appears to be as dependent upon metacognitive skills as other forms of high-level thinking. Consider, for example, the three components commonly associated with problem solving: goal, process, and mental activity. The essence of problem solving is to identify and initiate each component through mental interaction between the task and the individual's experience and knowledge. Two kinds of metacognitive awareness and skills appear necessary for this to happen.

First, it is important to recognize that problems are solvable through personal action and that problems are a normal part of life. In this sense, it is necessary to understand that general problem-solving strategies are available *and* can be applied in a variety of situations. Second, it is necessary to be aware that a particular problem exists and that it is definable as such. This appears to be a natural prerequisite to establishing a goal in the same way that a reader must be aware that meaning can be extracted (or constructed) from a text passage.

Monitoring skills also contribute to problem-solving effectiveness. Monitoring skills present some interesting challenges for investigation because they seem to be apparent in accomplished performers only when things are not going well (i.e., Anderson's automatic monitoring mechanism mentioned earlier). As a result, monitoring skills are not well understood except as conscious actions to assess operations. For example, in studying the water jug problems, Luchins discovered the *Einstellung Effect*, which is a routinizing of thought. Given a series of problems which required subtraction to solve, we could be stymied by one which required addition because it is outside of the success routine established. However, this effect appears rather easily modified through the exercise of cognitive control over problem-solving operations by simply warning the individual to not be too dependent upon subtraction or to "watch it" around number ______.

Certainly, it is unreasonable to expect an outside warning for every problem pitfall while solving an uncontrived problem. However, it is possible to develop executive cognitive abilities which can monitor the procedures and operations through which solutions are sought. When these are not going well, such as when a set effect is operating, this monitoring mechanism could ask, "Why don't you try another operation? This one is not working well."

Finally, the ability to take remedial action is an important skill for problem solving. It is quite reasonable that some alternative skills must be available if awareness and monitoring skills are to be useful. Alternatives have played an important role in problem solving but mostly as solution options from which a rational choice could be made. Perhaps alternative solution strategies and skills should also be a recognized part of the problem-solving process. These skills may range from seeking help in generating alternatives to identifying needed sources of information to allowing an idea to "incubate" (Silveira, 1971).

WHAT DOES THE FUTURE HOLD FOR PROBLEM SOLVING?

Recent research on cognition has suggested that sophisticated thinking consists of two general components. The first is an attitude characterized by confidence that understanding is possible. For problem solving this appears to include awareness of a general problem-solving process and recognition that problems get solved because we make an effort to solve them. The second is the executive skills that enable the attitude. That is, a set of metacognitive skills is needed through which the general process and its components can be monitored and adjusted to fit the unique challenge presented by a problem and the personal abilities of the problem solver. Successfully teaching or implementing problem solving or any form of sophisticated thinking appears dependent upon both.

Our understanding of these executive skills and how they operate in problem solving is incomplete. At the present, we do not know which component should come first or how either develops. However, some of the successes achieved in promoting comprehension of text, which may be viewed as a problem-solving task, have relied almost exclusively on teaching skills (Day, 1980). Baker and Brown (1984) indicate that "mature readers are those who practice thought experiments, question their own basic assumptions, provide counter examples to their own rules, and so on" (p. 383). These practices are not unlike those observed in good problem solvers. Such skills appear best learned in context; that is, while working on appropriate tasks. Bransford et al. (1985) remind us that Thorndike proposed an "identical elements theory of transfer" at the beginning of this century which stated that transfer was specific rather than general. Applied to problem solving, a successful approach may be to first identify the skills necessary to solve a particular class of problems and then provide models and instructional support to assist in learning these skills. The skills may then generalize or transfer to the general attitude associated with problem solving.

A final element of problem solving is knowledge. Simon and Gilmartin (1973) have provided convincing evidence that a major difference between good and expert chess players is their ability to use a vocabulary of chess moves to organize their knowledge. Unfortunately, research has not revealed the effects of continued knowledge acquisition on problem solving. However, it is likely that expertise in the sense of well-organized knowledge is a necessary component of any form of sophisticated thinking. The point is that we must carefully guide development so that it is more than adding experience. To be useful, experience must be repeatedly tested, evaluated, challenged, and organized. It is not a matter of how much experience but how individuals act on their experience which makes the difference. It appears that if we want to teach problem solving, it will be necessary to commit a considerable amount of time to helping people acquire, understand, and apply their knowledge using metacognitive skills to recognize, define, solve, and evaluate problems.

REFERENCES

Anderson, T. H. (1979). Study skills on learning strategies. In H. F. O'Neil, Jr., & C. D. Spielberger (Eds.), *Cognitive and affective learning strategies* (pp. 77-98). New York: Academic Press.

Baker, L., & Brown, A. L. (1984). Metacognitive skills and reading. In T. D. Pearson (Ed.), *Handbook of reading research* (pp. 353-394). New York: Longman.

Belmont, J. N., & Butterfield, E. C. (1971). Mining strategies as determinants of memory deficiencies. *Cognitive Psychology, 2*, 411-420.

Bransford, J. D., Stein, B. S., Arbitman-Smith, R., & Vye, N. J. (1985). Improving thinking and learning skills: An analysis of three approaches. In J. W. Segal, S. F. Chipman, & R. Glaser (Eds.), *Thinking and learning skills: Vol. 1. Relating instruction to research* (pp. 133-206). Hillsdale, NJ: Erlbaum.

Day, J. D. (1980). *Training summarization skills: A comparison of teaching methods.* Unpublished doctoral dissertation, University of Illinois, Urbana.

Duncker, K. (1945). On problem solving. *Psychological Monographs, 58*(270), p. 127.

Flavell, J. H. (1979). Metacognition and cognitive monitoring: A new area of cognitive-developmental inquiry. *American Psychologist, 34*, 906-911.

Ford, N. (1981). Recent approaches to the study and teaching of "effective learning" in higher education. *Review of Educational Research, 51*(3), 345-377.

Hayes, J. R. (1978). *Cognitive psychology*. Homewood, IL: Dorsey Press.

Lefcourt, H. N. (1976). *Locus of control: Current trends in theory and research*. Hillsdale, NJ: Erlbaum.

Luchins, A. S. (1942). Mechanization and problem solving. *Psychological Monographs, 54*(248).

Maier, N. R. F. (1931). Reasoning in humans: II. The solution of a problem and its appearance in consciousness. *Journal of Comparative Psychology, 12*, 181-194.

Newell, A., & Simon, H. A. (1972). *Human problem solving*. Englewood Cliffs, NJ: Prentice-Hall.

Polson, P. G., & Jeffries, R. (1985). Instruction in general problem-solving skills: An analysis of four approaches. In J. W. Segal, S. F. Chipman, & R.

Glaser (Eds.), *Thinking and learning skills: Vol. 1. Relating instruction to research* (pp. 417-452). Hillsdale, NJ: Erlbaum.

Pressley, N., & Levin, J. R. (1983). *Cognitive strategy research: Educational applications*. New York: Springer-Verlag.

Rotter, J. B. (1966). Generalized expectancies for internal vs. external control of reinforcement. *Psychological Monographs, 80*(609).

Segal, J. W., Chipman, S. F., & Glaser, R. (1985). *Thinking and learning skills: Vol. 1. Relating Instruction to research*. Hillsdale, NJ: Erlbaum.

Silveira, J. (1971). *Incubation: The effect of interruption, timing and length on problem solution and quality of problem processing*. Unpublished doctoral dissertation, University of Oregon, Eugene.

Simon, H. A. (1957). *Models of man*. New York: Wiley.

Simon, H. A., & Gilmartin, K. A. (1973). A simulation of memory chess positions. *Cognitive Psychology, 5*, 29-46.

David B. Palumbo
Ernest A. Vargas

Problem Solving: A Behavioral Interpretation

INTRODUCTION

A common problem everyone faces and tries to solve at some time or other is that of recalling someone's name. We know the person, talked to her only a few days ago, but now, in conversing with someone else, cannot say her name. This problem differs in no special way from any of those instances where we are attempting to state what we already know but at the moment cannot emit the proper response. We encounter such problems daily. Then, of course, there are those problems thrust upon us in test situations, all based on our having the proper prerequisite repertoire to solve them. We are instructed in calculus and, using what we know of that subject, are expected to solve problems presented to us. Another set of problems we initiate for ourselves is that posed by games. Games present problems; in fact, that accounts for most of the reason for their success. For example, millions of people spend hours playing chess. It requires a set of prerequisite skills: Necessary behaviors to make an effective response must be in place, and this repertoire makes it possible for the player to emit the proper response to any situation the game presents.

The examples point out a common feature of problem situations: We could emit the correct response if we could arrange to evoke it.

DAVID B. PALUMBO is a doctoral candidate, Educational Psychology, West Virginia University, Morgantown, WV 26506.
ERNEST A. VARGAS is Professor of Educational Psychology, West Virginia University, Morgantown WV 26506.

The authors wish to thank Julie S. Vargas, W. Michael Reed, and Lawrence E. Fraley for their comments and critical evaluation of an earlier version of this manuscript.

Such situations differ from those in which a response is not in our repertoire, and thus we cannot emit an effective response regardless of what we do and how hard we try. If we do not know someone's name, no problem is posed in trying to recall it since we cannot be placed in the situation of even attempting the solution. For those who do not know calculus, their problem-solving skills are irrelevant to a problem in that subject matter since they cannot begin to address the problem. We have not posed a problem in chess to someone who does not know how to play chess. We present legitimate problems only to those who know enough to solve them.

The prior examples illustrate the difference between learning and problem solving; that is, between shaping behavior and working effectively with behavior already shaped. Situations called problems and behaviors called problem solving depend on preexistent repertoires. Before we teach problem-solving skills, we must teach a repertoire appropriate to the subject matter of the problem.

PROBLEM SOLVING AND BEHAVIORAL PROCESSES

Once the individual has a response in place, he may face a situation in which he must emit that response but for any of a number of reasons he cannot. The *problem* is having behavior in one's repertoire, but not immediately available. The *solving* is manipulating the "reasons," or the events that increase or decrease the probability of emitting the previously unavailable response. Problem solving, then, is all those procedures in which we engage in order to increase the probability of emitting a response already in place but not immediately available.[1]

Both the existence of an appropriate response and its nonavailability are critical components of a situation defined as a problem. In short, a problem is defined not by the stimulus situation—a question is posed, a conundrum presented—but by the characteristics of a repertoire with respect to that situation. After repeated trials at executing a particular set of Logo commands to move an object across the screen, a student slams her fist on the table and her books on the floor, and finally asks her instructor for help. The instructor immediately shows her the correct series of commands, and the object then successfully moves across the screen. What she had to do did not present a problem for the instructor. He had a question from the student that could have been a problem but was not, as he had a response immediately available. If a computer gives an answer to a mathematical equation, it is not solving a problem. It simply gives an inevitable answer by following a set sequence of operations. This sequence was designed and put in place by someone for whom, perhaps, originally achieving the solution presented a problem. What characterizes problem solving is not that an answer is given or an effective response emitted (in short, not a product) but that behavioral processes are evoked that answer or that increase the probability of emitting the effective response.

Due to these processes, behavior becomes contingent upon a subset of the events before and after its occurrence. One class of behavioral processes increases the probability that a response will occur. When behavior becomes contingent on *prior* events and these antecedent events increase the probability of its occurrence (by altering its momentary strength), then these events are defined as *discriminative stimuli*. When behavior becomes contingent on events *following* its occurrence and these postcedent events increase the probability of its occurrence, then these events are defined as *motivative stimuli*. Problem solving consists of establishing conditions for others or oneself with respect to current events so that they become motivative or discriminative stimuli, thus increasing the probability of emitting a response that currently is unavailable.

Postcedent Processes

We manipulate motivative stimuli when we face the problem of not "feeling like" doing something we should do, and can do. The problem is a familiar one, and we can best exemplify how we solve it by looking at how we solve it with others. Consider for example the old saying: "You can take a horse to water but you can't make it drink." The problem, of course, is to get the horse to drink water—a motivational problem. There are a number of ways to solve this problem: We can deprive the horse of water for several days; we can give the horse salt just prior to taking it to water; we can make water drinking contingent upon some other action in which the horse is more interested; and so on. Or consider another familiar example. Drill-and-practice programs have been perhaps the most common uses of microcomputers in the educational system. Yet, until we establish the appropriate motivative stimuli, these drill programs may have little effect since students will not use them. Humphrey (1983) showed that feedback could be used effectively as motivative stimuli to increase the rate of responding on a computerized drill-and-practice math program. Such familiar examples illustrate solving problems with respect to motivating others. We solve those motivational problems not by motivating the person but by manipulating motivative events that affect the desired behavior. We increase the probability of emitting the required response (or set of responses) by delivering events that reinforce or punish contingent upon the response being emitted. A prior step is to establish operations that transform formerly neutral events into events that reinforce or punish, or events that increase the probability of the behavior occurring or not occurring (Michael, 1984).

We solve our own problems of motivation in like fashion. A typical set of problems with which most of us struggle in a health-conscious society are those of exercise and of eating. We are not jogging, or engaging in that daily walk, or playing as much tennis as we should; and, in addition, we may be smoking, drinking too much, or eating too much. These are common problems. So-called willpower, giving ourselves an instruction such as "Don't smoke any more" won't do; for, if it did, we would not have a problem. The common lay reaction when one observes that a behavior could have occurred with no restrictions of skill or restraint is to say that the person does not "want" to do it, and the analysis contains a bit of truth in it. The cigarette smoker may both "want" to quit and also to smoke. A common reaction on our part is to say, "That's the way we are. We can't help ourselves." Another common reaction, for we do not like to admit that we failed or that we are not in control of ourselves, is to say that we could have done it if we wanted to or, alternatively, that we can do it anytime we really want to. The behavior to be emitted is in our repertoire but is not emitted because the proper controls are not in place.

We engage in problem-solving activities similar to those involved in solving the problems of others when solving our health problems or any other problem of motivation. We establish certain events as reinforcers or punishers, and then make those events contingent upon emitting the proper behavior. Such a two-stage operation arranges postcedent contingencies to increase the probability that we will emit a certain response. Since in this article we concern ourselves primarily with behavioral processes that lie in the domain of events prior to responses, we will not further address problems, problem solving, and other behavioral processes in the postcedent domain.

Antecedent Processes

The traditional concern in problem solving addresses processes involving antecedent stimulus control. The typical problem situation portrayed assumes that the individual is motivated to solve the presented problem. Events occurring *prior* to a proper response must be manipulated before that response can be emitted. These events may be either the individual's own behavior or events external to it. Events that occur prior to the individual's response and increase the probability of that response by evoking it are discriminative stimuli. We increase the probability of available but not yet emitted responses by constructing discriminative stimuli for others and for ourselves.

We daily solve a number of problems by manipulating discriminative stimuli external to our behavior. If we encounter difficulty getting up in the morning, we set an alarm clock. If we wish to remember to do something, we tie a string around our finger. These solutions, where we manipulate events and objects to serve as discriminative stimuli, are so obvious and so common we rarely think of them as problem solving. Initially, we did not emit a ready response for manipulating clocks and strings to control our behavior. The first time we attempt to solve a problem by manipulating objects and nonbehavioral events, we may find ourselves in the position of those individuals in a room with two long cords suspended from the ceiling and with a pair of pliers on a nearby table. Neither cord can reach the other but the individual's problem is to tie them together. Many individuals find the problem difficult. Once one cord is moved so that it serves as an effective discriminative stimulus for the response that initiates the set of responses that solves the problem, the individual can tie them immediately on any future occasion. Problems such as obtaining a banana from the ceiling by moving boxes and sticks fall in the same category. This sort of problem solving, manipulating events and objects external to our behavior, is not addressed in problem solving with computers.

Dealing directly with our own behavior underlies the typical analysis of problem solving with the use of computers. We manipulate our own behavior as discriminative stimuli to increase the probability of other behavior that follows. This type of problem solving raises the traditional problem-solving issues. The most common analysis deals with verbal behavior, and it is that behavior that is of most concern to those who work with designing problem-solving materials using computers. We thus restrict our analysis to this type of problem solving: constructing discriminative verbal stimuli that increase the probability of emitting an effective verbal response.

PROBLEM SOLVING: ALGORITHM LEVELS I AND II

We thus see that a problem ensues when previously shaped behavior in our repertoire is not currently available. To increase the probability that the response will be emitted, we manipulate stimuli that control it by arranging for those stimuli to occur. We establish either motivative stimuli or discriminative stimuli. Discriminative stimuli can be verbal or nonverbal. A particular sequence of activities (a procedure) increases the probability of evoking an effective response where no response was previously evocable. Procedural steps for solutions are algorithms. There are two orders of algorithms. The first order of algorithms denotes those specific to the types of problems encountered. The second order of algorithms are those used to construct first order algorithms.

First Order (Level I) Algorithms

A large class of algorithms addresses specific sets of problems. Mathematics provides examples of many kinds of algorithms of this sort. We are taught to reduce a fraction to its simple form or solve a quadratic equation by going through a series of predefined steps (a first order algorithm usually supplied by a teacher). Thus when we are presented with these types of problems, we emit the particular algorithm that determines an effective response. (Unlike the computer, we continue to do this only if we are reinforced for doing so. These reinforcers need not be delivered by an agency external to us; in most cases, simply solving the problem acts as a reinforcer.) A problem with a specific characteristic increases the probability of a particular algorithm, a specific response sequence, being evoked. Once the initial response of the sequence is evoked, no further variation in the following responses occurs. Each response is closely controlled by the characteristics of the prior one. The control is sequelic (Vargas, 1986). The variables controlling succeeding responses are few in number and restricted to the characteristics of the prior responses. The results are close-ended. The procedure is essentially a mechanical one (though never completely so, for humans are not machines; they are governed by biological processes, such as reinforcement, that have no effect on, and thus no relevance to, the operations of machines such as computers). These typical algorithms are taught by teachers in logic, mathematics, and other subject matters where verbal material is well-ordered. These are also the algorithms that easily find their way into machines such as computers. Such algorithms are usually the result of long acquaintance by a culture, or by a particular verbal community within a culture, with certain classes of problems.

A variant of this type is a questioning technique used with verbal material. The student emits a sequence of questions, each the result of the answer to the former, with the final question being the discriminative stimulus that provides the momentary strength for a response, already learned but not until that point was made available, to solve the problem. Such an algorithmic sequence is an algorithmic tactic that can be used with any complex verbal material once the characteristics of that material are discriminated well enough. For example, consider the following analytical self-questioning procedures to identify examples of reinforcement from non-examples of reinforcement:

1. Is there an *increase* in the *rate* or *probability* of a behavior? (Does a behavior occur more frequently, or is a behavior more likely to occur?)
2. Does the *environmental change follow* the occurrence of a behavior?
3. Does the change in the *environment immediately* follow the behavior?
4. If the answer to all three questions is *Yes*, you have an *example of reinforcement.* (Bruce, 1986)

Second Order (Level II) Algorithms

Before a teacher gives a student a particular problem-solving technique, the algorithm itself has to be constructed. Before a programmer programs the algorithm that controls the computer's operations with respect to a particular set of questions, that algorithm has to be discovered and constructed. How does one engage in problem-solving techniques from which other problem-solving techniques will result? What does the individual do to arrive at a specific algorithm which that individual can thereafter apply to a particular type of problem? In short, what does level II algorithm behavior consist of and how are level II algorithms constructed?

Two aspects characterize level II algorithms: (a) The response desired is in one's repertoire but currently not available, a situation not unlike the level I algorithm situation; and (b) the specific events that lead to that response are not in place either; that is, the discriminative stimuli are not sequeled in such a way that they inevitably lead to the effective response. Level II algorithms are searches for such a sequeled set of procedures and the constructing of them. Descriptively, we might say that level II algorithms are open-ended problem-solving techniques that lead to "close-ended" algorithms. Metaphorically, we might call the first type of problem-solving techniques "manufacturing processes" and the second type "fishing expeditions."

Level II problem solving depends on providing supplementary stimuli that strengthen verbal behavior which leads to verbal practices to solve specific sets of problems. (Teaching then involves putting into place those verbal techniques by which other verbal behavior might be strengthened; that is, putting into place those techniques that might lead to a sequeled set of verbal discriminative stimuli appropriate to a particular set of problems.) The supplementary stimuli may be of two forms: (a) those supplementary stimuli that share some similarity in form with the response to be strengthened and (b) those supplementary stimuli, either verbal or nonverbal, that share no formal characteristics with the response to be strengthened. We call the first type *formal* supplementary stimuli, and the second type *thematic* supplementary stimuli (Skinner, 1953).

In some cases the effective response can be identified in advance; in other cases, it cannot. When an operator such as a teacher or a computer (and including the person himself) can identify the response in advance, the technique providing the supplementary stimulus is a *prompt*. A four-way classification of constructed verbal discriminative stimuli then ensues: formal prompts, thematic prompts, formal probes, and thematic probes. Asking the question, "Who was the sixteenth president of the United States?" and not getting an answer (or the correct answer), we could further state, "He's also known as The Great Emancipator—someone who freed the slaves," and such a hint exemplifies a thematic prompt, while the supplementary stimulus of "Can you *link* [emphasized] his name with what I told you?" is a formal prompt. Social inquiries provide many examples of probes. The inquirer does not know beforehand the answer but is nevertheless interested in it. When one is interested in finding out the name of a particular person at a party, he may ask someone else, "Do you know who she is?" The answer "no" may be followed by the response, "Isn't that the new girl from Ohio?" which acts as a thematic probe if it then evokes an effective response in identifying the person. The statement "Does her name start with C?" in the same situation would be an example of a formal probe if this then evokes the effective response (stating her name) and her name did in fact start with the letter C.

In solving a problem where the student knows what answer is desired but does not know how to obtain that answer, a level II algorithm procedure might be as follows. Say that a student has the difficult problem of ascertaining whether a statement is an explanatory fiction or not; that is, ascertaining whether a statement that is apparently true is true or is not true due to a variety of reasons mostly having to do with how language is used. The student could develop an algorithm that would provide a series of discriminative stimuli that would evoke the appropriate response as to whether a statement was or was not an explanatory fiction. The only way of asserting that a given algorithm is effective is to see if it does generate the appropriate discriminative stimuli to evoke the appropriate response. Therefore, by giving feedback (of which the stimulus features *may* act as reinforcers or punishers) as to whether or not a given response was correct in identifying an explanatory fiction, the student could continue to modify the algorithm until it was effective in evoking appropriate responses.

CONCLUSION

Figure 1 schematically summarizes the analysis discussed. The advent of the microcomputer into the education system has been greeted with great anticipation and promise. Yet some have recently said that perhaps it has offered more than it can deliver or at least that its promises have yet to be empirically demonstrated (Ginther & Williamson, 1985). With advancing computer technology, we should be more effective in shaping such complex behavioral repertoires as problem solving. The conceptual framework laid out in this paper, along with the available microcomputer technology, promises not only the means to a scientific analysis of problem solving but also the means to practical results. The computer can be

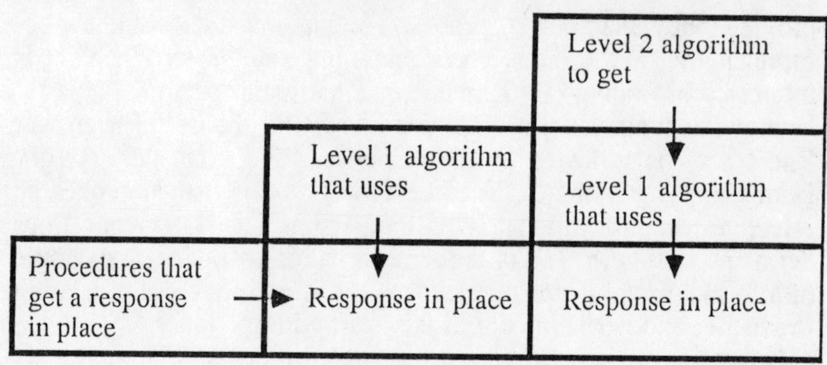

FIGURE 1. Levels of Problem Solving

more effectively used than it currently is as a tool to shape the development of both first- and second-order problem-solving algorithms. Computerized instructional systems can be developed to teach problem solving based on this analysis, and the authors are currently designing such a system.

FOOTNOTE

1. See Skinner's analysis of problem solving in the following books and journals: *Science and Human Behavior*, 1953, especially the chapters on "Thinking" and "The Analysis of Complex Cases"; *Verbal Behavior*, 1957, particularly the chapter on "Supplementary Stimulation"; *Problem Solving: Research, Method and Theory*, 1966, (Kleinmuntz, Ed.); chapter 4, with notes following, in *Contingencies of Reinforcement*, 1969; and the chapter, "An Operant Analysis of Problem Solving," including Skinner's comments following critiques by his critics, in *The Behavioral and Brain Sciences* issue, December 1984, co-edited by A.C. Catania and S. Harnad.

REFERENCES

Bruce, G. (1985, May). *Training problem-solving behavior: A questioning tactic to increase discriminative control*. Paper presented at the 12th annual convention of the Association for Behavior Analysis, Milwaukee, WI.

Ginther, D.W., & Williamson, J.D. (1985). Learning Logo: What is really learned? *Computers in the Schools, 2*, 73-78.

Humphrey, J.E. (1983). *A comparison of how paced and unpaced problems affect learning during CAI math drills*. Unpublished doctoral dissertation, West Virginia University, Morgantown.

Michael, J. (1984). Distinguishing between discriminative and motivation function of the stimuli. *Journal of the Experimental Analysis of Behavior, 37*, 149-155.

Skinner, B.F. (1953). *Science and human behavior*. New York: Macmillan.

Skinner, B.F. (1957). *Verbal behavior*. New York: Appleton-Century-Crofts.

Skinner, B.F. (1966). An operant analysis of problem solving. In B. Kleinmuntz (Ed.), *Problem solving: Research, method and theory* (pp. 133-171). New York: Wiley.

Skinner, B.F. (1969). *Contingencies of reinforcement*. New York: Appleton-Century-Crofts.

Skinner, B.F. (1984). An operant analysis of problem solving. In A.C. Catania & S. Harnad (Eds.), *Canonical papers of B.F. Skinner. The Behavioral and Brain Sciences, 7*, pp. 473-724.

Vargas, E.A. (1986). Intraverbal behavior. In P. Chase & L. Parrot (Eds.) *Psychological aspects of language: The West Virginia lectures* (pp. 128-151). Springfield, IL: Charles C Thomas.

James W. Garrison
C. J. B. Macmillan

The Erotetic Logic of Problem-Solving Inquiry

Problem solving has two aspects: (a) the *process*, or set of activities that guide the search for a solution, and (b) the *product*, or the actual solution. Most studies of problem solving have been experimental in design and have used scores on objective measures of achievement as the dependent variable. Relatively little empirical research has been done on the process involved in problem solving and virtually nothing on the logical activities present in the process. *Erotetic logic*, the logic of questions and answers, is one way of studying the underlying logical dynamics of problem solving.

This paper will introduce the basic ideas of erotetic logic and apply them to some of the principles that have been derived from research on cognitive psychology and information-processing models of problem solving. The introduction of erotetic logic into the literature on problem solving not only provides an alternative means for studying problem solving activity, but, more importantly, a "logical home" for a number of psychological ideas. The goal is not to eliminate empirical psychology from the study of problem solving; rather, the object is to reduce the amount of work required of psychology. By putting the mystery in the right place, we can better circumscribe the proper limits of empirical psychology while enlisting the rules of logic as a guide to empirical research. The truly psychological can never be reduced to the logical.

The logical world is clean, neat, and well-ordered. A high level of abstraction permits precision, but usually the price of precision is

JAMES W. GARRISON is Assistant Professor of Educational Philosophy, College of Education, Virginia Tech, Blacksburg, VA 24061.
C. J. B. MACMILLAN is Professor of Educational Philosophy, College of Education, Florida State University, Tallahassee, FL 32306.

content. The everyday empirical world, the real world, is commonly dirty, messy, and disorganized. Nevertheless, if we must be cast out of paradise, let us at least know what it is that we are missing.

INFORMATION, PROBLEMS, AND QUESTIONS

It is natural to conceive of a problem as a question that we cannot answer given the knowledge immediately available to us. Likewise, it is reasonable to conceive of a solution to a problem as a completely satisfactory answer to a putative question. It may surprise the reader to see how readily information theory may be used to provide a rigorous and precise formulation of the foregoing vague and intuitive erotetic equivalence between problems and questions.

Let us begin by distinguishing between questions posed *to* some agent, called the *inquirer*, by some source of problems, and questions posed *by* the inquirer to some source of information. We will refer to the "source" of both problems and information as the *oracle*. In practice the role of the oracle may be played by, among other things, the subject matter (curriculum), a teacher, mother (or father), nature, or a computer. For the sake of specificity, let us always refer to the *inquirer* as the student and the *oracle* as the computer. A question posed by the computer to the student that the student cannot answer constitutes a problem. Information theory permits us to specify a problem more precisely than this. John Dewey writes that whatever "perplexes and challenges the mind so that it makes belief at all uncertain . . . is a genuine problem, or question" (Dewey, 1933, p. 13). Understood thus, a problem is any uncertain and indeterminate situation. In terms of information theory, the student's uncertainty is defined and measured by the number of choices or alternatives to the actual situation that are compatible with what the student already knows or believes about the world. We may, following Hintikka (1976), refer to these compatible alternatives as *epistemic alternatives*.

Hintikka identifies the Inquirers' epistemic alternatives with "knowledge worlds" or "possible worlds." Let us refer to these possible worlds as possible solutions. The number of epistemic, alternative worlds compatible with what the student already knows (background knowledge) provides a measure of the student's uncertainty. The number of choices or alternatives to the actual situation that a given answer to a question *eliminates* provides an accurate measure of the answer's informativeness. Clearly, the student's questions to the computer are information-seeking questions, having as their ultimate goal the elimination of uncertainty. Likewise, the computer's verdicial answers, when forthcoming, provide information; that is, they eliminate uncertainty.

Some general, although important, observations may be made about the student's epistemic alternatives. First, not all alternatives need initially appear equally plausible to the Inquirer. Second, it is unlikely that the student will be explicitly aware of all the epistemic alternatives compatible with what the student knows. Rendering such tacit or implicit alternatives explicit is often crucial to successful problem solving. Third, false belief or inadequate knowledge on the part of the student may exclude the actual situation from the student's set of alternatives. In such situations the student must multiply alternatives before reducing them. This calls for productive thinking (Greeno, 1973). In one way or another the student needs either to "learn" more, "unlearn" false beliefs, or even "relearn" things that have been forgotten. Or, equivalently, gather information, eliminate noise and recover lost or poorly stored information.

THE EROTETIC LOGIC OF PROBLEM SOLVING: A PRECEDENT AND A PARADOX

Question-and-answer dialogues have been considered a method of inquiry and knowledge acquisition (information gathering) since antiquity. In the *Republic* (511b) of Plato, for instance, dialectic is conceived as a method of discovery, the highest form of inquiry. Likewise, Aristotle in his *Topics* (100a30 & 101a36-101b5) also takes dialectic as a means of discovery. These precedents are of more than mere historical interest, however. They provide us with one of the most immutable and intractable principles of all problem-solving inquiry.

It was Plato who first formulated the *Meno paradox*, after the Socratic dialogue known as the *Meno* (80e) where it was first introduced. The paradox goes like this: inquiry is possible. Why? Because either the inquirer already knows that which is sought, in which case there is no need to seek it, or the inquirer has no idea what the object of inquiry is like and therefore could not recognize it even if she or he were to chance upon it. Aristotle's solution to the paradox consists in declaring that "there is nothing to prevent a man in one sense knowing what he is learning, in another not knowing it" (*Posterior Analytics*, 71b5). What Aristotle (McKeon, 1941) means by this is indicated by the way he opens the *Posterior Analytics*. Aristotle writes, "All instruction given or received by way of argument [inquiry] proceeds from pre-existent knowledge" (71b5, p. 111). This idea is well ensconced in the field of cognitive and educational psychology (see Ausubel, 1968). Inquiry is impossible without sufficient prior information stored in long-term memory (LTM) to *recognize* and represent the problem well enough to anticipate, however inaccurately, the eventual solution. It is this simple but unassailable fact that makes atheoretical inquiry of any kind an impossibility (see Garrison, 1987).

Aristotle (McKeon, 1941) declares that "the pre-existent knowledge is of two kinds" (71a15, p. 110). They are "the meaning of the world and the existence of the thing [some matter of fact]" (71a15). For example, in geometrical inquiry, it may be enough simply to already know the meaning of the word *triangle*; that is, a three-sided figure enclosing a space the sum of whose interior angles equals 180 degrees. On a different occasion, it may be enough to know the fact that there is "this particular figure inscribed in the semicircle" (71a20-25, p. 110). Aristotle then goes on in the same context to describe one special kind of problem solution: "Recognition of a truth [a solution] may in some cases contain as factors both previous knowledge and also knowledge acquired simultaneously with that recognition" (71a17-18, p. 110). Aristotle gives an illuminating example:

> The student knew beforehand that the angles of every triangle are equal to two right angles; but it was only at the actual moment at which he was being led on to recognize this as true in the instance before him that he came to know "this figure inscribed in the semicircle" to be a triangle. (71a20-25, p. 110)

Here the solution turns on prior knowledge of "a meaning" and the recognition that some particular thing is an instance of it. Surprisingly, modern cognitive psychology takes a very similar view of "pre-existent knowledge." We will return to these matters shortly.

We will not concern ourselves with the deeper metaphysical and espitemological issues that arise from considering the implications of the Meno paradox. We will, rather, content ourselves with the fact, as well known to cognitive psychologists as to philosophers, that some form of prior knowledge is required in order to initiate problem-solving inquiry. We remain agnostic as to the ultimate origin of this prior knowledge.

In erotetic logic prior knowledge appears in the guise of the logical presuppositions of questions. All questions. For example, even so simple a question as "Who lives in that house?" assumes that there is a house in view (and not the stage set for *Gone with the Wind*) and that someone does indeed live in it. Presuppositions initiate, guide, and constrain problem-solving inquiry by determining *what* questions may be formulated, *how* they may be formulated, and in *which* order the questions are best formulated. The constraint provided by the presuppositions is the logical cash value of the old saw that says "A good question determines its own answer." Let us begin our investigation of the erotetic logic of problem-solving inquiry by examining how the logical presuppositions that initiate inquiry are represented in information-processing models.

EROTETIC LOGIC, COGNITIVE PROCESSING, AND INFORMATION THEORY

In cognitive psychology and information-processing models, information is understood to be stored in long-term memory (LTM). Information is usually taken to be stored in the form of *nodes*. A node represents a unit of information that may be interrelated in complex ways (Kintch, 1972; Schneider & Shaffrin, 1977). Some nodes contain sensory-perceptual knowledge of facts and others store semantic or propositional knowledge. The similarity between Aristotle's two kinds of pre-existent knowledge and the kinds of information stored in LTM is striking. This information may be stored in LTM by highly organized and interconnected conceptual networks (Anderson, 1981; Puff 1979) wherein concepts may be represented as nodes and lines connecting the nodes stand for meaningful associations between concepts (Frederiksen, 1984, p. 364). Since, on the Hintikka version of erotetic logic, the presuppositions of questions *are* the conceptual presuppositions, it is natural to consider the conceptual network stored in LTM as comprised of the logical presuppositions of questions and their connections. Information in the form of presuppositions stored in LTM provides the requisite prior knowledge for initiating inquiry.

In cognitive psychology matters dealing with the initiation of inquiry are discussed in terms of the *problem representation*. Newell and Simon (1972) divide problem representation into the concepts of *task environment* and *problem space*. The task environment is, on their model, comprised of facts, concepts, and their relationships that make up the problem: the question posed by the computer. The problem space is defined by Newell and Simon as the problem solver's (student's) mental representation of the task environment. The facts, concepts (meanings), and their relationships comprising the Inquirer's problem space must initially be drawn from LTM. These constraints on the initial construction of the problem space are precisely the same as the constraints of pre-existent knowledge described by Aristotle. Erotetics renders the notion of problem space precise, at the price of mental content perhaps, by depsychologizing the notion of problem space in terms of logical space.

Inquiry is initiated from the presuppositions and their relationships, along with any facts available to the student. Conceptual presuppositions and facts are not independent. In recent years philosophers of science have spoken of the "theory-ladenness" of phenomena, data, or facts (Hanson, 1958). The argument is that there are no theory-independent facts, but rather that facts are dependent on the theory; or, more exactly, facts are dependent upon the concepts that comprise the theory. It is theory that allows us to recognize and interpret phenomena *as* something. Rather than speak of the theory or even concept-ladenness of observation, we would rather follow Hintikka and Hintikka (1982, p. 66) and speak of the question-ladenness of observation. Psychologists usually speak of what we are calling question-ladenness as "selective attention." We generally prefer the linguistic notion of question-ladenness to that of the psychological notion of "selective attention," although we can loosen this restriction to explore the boundary between the logical and the psycho*logical*. In any event, the student must initiate the inquiry from those presuppositions (and perceptions that the presuppositions make possible) that constitute the student's problem space. The presuppositions present within the problem space comprise the pre-existing knowledge necessary to overcome the Meno paradox and initiate inquiry.

An inaccurate, inexact, or ambiguous problem representation may make it more difficult, if not impossible, to solve a given problem. Let us consider some of the more obvious logical possibilities. If the student finds the question posed by the computer conceptually confused and/or the putative "facts" referred to by the question false, the Inquirer is likely to reject the question rather than attempt to answer it. The student will seek to dissolve, rather than solve, such a problem. The question "How high can a unicorn jump?" to us, at least, is, in Aristotle's terms, meaningful in the sense that we know the meaning of the words. But we don't believe unicorns exist, so we reject the question. Likewise, we find the question of how many "slithy toves did gyre and gimble in the wabe?" (Dodgson, 1967, p. 501) grammatical but meaningless; and, since we don't know the meaning of the words, we are skeptical, without good reason perhaps, about the existence of their referents. Do "slithy toves" exist? Likewise, conceptual confusion and false presuppositions on the part of the student can confound inquiry. Perhaps unicorns exist and are in fact the cause of quantum leaps in physics. Perhaps an occupant of the looking glass world, say Humpty Dumpty, would know what a "tove" is. The prominent nineteenth-century logician C. L. Dodgson provided perhaps the most famous example of the difficulties and dangers of inquiry in regions where our everyday presuppositions fail to hold. We have in mind *Alice in Wonderland*.

The gap within the problem representation that lies between the student's problem space and the task environment set by the computer's question may be said to constitute, in terms of cognitive psychology, a cognitive gap. The student's task is to completely close this gap.

It does not stretch credibility at all far if we identify the problem space with the premises (in a very loose sense of the term) available to the student in carrying out a deduction or proof of some theorem or conclusion. Nor is it unnatural to equate the task environment with the final conclusion of some logical deduction or proof. If we look at things this way, we may think of the student's intellectual predicament as being the task of eliminating uncertainty by closing the "logical gap" between premises and conclusion.

Admittedly, this identification is partial and incomplete, but once we begin to allow the student to make interrogative moves, that is, ask information-seeking questions to the computer, the difference between the logical and cognitive situations becomes less pronounced. Nevertheless, the difference between a logical and a cognitive gap does not disappear. The logical represents an ideal that may be grasped a priori whereas the psycho*logical* requires empirical, a posteriori, considerations. The similarities between the two situations, however, permit us to construct a logical home for cognitive psychology that helps us better understand the enterprise of cognitive research. For one thing this similarity will allow us to study some of the erotetic teaching "moves" available as strategical options in the *process* of problem solving. Another, and unexpected, result is that the overlap between the notions of logical gap and cognitive gap allows us to offer some measure of a problem's difficulty. Developing such a measure has remained a recalcitrant research problem for cognitive researchers into problem-solving activity. The ability of erotetic logic to make some headway regarding the problem of measuring a problem's difficulty provides good reason to pursue the idea of erotetics and problem solving further.

AN EROTETIC MEASURE OF A PROBLEM'S DIFFICULTY

If we conceive the student's intellectual predicament to be the elimination of uncertainty by closing the gap between the problem space and the task environment within the problem representation, we may think of the width of the logical (epistemological or cognitive) gap as providing an intuitive indication of a problem's difficulty. The question is, How may we provide a definite measure of cognitive distance?

In order to measure anything, it is necessary to have something to compare and count. What we will compare and count are the presuppositions of problems. The problem space is comprised of presuppositions, their relations, and the facts that the interrelated presuppositions make it possible to recognize. The same, of course, may be said of the task environment, since it is itself a question posed by the computer to the student. Inquiry must begin with the confines of problem space, since the only questions that can be asked by the student to the computer must be those formulated from the presuppositions found there. A first approximation to a measure of the difficulty of a problem is to count the number of presuppositions found in the task environment. The measure of a problem's difficulty would then be the number of presuppositions present in the task environment missing from the problem space. A more refined notion would be to count the number of presuppositions and their relations in the task environment. The measure of a problem's difficulty would then be the number of presuppositions and their relations in the task environment that are missing from the problem space. This helps, but it is still not nearly good enough.

What remains to be taken into consideration is that it will oftentimes be necessary, in order solve a problem, to introduce additional presuppositions that do not appear either in the problem space (premises or axioms) or the task environment (conclusions or theorems). An example is when we introduce "auxiliary constructions" in solving geometrical problems. Another is when we introduce "auxiliary variables" in order to obtain as many variables as equations in solving an algebraic problem. We will make use of the geometrical example below.

Simon (1973, 1978) distinguishes between *well-structured* and *ill-structured* problems. Well-structured problems only require the information (presuppositions) contained in the task environment and problem space, including what is readily retrievable from LTM. The criteria defining ill-structured problems are that they (a) are more complex and have less definite criteria for determining when the problem has been solved, (b) do not provide all the information necessary to solve the problem, and (c) have "no legal move generator" for finding all the possibilities of each step.

Greeno (1973) distinguishes *productive* from *reproductive* thinking. Reproductive thinking (or inquiry) only requires the application of a rule or algorithm readily retrieved from LTM. Productive thinking requires that additional information be gathered or old information be organized in fresh new combinations. Frederiksen (1984) suggests that the views of Simon and Greeno might be combined to yield three categories. The first type of problem Frederiksen calls "well structured." These problems are clearly formulated, some algorithm for their solution is well known, and criteria are available for testing the correctness of the solution. Frederiksen gives the example of finding the area of a right triangle. The second type of problem labeled "structured problems requiring productive thinking" is similar to well-structured problems except that "the problem-solving procedure, or some crucial step in the procedure, must be generated by the problem solver" (Frederiksen, 1984, p. 367). Frederiksen refers to Greeno's geometry problems "that require the addition of construction lines to generate a proof" (p. 367), as an example. Finally, the third category contains the ill-structured problems that "lack a clear formulation, a procedure that guarantees a correct solution, and criteria for evaluating solutions" (Frederiksen, 1984, p. 367). Frederiksen observes that most social and political as well as many scientific problems fall into this category. There is, as we are about to see, a third geometrical example for this category as well. Frederiksen concludes by noting that the category a problem falls in is, in part, relative to the *background knowledge* of the problem solver.

It is possible to illustrate each of the three levels of problem-solving difficulty by means of a geometrical example. Geometrical problem solving has long been considered a paradigm example of problem solving in general. Since, as we are about to see, there exists a fairly sharp measure of the difficulty of a geometrical problem, it is possible, mutatis mutandis, to provide a reasonably accurate measure of any problem.

Geometrical constructions, traditionally auxiliary constructions by geometers, represent the introduction of geometrical presuppositions that are not found either in the statement of the theorem (or problem) or in the original axioms (background knowledge). In what follows we propose to generalize the notion of geometrical presuppositions to conceptual presuppositions in general. Similarly, the idea of axioms will be expanded to mean the presuppositions possessed by the student within the initial problem space from whence inquiry is to proceed. The idea of a geometrical theorem will likewise be generalized to include the extent of any task environment. Nor is this generalization farfetched, since antiquity geometrical proof has been taken as the paradigm of problem-solving activity. As it turns out, geometry will show itself to be but a shining example of a more general pattern.

Geometrical problems that require no auxiliary constructions are well structured and require only reproductive thinking to solve. This does not mean that there is no gap to be bridged by thinking, only that the student will not need to produce anything beyond what is already available in the axioms in order to prove the theorem. Nothing new is required to close the gap between the student's problem space and the task environment of the problem. An instance of closing such a gap was given by Aristotle earlier where the student recognized "this figure inscribed in the semicircle" (71a20-25, p. 110). We might say the student already possessed the algorithm or solution schema, but she was unable to recognize the particular instance of it before her. Well-structured, reproductive problems require that no new presuppositions be introduced into the original problem representation, although it may still be necessary to structure them in an unfamiliar way in order to solve the problem.

A second class of geometrical problems requires the introduction of one or more auxiliary constructions in their solution. These problems are clearly productive. Following Hintikka and Remes (1974), we might say that the number of requisite auxiliary constructions are a measure of the non-triviality of the reasoning requisite to proving the theorem from the given axioms. More generally, we might say that the number of presuppositions that must be introduced into the original problem representation in order to solve the problem provides a fairly precise measure of a problem's difficulty.

In the course of carrying out the concomitant proof of a geometrical theorem in first-order logic, it is often necessary to introduce auxiliary *individuals* in the intermediate stages of the proof between the axioms and the theorem to be proved, just as it is necessary to introduce auxiliary variables and constructions in algebra and geometry. It can be shown (as a consequent of the Church corollary to the Gödel incompleteness theorem), that the number of these additional individuals cannot always be predicted recursively on the basis of the theorem. When this occurs, there is no decision method, or recursive procedure; in other words, there is "no legal move generator."

Infinite register machines, that is, computers, operate recursively (following primarily first-order logic). Category three problems are not computable. This does not mean the problems are insoluble; a human operator might solve such a problem quite readily. It only means that the problem is ill structured from a computability perspective. Let us designate category three problems as those problems calling for productive thinking that are not Turing machine computable.

Computer problems can, of course, be of all three types. Artificial intelligence researchers are working on heuristic strategies to help computers mimic human intelligence in solving category three problems (e.g., chess playing programs). Nevertheless, it still remains a rare day that a computer beats a chess master, whether or not the problem is recursively decidable.

The measure of the difficulty we have developed is ex post facto; but then, except for the most trivial problems, we do not know until after the fact whether the theorem or problem is true, much less solvable. Goldbach's conjecture that every even number greater than six is the sum of two odd primes is easy to state, but it has remained unproven either way for hundreds of years.

To summarize, we may say that a well-structured, nonproductive problem will require for its solution no additional presuppositions beyond those found in the original problem space. Well-structured productive problems are recursively decidable, but will require, at some stage of their solution, the introduction of at least one additional presupposition not found in the problem space. The degree of difficulty may be gauged by the number of new presuppositions that must be introduced in the course of the proof. Finally, ill-structured problems may be considered as problems that are recursively undecidable.

Let us close with a brief note on why it is necessary to ignore the production of novel, conceptual presuppositions, as such, in developing our measure of a problem's difficulty.

Productive thinking that requires the production of novel conceptions, that is, new "meanings," cannot be measured. In this sense they may be said to constitute a fourth distinct category. The introduction of such concepts as the sum of the interior angles of a triangle is greater (or less) than 180° or the fundamental processes of nature occur by quantum leaps represent distinctly *qualitative* changes in inquiry. The production of new meanings revolutionizes thinking in the sense popularized by Thomas Kuhn (1970) in his book *The Structure of Scientific Revolutions*. In such circumstances Jabberwocky begins to make sense. We might even begin to look for "slithy toves" or massless particles. New meanings redefine and redirect the line of inquiry in unpredictable ways.

THE LOGICAL HOME OF THE PROBLEM-SOLVING PROCESS

In what follows we will concentrate on some of the logical constraints placed upon and strategical possibilities open to the student in the course of seeking an answer to the initial question posed by the computer. Let us call the initial question the "big" question to distinguish it from the smaller questions the student might ask in answering the initial question. To help fix our thinking, we may conceive of the initial question as a conclusion the student seeks to "prove" from the set of presuppositions available in the problem space. To carry out this proof the student has two basic moves available. They are (a) deductive moves and (b) interrogative moves. Deductive moves are the usual steps of inference made in genuine deductive proofs, and interrogative moves are questions posed to some source of information; that is, the computer. (Unlike genuine deductive proof, interrogative moves are information seeking.) Interrogative moves introduce an inductive element into the inquiry. If the question is well-formulated and the source of information answers and answers honestly, the student knows more than before. For instance, the student may acquire new presuppositions that amplify and help propel the inquiry forward to a successful solution. We assume that the computer is always veridicial.

The constraints and possibilities are largely determined by the presuppositions necessary to formulate an appropriate question. Certainly the golden rule of asking information-seeking questions is to ask the question that provides the most information, that is, reduces the most uncertainty for the student, or equivalently, to ask the question that eliminates the most alternatives compatible with what the student already knows. One might wonder, then, why the student doesn't always just ask the computer the "big" question outright? The answer is that the student may simply not have all the presuppositions requisite to formulating the question available in the original problem space. Classically the error of posing a question before first establishing its presuppositions is known as "the fallacy of begging the question." An ancient Greek tragedy would commonly involve the tragic hero misinterpreting an ambiguous question he had posed to the Oracle at Delphi. Common sense counsels against jumping to conclusions.

As we have seen in our discussion of Aristotle's solution to the *Meno* paradox, it is possible in one sense to know something and in another not. Let us discuss two erotetically interesting ways in which this can happen. The first way involves the use of questions to elicit *tacit* knowledge. Tacit knowledge is simply knowledge already stored in LTM that must be retrieved and placed in short-term (STM) or working memory. Working memory contains information that is actively being used. Failure to activate presuppositions stored in LTM would needlessly deplete the information available in the original problem space and thereby give rise to unnecessary difficulties in problem resolution.

Tacit knowledge is elicited by the Inquirer posing a question to himself or herself. Self-directed questioning is, in the language of cognitive psychology and information processing, an instance of a *metacognitive* or *executive* processing function. Another use of metacognitive questions is to elicit *implicit* knowledge.

Because of the interconnections between presuppositions or nodes in LTM, it is possible to derive more information from LTM than was, in one sense, originally stored there (Bower, 1978). No one is logically omniscient. That is, no one is consciously aware of all of the deductive consequences of everything he or she knows. Sometimes, if the student can recognize structural relations between concepts, it is possible to *derive* additional information from LTM. One way of accomplishing this is by the student engaging in a self-questioning activity by means of information-ordering questions. Such questions will have an "if-then" or some other logical structure.

New presuppositions open up new lines of inquiry. One way of obtaining such new presuppositions is, as previously indicated, from the answers to earlier questions. Another way is to simply guess, that is, formulate questions containing a *hypothetical* presupposition. Hypothetical questioning arises in the context of problems requiring productive thinking. Such questions can be quite effective in drawing out implicit knowledge by placing the hypothesis in the antecedent ("if") position in an if-then question asked of one's self. Similarly, in science, this strategy manifests itself in the hypothetico-deductive method wherein the student postulates an hypothesis, deductively draws some empirical consequences from the hypothesis and other already-present presuppositions, and then asks nature an experimental question. A favorable answer is then said to confirm the hypothesis. Cognitive psychologists (e.g., Moshiman, 1978; Mynatt, Doherty, & Tweney, 1977) have demonstrated a dangerous "confirmatory bias" in solving problems that required hypotheses for their solution. This bias poses a serious threat to successful inquiry (see also Bruner, Goodnow, & Austin 1956).

False presuppositions may arise in many different ways: "Confirmatory bias" is just one; false instruction is another. There are others. False presuppositions need not prove fatal to inquiry, although they often are. It is possible to be right for the wrong reasons. False presuppositions do not preclude the inquiry from succeeding, as the history of science amply testifies, but it does limit the number of questions that can be answered correctly and must eventually misdirect inquiry and mislead the student. Detecting and correcting such false presuppositions and the relations they enter into is not unlike debugging faulty problem-solving programs (e.g., see Brown & Burton, 1978).

Newell and Simon have found that many problem solvers will spontaneously gravitate toward a heuristic they call *means-ends analysis*. In this heuristic the Inquirers will repeatedly compare their present state with the desired end state and attempt to determine the size of what we have been calling the logical gap between where the student is and where the student would like to be in the hope of determining what can be done to close the gap. The inquiry is linear and proceeds sequentially with each step intended to draw the Inquirer ever closer to the solution. In the logic of questions and answers, each step would correspond to asking "smaller" information-seeking questions in the hopes of eliminating some of the epistemological alternatives to the actual situation; that is, the answer to the "big" question. The logic of *means-ends analysis* is captured by what we called in an earlier chapter, a chain of questions.

Some of the shortcomings of *means-ends analysis* is that it is usually only effective with well-structured problems and that it rarely provides for the induction of novel concepts. Erotetic logic illuminates these shortcomings. First, we note that, if the actual solution is not in the initial set of epistemological alternatives, *means-ends analyses*, proceeding by smaller information-seeking questions intended to eliminate alternatives, will not generate these alternatives and so will not turn up the answer. Recall, however, that dialectic has been viewed as a logic of discovery of sorts since antiquity. The reason is twofold. First, we may introduce new presuppositions by hypothesis. Second, answers from computer Oracle may introduce new presuppositions into the inquiry. New presuppositions alter the set of epistemological alternatives compatible with the presuppositions of the student and, hopefully, the actual situation may be found in the altered set. Productive thinking calls for divergent as well as convergent thinking.

Perhaps the best known problem-solving heuristic consists in merely instantiating the problem statement—that is, providing a visual concrete image in place of an abstract linguistic statement. In the logic of questions and answers, this is tantamount to instantiating some of the presuppositions available in the problem space. This is, of course, precisely what the ancient geometer did when he or she drew a geometrical figure upon the slate or in the dust. Presuppositions may be instantiated so as to formulate a question. This is commonly the case when the student instantiates hypothetical presuppositions as when the student "tries" an auxiliary construction or sets up an experiment (a question put to nature), usually with the hypothesis as the dependent variable. Remarkably, those who study problem solving tend to ignore this heuristic altogether. It is, however, easy to grasp why this heuristic works. By representing the stored information in external space, it is no longer necessary to store it in working memory ("mental space") whose limited storage capacity (7 ± 2 items) may then be freed to process other information.

The foregoing represents but a small sample of some of the strategical possibilities and logical constraints on problem solving that may be mapped out using the logic of questions and answers.

Finally we conclude by noting the concept of feedback plays a crucial role in cognitive theory and information-processing models of inquiry. In erotetic inquiry the role of feedback is fulfilled by the computer's answer to the student's information-seeking questions.

Atkinson (1976), reflecting on why psychology has not had a great impact on education, argued that what is required is not only theories about how skills and facts are learned, but also about how knowledge structures are acquired. He indicates "how knowledge is represented in memory, how information is retrieved . . . how new information is added to the structure, and how the system can expand that structure by self-generative processes" (p. 82). Hopefully this paper has made some contribution toward answering these difficult questions about psychological structure by exposing some of the underlying and oftentimes hidden logical structure.

REFERENCES

Atkinson, R. C. (1976). Adaptive instructional systems: The learning process. In D. Klahr (Ed.), *Cognition and instruction* (pp. 81-108). Hillsdale, N.J.: Erlbaum.

Ausubel, D. P. (1968). *Educational psychology: A cognitive view*. New York: Holt, Rinehart, & Winston.

Bower, G. H. (1978). Contacts of cognitive psychology with social learning theory. *Cognitive Therapy and Research, 2*, 123-146.

Brown, J. S., & Burton, R. R. (1978). Diagnostic models for procedural bugs in basic mathematical skills. *Cognitive Science, 2*, 155-192.

Bruner, J. S., Goodnow, J. J., & Austin, G. A. (1956). *A study of thinking*. New York: Wiley.

Frederiksen, Norman. (1984). Implications of cognitive theory for instruction in problem solving. *Review of Educational Research, 54*(3), 363-407.

Garrison, J. W. (in press). The impossibility of atheoretical educational research. *Journal of Educational Thought*.

Greeno, J. G. (1973). The structure of memory and the process of solving problems. In R. Salso (Ed.), *Contemporary issues in cognitive psychology* (pp. 103-131). The Loyola Symposium. Washington, D.C.: Winston.

Hanson, N. R. (1958). *Patterns of discovery*. New York: Cambridge University Press. (See especially pp. 4-11 and 15-49.)

Hintikka, J. (1976). The semantics of questions and the questions of semantics. (Monograph Series). Amsterdam, The Netherlands: North-Holland Publishers.

Hintikka, J., & Hintikka, M. B. (1982). Sherlock Holmes confronts modern logic: Toward a theory of information-seeking through questioning. In E. M. Booth & J. L. Martens (Eds.), *Argumentation approaches to theory formation* (pp. 55-76). Amsterdam, The Netherlands: John Benjamins.

Hintikka, J. & Remes, U. (1974). *The method of analysis*. Dordrect, Holland: D. Reidel Publishing.

Kintsch, W. (1972). Notes on the structure of semantic memory. In E. Tulving & W. Donaldson (Eds.), *Organization of memory* (pp. 247-308). New York: Academic Press.

Kuhn, Thomas S. (1970). *The structure of scientific revolutions*. Chicago: University of Chicago Press.

McKeon, R. (Ed.) (1941). *The basic works of Aristotle*. New York: Random House.

Moshman, D. (1979). Development of formal hypothesis-listing ability. *Developmental Psychology, 15*, 104-112.

Mynatt, C. R., Doherty, M. E., & Tweney, R. D. (1977). Confirmation bias in a simulated research environment: An experimental study of scientific inference. *Quarterly Journal of Experimental Psychology, 29*, 85-95.

Newell, A., & Simon, H. A. (1972). *Human problem solving*. Englewood Cliffs, NJ: Prentice-Hall.

Plato, All references to passages from Plato are taken from *The Collected Dialogues of Plato*. (1961). Edith Hamilton & Huntington Cairns (Eds.) Princeton, NJ: Princeton University Press.

Puff, C. R. (Ed). (1979). *Memory organization and structure*. New York: Academic Press.

Simon, H. A. (1973). The structure of ill-structured problems. *Artificial Intelligence, 4*, 181-201.

Simon, H. A. (1978). Information-processing theory of human problem solving. In W. K. Estes (Ed.), *Handbook of learning and cognitive processing: Vol. 5. Human information processing* (pp. 271-295). Hillsdale, NJ: Erlbaum.

L. Pend Armistead
John K. Burton

Creative Computer Problem Solving

In recent years, there has been increased interest in the development of artificially intelligent systems. The research on artificial intelligence has produced computational models for such complex processes as "vision, language comprehension, knowledge representation, learning, inferring reasoning, planning, and language production" (Wilson & Bates, 1981, p. 336). Further, systems such as PILOT, TICCIT, AND GNOSIS are capable of "understanding" course content, possess interactive processing abilities, and can adjust to fluctuating thought processes (Brown & Burton, 1978). Unfortunately, the critical questions and observations have risen concerning the construction of these superhuman faculties (Longuet-Higgins, 1982, p. 225). As noted by Wilson and Bates (1981), for example, although these systems possess an "impressive amount of intelligence" (p. 337) their expertise is in limited domains and imperfections are vast. Perhaps, however, these weaknesses stem not so much from a failing in the technology of artificial intelligence, but from a lack of understanding of how intelligence is applied to solving problems creatively.

As defined by Ausubel, Novak, and Hanesian (1978), problem solving is "hypothesis-oriented discovery learning requiring the transformation and reintegration of existing knowledge" (p. 556) to fit the demands of a means-end relationship. It involves discovery learning in the sense that prior learning experiences or schemata are combined with components of a current problem to create "a transformed or reintegrated knowledge base" (p. 566).

Creativity, involving "novel or original transformation of ideas"

L. PEND ARMISTEAD is Assistant Dean of Instruction, John Wood Community College, Quincy, IL.
JOHN K. BURTON is Associate Professor, Educational Psychology, Education Microcomputer Lab, Virginia Tech, Blacksburg, VA 24061.

and the generation of new "superordinate and explanatory principles" (Ausubel et al., 1978, p. 556), may be viewed as the highest expression of problem solving. Newell and Simon (1972) state that problem solving is termed creative when the problem solved is of a new and different context.

CREATIVITY

As noted by Amosov (1967), "creativity is the most important feature distinguishing man from the lower animals" (p. 137). Generally, the human process is assumed to involve a certain flash of insight which reveals solutions to problems that have been worked on over a period of time. Yet, according to George (1979), there seems to be no reason that the processes and characteristics of human creativity cannot be employed in the constructs of an artificial system. However, there are some theoretical and logistical conflicts that are in need of consideration (George, 1979; Wolfe, 1983).

Definitions of creativity are often misleading with none being universally agreed upon (Lesner & Hillman, 1983; Taylor, 1975). Earlier definitions tend to be unitary in nature, focusing solely on sources or origins of creativity. Morgan (1953) compiled a list of 25 definitions of creativity, most of which imply that the concept is a process of establishing unique development. Spearman (1931), for example, describes creativity as "the power of the human mind to create new content" (p. 18). Jung, as cited by Lesner and Hillman (1983, p. 103), expands upon a principle of synchronicity. This concept suggests the simultaneous joining of two meaningful but not causally connected events, which in final form produces a unique construct.

If we strictly apply most definitions of human creativity to artificially intelligent system, such systems will never be deemed creative. However, as Wolfe (1983) contends, there are distinct levels of creativity represented by a three-level hierarchy:

1. The independent structuring of primarily imitative ideas into a unified whole such that the same pattern of ideas is never exactly replicated at a different time or effort.
2. The evolution of ideas that are original relative to the person or machine generating those ideas.
3. Fully original ideas that have no precedence in human culture. (p. 59)

From this perspective present artificial intelligence (AI) systems are incapable of original processing but can accomplish the first order task of imitation. However, by focusing on the first level or lowest order, what is essential to the ability to create within the grasp of AI capabilities is the ability to imitate. This ability is exemplified by the act of random selection, a component of the algorithmic principles (Wolfe, 1983).

Nominally at best then, under Wolfe's (1983) specifications, one can state that an AI system is able to create. Presently, however, there are still many more human tasks that are not in the realm of machine creative capabilities such as artificial matching of human inconsistencies in thought patterns. This problem becomes of greater magnitude when the systems acquire greater utilization in areas requiring something more than logical, low level, creative thoughts (i.e., air traffic control, air defense, and nuclear power). Generally, definitions suggest two primary components of creativity which differentiate and distinguish human creative thinking from AI creativity: process and product (Taylor, 1975).

PROCESS

According to Getzels (1975), definitions of creativity are formulated in terms of an underlying process. Ghiselin (1952) speaks of creativity as a process of change and development in the "psychic life of an individual leading to invention" (p. 6). In Wallas' 1976 work entitled *Art of Thought*, the author cites four stages in forming a unique thought: (a) preparation (information is gathered), (b) incubation (unconscious work is going on), (c) illumination (inspired solutions emerge), and (d) verification (solutions are tested and elaborated). In a similar context, Gordon (1961) has developed a process based upon synectics. This model involves considerable use of analogies and metaphors as tools to develop the problem-solving technique of inventive strategy. Therefore, as noted by Getzels (1975), methods for facilitating creativity rest upon the assumption that the process of thinking can be separated from the content of thought so that one can learn a general cognitive strategy outside the confines of a particular structure of knowledge. In a similar context, Taylor (1975) cites Rossman who proposes a more detailed set of steps, including:

1. an initial need or difficulty observed,
2. problem formulated,
3. available information surveyed,
4. solutions formulated,
5. solutions critically examined,
6. new ideas formulated, and/or
7. new ideas tested and accepted. (p. 197)

Thurstone (1962), in a definitive approach, assumes that the creative performance is "characterized by the moment of insight which is often preceded by nonverbalized prefocal thinking" (p. 52). Ribot (1900) describes creativity as "a process of association by which mental states become joined together so that one state tends to involve the other" (p. 649).

Although exact analogies cannot be definitively drawn between the processes of human problem solving and creative thought to the same processes of artificially intelligent systems, significant strides have been made. First and foremost, Longuet-Higgins (1982) states that by attempting to describe the process of human thinking in algorithmic terms, psychologists are able to formulate a more explicit theory of cognitive skills. Furthermore, the concept of an *effective* procedure is also of great importance. In a related context, evaluation and inquiry into scientific theory are enhanced. Artificially based observations disallow the vagueness once attributed to human errors. Thus, retention or rejection of hypotheses can be made with a greater degree of assurance.

PRODUCT

Researchers have also attempted to define or identify creativity by way of its product. Ghiselin (1952) states that a creative product is "intrinsically a configuration of the mind, a presentation of constellated meaning, which at the time of its appearance in the mind was new in the sense of being unique, without a specific precedent" (p. 7). Taylor (1975) cites Spricker, who contends that the product "has the characteristics of being itself creative in the sense that it generates additional creative activity" (p. 19). Placing additional criteria on the term, Jackson and Messick (1965) posit that the generated concept must be novel before it is defined as creative. Furthermore, it must make sense in light of the demands of the situation and the desires of the producer. A third criterion pertains to products of transformation. This criterion involves the extent to which the product reformulates a situation or field. That is, it is concerned with the "power to transform the constraints of reality [which suggests] a defiance of tradition to yield a new perspective" (Jackson & Messick, 1965, p. 312). Finally as noted by Jackson and Messick (1965) and Taylor (1975), the product must unify a great deal of information and be expressed in a highly condensed form.

Researchers of artificial intelligence have recently challenged the issue of novelty. George (1979), in an extension of earlier work by Newell and Simon (1972), speculates that there is no such thing as a new concept existing in the environment other than the expansion of an individual's sensory experience. His contention implies that creative thought is dependent upon the individual's past sensory experience. And it is difficult to imagine providing an artificial system with the processes and experiences necessary to generate thought by any means other than randomization. As such, this trend of thought is consistent with Wolfe's hierarchy, which suggests that AI systems are limited to the imitation level of thought.

A second counterpoint is whether an artificially constructed system can actually manufacture a creative work. As observed by Wolfe (1983), although AI systems such as those able to master a game of checkers or solve I.Q. questions have displayed a degree of creative thought, "a machine has yet to win a composition contest or even compose a first-rate sonnet" (p. 61). Furthermore, if a machine is capable of writing poems or drawing pictures, it is simply producing what is implicit in the instruction of the program. Therefore, what creativity exists is composed by human mentality and not by machine (George, 1979).

One reason for this lag in progress is the nature of creative intelligence. In contrast to the highly logical, convergent, and well-defined traits of rational thinking, creative thought is abstract and intuitive. Thus, in a mechanical sense, it is much more difficult to program. In terms of the earlier accepted definitions of problem solving involving the operations of synthesis and interpretation, the task of analytic composition is obtainable. However, if a creative product is developed by way of ambiguity, emotion, and illogical choices, then AI systems encounter limitations. Contrary to this position and contingent upon the accepted definition of creativity, several authors (Michie & Johnston, 1984; Wolfe, 1983) contend that AI systems can create.

Michie et al. (1984) state that when expert systems were first developed, they were intended to act simply as substitute human experts. It was not believed or suggested that the input would be modified in any capacity. In contrast AI systems have actually helped to modify and improve expert human knowledge (Michie et al., 1984) by taking what was once fragmented and inconsistent and turning it into precise and comprehensive knowledge.

THE DEVELOPMENT OF COMPUTER CREATIVITY

The issue of what constitutes a creative act is controversial. However, it is accepted that many AI programs have the capabilities of simulating thought (Wilson & Bates, 1981). These heuristic procedures (which range from simple randomization to rule-governed processes) are exemplified in a variety of programs. Barr and Feigenbaum (1982) cite expert systems whose creative capabilities cannot altogether be refuted. SCHOLAR is a computer-based tutoring system which has a number of strategies for composing relevant questions, determining the appropriateness of students' responses, and answering a wide realm of questions from the student. Similarly, SOPHIE guides the student through a series of problem-solving strategies, proposing alternative solutions. In cases where the student follows no logical progression, SOPHIE is able to generate counter examples and critiques. And, as observed by Barr and Feigenbaum (1983), the system combines domain-specific knowledge and domain-independent inferencing mechanisms to provide solutions that "even human tutors might find extremely difficult to answer" (p. 252). Similarly Roberts and Park (1983) offer a system which is representative of structured knowledge. SPADE, through use of formal grammars, provides a basis for characterizing and structuring problem-solving sequences. SPADE maintains a tree-structured phase of a user's problem-solving activity that is used to monitor the student's behavior and to assist in developing "adequate problem-solving skills" (Roberts & Park, p. 107).

In general, AI research has only begun to investigate problems of representing the human creative processes. Continued development on expert systems could possibly offer a more definitive unyielding answer to the question: Can computers create? As recognized by Barr and Feigenbaum (1982), extant systems allow for interactive techniques through various reasoning and inferencing processes. Further research will provide expert systems with the capabilities of offering solutions to questions from an entirely new domain, through generation of original thought.

REFERENCES

Amosov, N.M. (1967). *Modeling of thinking and the mind*. New York: Spartan Books.

Ausubel, D.P., Novak, J.D. & Hanesian, H. (1978). *Educational psychology: A cognitive view*. New York: Holt, Rinehart & Winston.

Barr, A., & Feigenbaum, E. A. (1982). *The handbook of artificial intelligence, II*. California: Heuristech Press.

Brown, J.S., & Burton, R.R. (1978). Diagnostic models for procedural bugs in mathematics. *Cognitive Science, 2*, 176-204.

George, F.H. (1979). *Philosophical foundations of cybernetics*. Kent, Great Britain: Abacus Press.

Getzels, J.W. (1975). Creativity: Prospects and issues. In I.A. Taylor and J.W. Getzels (Eds.), *Perspectives in Creativity* (pp. 326-344). Chicago: Aldine Publishing.

Ghiselin, B. (Ed.) (1952). *The creative process*. Los Angeles: University of California Press.

Gordon, W.J.J. (1961). *Synectics: The development of creative capacity*. New York: Harper.

Jackson, P.W., & Messick, S. (1965). The person, the product, and response. *Journal of Personality, 35*, 309-329.

Lesner, W.J., & Hillman, D. (1983). A developmental schema of creativity. *Journal of Creative Behavior, 17*, 103-113.

Longuet-Higgins, H.C. (1982). A new theoretical psychology. *New Universities Quarterly, 36*, 225-229.

Michie, D. & Johnston, R. (1984). *The creative computer: Machine intelligence and human knowledge*. New York: Viking Press.

Morgan, D.N. (1953). Creativity today. *Journal of Aesthetics, 12*, 1-24.

Newell, A., & Simon, H. (1972). *Problem solving*. Englewood Cliffs, NJ: Prentice-Hall.

Ribot, T. (1900). The nature of creative imagination. *International Quarterly, 1*, 648-675.

Roberts, E.C., & Park, O. (1983). Intelligent computer-assisted instruction: An explanation and overview. *Educational Technology, 23*, 7-11.

Spearman, C. (1931). *Creative mind*. New York: D. Appleton.

Taylor, I.A. (1975). A retrospective view of creativity investigation. In I.A. Taylor & J.W. Getzles (Eds.), *Perspectives in creativity* (pp. 1-36). Chicago: Aldine Publishing.

Thurstone, L.L. (1962). *The scientific study of inventive talent*. New York: Scribner's.

Wallas, G. (1976). *The art of thought*. New York: Harcourt Brace.

Wilson, K., & Bates, M. (1981). Artificial intelligence in computer-based language instructions. *Volta Review, 83*, 331-348.

Wolfe, George, (1983). Creative computers—Do they think? *Music Education Journal, 69*, 59-62.

W. Michael Reed

A Philosophical Case for Teaching Programming Languages

The educational computing community has slowly recovered from earlier claims that students need to be taught programming languages to be prepared for the future job market. This earlier sentiment was based on the observation that computers were becoming more and more a part of our lives (Kelman, 1984). Having thought through this particular issue more carefully and having more accurately observed the nature of the advent of computers, proponents now agree on two crucial points: (a) that computers are, at an alarming rate, becoming routine features of our lives, but (b) that they are becoming more user friendly and, thus, are requiring less knowledge about them. Simply put, there is a negative relationship between the advent of computers and what people need to know about them. Given this recent observation, it makes little sense to teach programming languages to students to prepare them for a future job market. A very small percentage of future jobs will require programming knowledge, and that preparation will be left to undergraduate and graduate computer science programs and professional schools.

So, if preparing students for future jobs is not a valid reason for teaching programming languages, is there a valid reason? The answer is an emphatic yes.

The support for such a contention centers on the reasons we teach what we teach in any content area. One pervasive curricular truism is that we don't teach what we teach because we really think the content is important for our students to know in the future, but rather, we have them use the content to develop thinking skills. A simple test of this line of reasoning can be made by posing and

W. MICHAEL REED is Assistant Professor of Computer Education and English Education, West Virginia University, Morgantown, WV 26506.

reacting to the following scenarios. You can ask most nonscience people what the stages of photosynthesis are, and they most likely will verbally stumble around. You can likewise ask nonmath people about algebraic formulas, and comparable stumbling around will occur. Or, you can ask non-English people where *Hamlet* took place, and they will probably not be able to recall the word *Elsinore*. We were taught these bits of information and had test items—perhaps even verbatim—on the scenarios posed above. The vital point here is not where did the ideas go, but rather why were we taught them and how were we held accountable for them?

Hopefully we were taught them to develop thinking processes. We became aware of the stages of photosynthesis as a series of logical steps of a natural system, how one event affects another, and the similarities between this process and others. We learned algebraic formulas to obtain a sense of variables, how one thing represents another, and even perhaps how the mathematical variable can be compared to the literary symbol. When we studied *Hamlet*, we were asked to write a character analysis, or we became better informed about a historical period, or we increased our awareness of our language, improved our reading ability, became more critical of literature, and practiced our writing skills. Hopefully, the content was used to promote such thinking processes as comprehension, analysis, synthesis, and evaluation; hopefully, we were not held accountable for the ideas for the sake of merely knowing the ideas.

If developing generic strategies to deal with new situations is our major curricular goal, teaching programming languages should not only be in the curriculum but should dominate it, not only because of the thought processes required but also because of their content-free nature (Reed, 1986). The learning of programming languages has a vital place in the curriculum, as much as, and perhaps more than, a goodly portion of any subject area that is presently being taught.

Regardless of the programming language developed primarily for educational purposes—for example, BASIC, Logo, or Pascal—each has a syntax void of any specific content. Because of this "content-voidness," developing thinking processes may even be more possible with programming languages because the content itself does not get in the way as much.

Programming languages are based on operational logic, an area that "modern education has overlooked" (Galanter, 1984, p. 31). Galanter distinguishes operational logic from formal deductive and inductive logic by stating that operational logic involves "the logic of planning and the rational execution of action" (p. 30). Galanter goes on by claiming that programming languages may easily be the language for operational logic: "We have long needed a language for operational logic, and programming languages offer such a structure" (p. 31). Such a line of reasoning is not impractical since "the talk of lawyers, doctors, and psychologists [has been] tailored to their specific tasks" (p. 31).

Much research investigating the link between programming languages and problem-solving skills has been conducted. At best, the results have been inconclusive. In defense of those who feel that a relationship exists, there have been such research design problems as dependent measures and treatment (see Burton & Magliaro, this issue). Although there has been little support for claiming such a relationship, feeling that such a relationship doesn't exist should be held at a standstill until sounder researcher is conducted. Research in any field has gone through early stages of growing pains.

Fortunately, during the last few years, computer proponents have abandoned the sentiment that learning programming languages is essential for the future job market. Rather, they have recognized the potential relationship between learning a programming language and the tapping, developing, and fine-tuning of problem-solving skills. Such an orientation may make us re-think what we teach, how we teach it, and how we should hold our students accountable for the bodies of knowledge that we pass on to them.

REFERENCES

Burton, J.K., & Magliaro, S. (1988). Computer programming and generalized problem-solving skills: In search of direction. *Computers in the Schools, 4*(3/4), Fall/Winter 1987.

Galanter, E. (1984). Homing in on computers. *Psychology Today*, pp. 30-33.

Kelman, P. (1984). Computer literacy: A critical re-examination. *Computers in the Schools, 1*(2), 3-18.

Reed, W.M. (1986). Teachers' attitudes toward educational computing: Instructional uses, misuses, and needed improvements. *Computers in the Schools, 3*(2), 73-80.

RESEARCH ON COMPUTERS AND PROBLEM SOLVING

One of the most intensely investigated topics in educational computing research is the speculated link between learning programming languages and the development of problem-solving skills. One of the most consistent findings from such research has been virtually no support of such a link.

This section begins with John Burton and Sue Magliaro's critical review of many of the studies to date. Their premise is to determine whether such studies have been as soundly constructed as they should be. Some of the weaknesses they have identified are (a) inadequate length of treatment, (b) whether a language was, in fact, actually taught or learned, (c) lack of ideationally rigorous treatment, (d) use of insufficiently sensitive and/or inappropriate dependent measures, (e) lack of a theoretical, problem-solving basis for conducting the studies, and (f) whether the samples were developmentally capable of learning the language to the extent that problem-solving skills might be affected.

The next three research reports reflect a series of studies that investigate the purported link between problem-solving skills and programming languages. The first study, by W. Michael Reed and David Palumbo, centers on the effect of eight weeks of BASIC programming language instruction on problem-solving skills and computer anxiety. They used the guidelines posed by John Burton and Sue Magliaro when constructing their study, with the intent to construct a design that was more sound than the designs of some of the previously conducted research. They found significant problem-solving gains after eight weeks or approximately 81 hours of working with the language. Additionally, they found significant decreases in computer anxiety from pretest to posttest and a significant negative relationship between problem-solving skills and computer anxiety. They also determined relationships between "internal" factors such as positive relationships between prior experience with BASIC and (a) problem-solving skills, (b) debugging competence, and (c) programming performance and negative relationships between computer anxiety and (a) prior experience with BASIC, (b) debugging competence, and (c) programming performance.

The second study, by W. Michael Reed, David Palumbo, and Aletha Stolar, poses two questions: Does learning a programming language affect problem-solving skills? If so, which language—BASIC or Logo—affects problem-solving skills more? As in the first study, they found that both BASIC and Logo do positively affect problem-solving skills, after eight weeks and approximately 81 hours of working with both languages. They also found that one language does not significantly affect problem-solving skills more than the other.

The third study, by David Palumbo and W. Michael Reed, is an attempt to determine at what point problem-solving skills might be measurably affected. They have added another factor to the notion of rigor of treatment identified by John Burton and Sue Magliaro in defining the term, *intensity of treatment*: (a) length of treatment, (b) rigor of treatment sessions, and (c) proximity of treatment sessions. Their treatment focused on BASIC instruction and paralleled the treatment of their previous two studies: approximately 81 hours over an eight-week period. They used the two-stage, problem-solving concept as a design framework: (a) Time must first be spent to establish a linguistic base and to overcome potentially debilitating factors such as anxiety toward computers; and (b) once a linguistic base has been established, the problem solvers can begin to apply and fine-tune strategies. They decided that an appropriate measurement point to determine if problem-solving skills were affected would be the midpoint, or after 40 hours over a four-week period. At midpoint, problem-solving skills had not significantly improved, although computer anxiety had significantly decreased. Such a finding supports their notion that time must be spent simultaneously to build a linguistic base and to overcome potentially debilitating factors. From midpoint to posttest, problem-solving skills had significantly improved, whereas computer anxiety had not decreased significantly. Such findings support the belief that, once a linguistic base is established, students can then use the language for solving problems that might affect problem-solving skills. Although they did not isolate the exact moment problem-solving skills significantly changed, the authors' finding does indicate that many of the treatments in prior studies that have not shown a significant effect on problem-solving skills have either been too brief, not sufficiently rigorous, or both.

The next study is one on adolescents' chunking of computer programs by Susan Magliaro and John Burton. They compared ability of student programmers of differing programming language backgrounds—novice, intermediate, and advanced—to recall lines and chunks of lines of coherent and scrambled programs. They found that all three groups of programmers recalled more program lines and chunks from coherent programs than from scrambled programs. Also, intermediate programmers were more successful at recalling lines and chunks of coherent programs than both novice and advanced programmers. One reason for the superior performance by the intermediate programmers over advanced programmers was that intermediates were being instructed in BASIC and the advanced programmers were being instructed in Pascal; the test was on BASIC. The advanced programmers outperformed the novices and intermediates on the scrambled-program task.

Mike Orey and David Miller's study centers on computer programs constructed to aid in the detection and analysis of student bugs in arithmetic and computer programming problems. They give reasons why none of these systems is adequate in and of itself and explain how a superior system could be constructed through the combination of several of the strategies that are explored. They support some of their points with an analysis of mathematical decisions made by a student research-participant.

Leah McCoy and Mike Orey investigated the effect of computer programming on problem-solving ability and the relationship between ability and problem-solving scores with computer programming achievement. The 120 middle school and high school students received daily instruction on the BASIC programming language for one semester. The results conclude that (a) the problem-solving skills of both middle school and high school students increased significantly from pretest to posttest; (b) programming achievement for both groups likewise increased; (c) problem-solving ability was the only significant correlate of programming achievement for the middle school students; (d) both problem-solving ability and verbal reasoning, however, were significant correlates of programming achievement; and, (e) the only significant predictor variable for programming achievement was general problem-solving ability.

This section ends with another study by Leah McCoy who examined the relationships of six variables: gender, age, developmental level, mathematics background, ability to use mathematical variables, and mathematical problem solving. The research participants were 21 students, ages ranging from 10 to 17 years, enrolled in a two-week computer camp who received instruction on the BASIC programming language. She found a significant relationship between mathematics (higher mathematics courses, mathematical problem-solving ability, and the ability to use mathematical variables) and computer programming achievement. However, the only significant predictor of programming achievement was the ability to use mathematical variables.

The research reported in this section sheds some new light on the link between learning programming languages and developing problem-solving skills. As John Burton and Sue Magliaro point out in their review, researchers must soundly construct their designs before findings can be acceptable guidelines. The subsequent studies indicate that the treatment (or instruction) must be rigorous, have depth, and be applied for a certain period of time. One reason for the promising results of the research in this section may be the developmental capability of the research participants; it may very well be that student programmers must be of a certain developmental age before they can learn a language to the extent that problem-solving skills might be affected. Although much work on the link between programming languages and problem-solving skills still needs to be conducted, these studies are significant contributions to this area.

John K. Burton
Susan Magliaro

Computer Programming and Generalized Problem-Solving Skills: In Search of Direction

Over the course of the last three decades or so, a new field of study, cognitive science, has emerged and developed. As Wilkinson and Patterson (1983) have characterized it, cognitive science is "a field of study at the intersection of linguistics, artificial intelligence, and psychology" (p. 4). Although it may be argued that other disciplines are also at this intersection, particularly anthropology and philosophy, there can be little argument with the notion that the new area represents an interdisciplinary synergy. As such, cognitive science has always been grounded in the basic theories, paradigms, and evidentiary proofs of the elemental disciplines that contribute to it. Not surprisingly, cognitive science has also had a great impact on the conceptual symbols and explanatory patterns found in the parent disciplines, most particularly, on the information-processing framework of cognitive psychology.

Coinciding with the last decade of this development, commercially available microcomputers began to make their way into public school classrooms. Due to the relative low cost of the micros, schools began gathering any and all available resources to permit these devices to be included in the curricula. Since the beginning of the subsequent movement to the present, there has been much said and written about the use of microcomputer programming instruc-

JOHN K. BURTON is Associate Professor of Educational Psychology, Education Microcomputer Lab, Virginia Tech, Blacksburg, VA 24061.
SUE MAGLIARO is a doctoral candidate, Educational Psychology; Center for Reading Diagnosis, Evaluation, and Remediation; Virginia Tech; Blacksburg, VA 24061.

tion as a device to teach higher level cognitive skills (see, e.g., Papert, 1980). In fact, for many of us now engaged in educational cognitive science, this possibility, as well as the potential to model such processes through expert systems, has become a major reason for our decision to forsake the more traditional thrusts of our respective disciplines. From powerful ideas (e.g., Papert, 1980) to fifth-generation prospects (e.g., Feigenbaum & McCorduck, 1984), the claims vary widely but Feurzeig, Horwitz, and Nickerson (1981, as modified by Pea & Kurland, 1984b) offer a reasonable summary of proposed outcomes:

1. rigorous thinking, precise expression, recognized need to make assumptions explicit;
2. understanding of general concepts such as formal procedure, variables, function, and transformation;
3. greater facility with the art of "heuristics," explicit approaches to problems useful for solving problems in any domain, such as planning, finding a related problem, solving the problem by decomposing it into parts, etc.;
4. the general idea that "debugging" of errors is a "constructive and plannable activity" applicable to any kind of problem solving;
5. the general idea that one can invent small procedures such as building blocks for gradually constructing solutions to large problems;
6. generally enhanced "self-consciousness and literacy about the process of solving problems"; and,
7. enhanced recognition that for domains beyond programming there is rarely a single "best" way to do something, but rather different ways that have comparative costs and benefits with respect to specific goals. (p. 8)

Obviously, the critical words and phrases are "the general idea," "domains beyond programming," and "in any domain" which imply transfer of programming gains to other problem-solving areas and the development of general problem-solving skills. Unfortunately, we are as short on evidence as we are long on claims (see also Patterson & Smith, 1986). As computer systems become friendlier, the need to understand languages and operating systems to be literate diminishes. And, as the "gee whiz" factor that characterized the introduction of computers into the schools begins to fade, critics are beginning to voice concern over the lack of evidence to substantiate the promises (e.g., Ginther & Williamson, 1985). We perhaps underestimated the speed at which the public schools would invest in computer systems and thereby underestimated the length of time by which our promises would be called due. As Maddux (1985) points out:

> Singing uncritical praises may be a necessary first step in stimulating curriculum change. If such behavior was ever appropriate, however, it no longer is. Promising more than we can deliver and document is dangerous. We, as computer-enthusiastic educators have been guilty of this in educational computing in general. As a result, we are beginning to see the start of a great backlash of reaction against computers in education. We are being told to justify our claims about the benefits of educational computing. The only convincing way for us to respond is with evidence. (p. 10)

In response to such criticisms, those of us who believe in programming as a device to teach problem-solving skills and processes have rushed to provide evidence, and, in the process, conducted research which was poorly conceived and executed. As a result, much of our evidence is negative or at best inconclusive. Our purpose is to discuss some major problems in the research. Moreover, it is a call for those of us in educational cognitive science and educational computing to pull back from prophecy and return to our laboratories, to cease our attempts at "easy proof" and return to the principles of our root disciplines.

AN INFORMATION-PROCESSING VIEW OF PROBLEM SOLVING

In order to set a context for our remarks it is necessary for us to give a brief overview of the current thought and research in problem solving which has emanated from Newell and Simon's (1972; Simon, 1978) information-processing theory of human problem solving. Since this view of the human system was initially grounded in the computer as a metaphor for the human memory system, the information processing framework has particular appeal as a framework for research on computer programming and problem solving. According to this framework, problem solving is characterized as a complex mental activity that involves the interaction between a task environment and the individual problem solver (Newell & Simon, 1972). The task environment is the description of the problem as presented to the individual. This description includes the information, assumptions, and constraints, as well as the context in which the problem is presented. Based on the perception of the problem and the declarative (facts) and procedural (processes) knowledge that has been learned and stored from past experiences, the problem solver then forms a mental representation or problem space of the problem. It is in this space that the solver evaluates the possible choices, hypotheses, and strategies that may be used to reach a solution.

As a complex thinking process, problem solving is a goal-directed activity that involves a sequence of stages (Polya, 1957). Polya (1957, 1968) outlines four general stages of the processes: (a) understanding the problem, (b) devising a plan, (c) carrying out the plan, and (d) looking back. During this multi-stage course of solving a problem, the solver progresses through a sequence of knowledge states. Each knowledge state contains the information, from the task environment and long-term memory, that is available to the solver at that point in time. Knowledge states are transformed (in this progression) by applying the mental operations deemed appropriate by the solver for that particular state.

Problem solving is influenced by properties of the information-processing system (Kahney, 1986). Perceived information first enters the sensory store, where it is held in its original form for only a brief period of time – less than 250 milliseconds for visual or iconic images (Sperling, 1960) and less than 4 seconds for auditory or echoic sounds (Darwin, Turvey, & Crowder, 1972). Thus, the perceiver must be able to quickly recognize salient cues that will activate relevant information from long-term memory. Short-term memory, the "workbench" (Klatsky, 1980) in which information may be rehearsed, elaborated, and used for decision-making, is limited in both the length of time it can hold information and the amount of information that it can retain (Miller, 1956). If short-term memory is capable of holding only a few units of information, but optimal performance on a task requires that more environmental cues, relevant information, and strategies need to be considered, performance is likely to be less than optimal (Kahney, 1986). Long-term memory, our relatively permanent storage component, is organized according to the way in which information was encoded

(Tulving & Thomson, 1973). Consequently, information that was encoded in ways that differ from the contexts or cues present at retrieval may not be accessed easily, if at all.

In addition to the constraints of the human memory system, individuals differ in the way they solve problems and the success in their activity for a number of reasons. First, people differ in the amount of experience they have had with a particular type of problem. Some individuals may be relative novices, thus having rather simple cognitive structures or organized memories of that specific problem or content area (Norman, 1978). They have not developed the automatic associations between the critical cues in the environment and the relevant stored knowledge. They focus on only superficial or surface features of the problem, often missing those aspects of the task that would allow them to access the appropriate information quickly, thus, leaving them to search their long-term memory in a random or inefficient manner (e.g., Chase & Simon, 1973; Egan & Schwartz, 1979; Larkin, McDermott, Simon, & Simon, 1980).

Second, individuals employ different strategies in solving a particular type of problem (Kahney, 1986). This may be related to the fact that they have not had enough experience to implement a sophisticated versus an elementary solution. Or, through differing past experiences, individuals may have learned different, yet equally efficient, strategies for solving the same problem.

Finally, individuals may pay attention to different aspects of the problem structure based on their conceptions or convictions about what is more important. For example, reading diagnosticians focus on different aspects of a child's reading according to their perception of how people learn to read and what they think is important about the reading process (Leu & Kinzer, 1987).

One concept of human problem solving that underlies the main focus of this critique is the notion of transfer. Transfer of problem-solving skills from one domain to another requires the recognition of related patterns in the alternate domain and the subsequent application of related knowledge or strategies (Greeno, 1980). A distinction must be made between near transfer, which involves new applications that are like the original in many important features (e.g., Dalbey & Linn's [1984] use of a robot rather than a spider which employed a similar computer language syntax), versus remote or far transfer which involves an extension of the learned principle (e.g., Pea & Kurland's [1984a] transfer of knowledge about planning a computer program to developing a plan to clean up a classroom) (Mayer, 1983). It is also useful to distinguish between specific transfer (within a given domain) and generalized or nonspecific transfer (see, e.g., Hudgins, 1977).

The evidence for the transferability of knowledge and skills to new contexts, domains, or task situations is very mixed (Simon, 1980). Problem-solving skill is generally viewed as "specific to a relatively narrow area of expertise, such as algebra, mechanics, or chess" (Frederiksen, 1984, p. 39). In fact, in his review of the problem-solving literature, Frederiksen (1984) reports that "there appears to be little if any transfer from one domain to another; being an expert in chess apparently does not transfer to *go* and skill in solving physics problems does not transfer to politics or economics" (p. 391). Specific to programming is Ginther and Williamson's (1985) observation:

> In contrast to Papert's claims, decades of research on problem solving, with both animal and human subjects, has shown that transfer of general problem-solving skills is difficult to achieve. There is no reason to believe that Logo offers a magical exception to this well-supported generalization. (p. 76)

One area of research that offers some hope to this transfer dilemma is the *explicit* instruction of strategic knowledge within the domain (Greeno, 1980). While this hypothesis needs further study, the general idea of teaching explicitly how to analyze, for example, the relevant features of problem domains and identify those features seems to be a promising avenue.

While this outline of the areas of problem solving and transfer is admittedly brief, we hope that it establishes our orientation and a context for the comments and directions we offer in this paper.

A PRELIMINARY PROBLEM

In reviewing the literature that attempts to relate computer programming and problem solving, it becomes obvious that much of the work has not gone through the usual peer review process. Many citations used in support of the proposed link are derived from books, paper presentations, technical reports, and unpublished dissertations. Clements (1985), for example, includes a brief review of problem solving in his larger review of computer effects. He reviews some 22 sources: eight paper presentations, three technical reports, three unpublished dissertations, one collection of unpublished memos, one book, one book chapter, one article submitted for publication, one in-press article, and three journal articles (one each in the *AEDS Journal, The Bulletin of the Psychonomic Society*, and *Educational Computer*). Similarly, Dalbey and Linn (1985) reviewed 108 sources relating to the demands and requirements of computer programming. Within this larger context, these reviewers cited 11 sources they felt dealt directly with the transfer of problem-solving effects and strategies from programming to other tasks. Of these 11, five are *American Educational Research Association* (AERA) papers, one is an unpublished doctoral dissertation, one is a technical report, one is a book, and three are journal articles. Both reviews are well written and comprehensive given the breadth of their scope. Presumably each review author selected the best sources available given the few pages allocated to generalized problem-solving skills. Yet each found (as we did) that the literature in the area is at present rather informal. Unfortunately, as authors include such works in published works, these informal works gain in weight and credibility. To make our points, we have included many of the more commonly cited works as part of this review. Be assured that many papers were intentionally not included in this review.

THE RESEARCH-RESEARCH GAP

As we prepared to study the suggested link between computer programming and problem solving, we initially tried to categorize the research in the area into some sort of matrix or organizer. Our initial feeling was that a continuum anchored by experimental studies on one end and anthropological or ethnographic studies would likely be the easiest with which to work. Immediately we discovered that, with few exceptions (e.g., Mayer, 1975; McKeithen, Reitman, Reuter, & Hirtle, 1981; Pea & Kurland, 1984a), there were few studies at the experimental end and only one study that we could find (Hawkins, Homolsky, & Heide, 1984) at the interpretive end. (Karen Sheingold and her colleagues [Sheingold, Kane, Endreweist & Billings, 1981; and Sheingold, Hawkins & Char, 1984] have conducted some excellent examples of this genre of research in the area of the social aspects of computers in classrooms, but none focused on problem solving.)

Most of the studies tended to cluster in a zone running from quasi-experimental through descriptive (our center-point) to correlational analyses. It was at this point that we discovered for ourselves what Amarel (1983) has called the "research-research" gap (p. 16). Briefly, Amarel contends that, as a result of trying to close the gap between research and practice, "investigators began to turn to the classroom in the hope that disciplined inquiry into its phenomena would yield a double dividend—gains in general understanding of learning and teaching, and a better grasp of their particular manifestations in schools" (Amarel, 1983, p. 17). We agree with Amarel that the best of these works (such as Barr & Dreeben, 1977; Doyle, 1977; Evertson, Anderson, Anderson, & Brophy, 1980; Kounin, 1970) have made significant specific contributions, as well as general contributions, to our understanding of the complexity of the classroom as a teaching/learning system. It may be that, as Amarel (1983) suggests, these contributions brought an unwelcomed side effect:

> Research conducted in schools diverged from the work going on in more controlled and controllable settings, and further fragmented a weakly integrated field. This development should have been anticipated, as the choice of a particular research setting both reflects and shapes the questions studied, predisposing, at the same time, the class of answers that will result (Shulman, 1981). The benefits, even the necessity, of taking multiple routes to understanding educational phenomena are not at issue; the integration of knowledge derived from the multiple research traditions, however, is a challenge yet to be met. The relationship between instructional events and the students' cognitive activities that mediate learning is not well enough understood to guide teachers' decisions, nor are the effects of different classroom organizations sufficiently clear to determine the design of these settings. Yet, the development of pedagogically sound and classroom-friendly computer instruction is contingent on such understandings—the technology per se does not benefit education. (p. 17)

Although we are not prepared to agree in toto with this analysis, it does appear that the innovative attempts of the researchers mentioned may have been misconstrued to the point that the traditional "rules" were perceived to be relaxed or suspended. In fact, the "disciplined inquiry" these pioneering investigators brought to the classroom was their strength and the source of the ultimate impact that their work has had on the field of teacher education. We recognize valuable work along all areas of the continuum. Like Smith and Heshusius (1986), however, we are concerned at the movement toward qualitative-quantitative detente. We can value an interpretivistic orientation to problem solving and computers (e.g., similar to work involving the ability or inability to solve the same math problems in specific problem-solving contexts such as Brenner, 1985; de la Rocha, 1985; Murtaugh, 1984; Lave, 1985), as well as we can value the theory-based experimental work such as Mayer (1975) and Pea and Kurland (1984a).

We do, however, have some problems with notions such as those expressed by Saloman and Gardner (1986). For example, while we agree that research on computers should be grounded, we are more comfortable (in this case, at least) with grounding the work in problem-solving theory rather than communicational symbol systems. Moreover, while we might concede that "open-ended holistic research" (p. 15) might be a valuable, preliminary first step for many researchers (perhaps even to be shared in informal paper sessions), we find that too much of this work finds its way into the literature and dilutes the accepted body of knowledge. In this context we find descriptive studies such as Bell (1978) to be excellent exemplars of preliminary investigation (in this case, an attempt to describe the incidence and type of programming errors committed by novice programmers). Nor do we question the straightforward correlational reports such as Fisher and Mandinach (1985) which primarily focus on the relationships among a large array of individual difference variables and programming performance. Such studies are conducted and reported "within themselves"; they are consistent with the purposes and assumptions of such research. Many of the studies we reviewed, however, appear to fall squarely within Amarel's (1983) research-research gap. In general, we contend that research that purports to combine both qualitative and quantitative paradigms is obliged to meet the assumptions and standards of *both* orientations.

THEORETICAL AND/OR LITERATURE BASE

Probably the most striking problem with the research involving computer programming and problem solving is the lack of any real basis for the studies and, as a result, the lack of any anchor points to tie the findings back into the literature. In some cases this is because problem solving emerges more as an afterthought or throw-in variable than as a focus of the study (e.g., Brooks, 1973).

In other cases, the failure to consider relevant literature may be because computers and computer programming are considered to be self-justifying. Clements and Gullo (1984), for example, studied the effects of computer programming (24, 40-minute Logo classes versus 24 exposures to computer-assisted instruction [CAI]) on cognitive style, metacognition, cognitive development, and directionality without a single citation in the areas of cognitive style, metacognition, cognitive development, or directionality. In part, this lack of a literature base leads the authors to a "kitchen sink" approach, using 8 tests (actually some 18 subtests and totals) (c.f. Saloman & Gardner, 1986; "experimentation that casts a wide net of measures ought to be carried out" [p. 17]). In a similar fashion Soloway, Lochhead, and Clement (1982) investigated programming effects on problem solving without reference to the problem-solving literature; Spider World is developed, described, implemented, and reported (Dalbey & Linn, 1984) without reference to the problem-solving literature; and Dillashaw and Bell (1985) investigated programming and logical thinking without reference to the logical reasoning literature. On the other hand, researchers such as Gorman and Bourne (1983), Mayer (1975), McKeithen et al. (1981), Pea (1983), Pea and Kurland (1984a), and Pohl and Nutter (1985) do establish such a base and the "payoff" (not surprisingly) is in "tighter" hypotheses and methodology as well as conclusions which can be interpreted.

It is beyond the scope of this work to review all the relevant literature for such studies but consider briefly the issue of whether in Dillashaw and Bell's (1985) concluding words, "10 weeks (34 hrs.) may be too short a time period to expect much growth in logical thinking skills" (p. 10), or, for that matter, 15 hours (Webb, 1984a), or 8 sessions from 5-20 minutes over 2 months (Sprigle & Schaefer, 1984), or 30 hours over 1 year (Pea & Kurland, 1984a), or 16 hours over 12 weeks (Clements & Gullo, 1984).

Development of expertise in a complex area is estimated to require between 5,000 (Norman, 1978) and 10,000 hours of practice with feedback (Simon, 1980). Computer programming is generally considered to be a complex skill (Bell, 1978; Brooks, 1977; Pea & Kurland, 1983). Even the most liberal estimate of expertise in programming (Linn, 1985) is at least 500 hours, and this figure is apparently derived from Kurland, Mawby, and Cahir's (1984) study in which six "*very bright* boys" (p. 13), identified as programming experts, reported 550 to 3,850 hours as their total programming time. Norman (1978) characterizes the first third of the development of expertise, accretion, as a period of knowledge accumulation marked by low transfer. The participants in the majority of the studies cited in this paper would be classified as novices (see e.g., Dreyfus & Dreyfus, 1986; Egan & Schwartz, 1979). Kurland, Mawby, and Cahir (1984) note that "many students fail to achieve even a modest understanding after one or two programming courses" (p. 2). Even adult novices in any given domain typically are able to identify only some of the relevant symbols by name (e.g., Egan & Schwartz, 1979). Linn and Dalbey (1985) studied six schools that taught computer programming for between 25-84 hours and noted that a "striking finding was that the majority of students made very limited progress in programming" (p. 202).

Consider the fact that many participants in the programming studies are children, most of whom are still in the concrete operational stage or at the brink of the formal operations stage of cognitive development (Piaget, 1970; and as noted by Dillashaw & Bell, 1985). Moreover, consider that these children presumably lack the prior knowledge gathered by adulthood. As such, any expectation of a measurable change in a higher order cognitive skill after a 15- to 30-hour computer language learning experience is suspect. Further, our present understanding of cognitive development indicates that children's problem solving is "mediated by sub-processing deficiencies" (Gross, 1985, p. 157). For example, children may not have developed the strategies to differentiate between stimulus dimensions (Gross, 1985). They may learn strategies on a rote level (i.e., mimic adult behavior), but there is some question about their ability to understand and be able to evaluate what they have learned (Gross, 1985). Thus, apparent problem-solving gains after a short computer-related treatment may not be a function of the computer at all. It is possible that the participants may not have the cognitive abilities required for such a complex skill but have merely memorized the programming task. Kurland and Pea (1985), for example, reported that children were able to construct programs with complex operations such as variables and recursion but could not explain the flow of control or the process supporting these operations.

Problem-solving researchers using computer language learning (usually Logo) as a "treatment" with young children should also consider the findings of researchers such as Gholson (1980) and Eimas (1969) which indicate that children do not spontaneously use hypotheses until second grade; and, moreover, kindergarten and first graders do not profit from *direct* instruction in a problem-solving strategy (e.g., focusing or scanning). In other words, first graders cannot demonstrate the strategies *in the context in which they were taught*, let alone transfer such strategies (see also, e.g., Canton & Spiker, 1978; Phillips & Levine, 1975).

It should be noted that, while none of the researchers we read dealt in any extensive way with the issue of time in the rationale/literature review of their study, many issued "disclaimers" in their discussions of results. While we agree that this explanation is often a reasonable alternative interpretation to offer, we are somewhat surprised that it continues to be proffered as an explanation. Statz's (1973) widely cited dissertation reported a high correlation between experience and degree of mastery and, with a relatively long treatment (her high experience 10-year-olds averaged 61 hours), found few students (2 of 52) who reached her Stage Four (the child uses the concept in similar cases) on all six of her concept areas and many concepts for which half or less reached her Stage Three (the child can use the concept but does not know when to use it). While every one of her students achieved at least Stage Four on two concepts (procedures and editing), over half did not reach above Stage Three on any of the other (arguably more important in this context) four concepts (recursion, inputs, conditionals, and variables). Statz concludes that her results show "promise for transfer of specific skills, if not for a general problem-solving ability" (p. 204). Yet over a decade later we continue to find insufficient time of treatment offered as an explanation.

METHODOLOGIES

Qualitative Techniques

A number of studies have examined the effects of computer programming on children's problem solving from a qualitative perspective. For the most part, qualitative educational research has employed the techniques of two methodologies—ethnography (e.g., Denzin, 1978; Erickson, 1986; Spradley, 1980) and protocol analysis (e.g., Afflerbach & Johnston, 1984; Ericsson & Simon, 1984). Ethnographic methods examine the participant within the relevant context in order to gain an understanding of the phenomenon from his or her point of view (Spradley, 1980). This approach requires a systematic and sequential analysis of data that emanates from a variety of sources within the context (e.g., observations, interviews, documents). The components of these data are then examined for themes or constructs that undergird the meaning the participant has for the phenomenon.

Hawkins, Homolsky, and Heide (1984) investigated the negotiation of children as they solved group programming problems using this qualitative process. Their study, which spanned two, one-year cycles of data collection, revealed that children did not engage in more or more successful negotiations after a year's instruction in Logo. Of particular relevance to the present argument is the rich and coherent description of the group processes the researchers were able to extract from the data in terms of the patterns of interactions that may have contributed to the findings. Unfortunately, descriptions such as these do not frequently appear in the literature. Instead, the descriptions often consist of anecdotal reports of random observations of students interacting with the computers (e.g., Blitman, Jamile, & Yee, 1984; Chiang, Thorpe, & Lubke, 1984). Typically, the anecdotes resemble the following: "At times, I could almost 'see' the children 'think' and that's a thrill" (Blitman et al., 1984, p. 19).

Over the past two decades, the second major qualitative technique, *protocol analysis*, has gained increasing support as a way of examining the mechanism and internal structure of cognitive processes (Ericsson & Simon, 1984). Typically, data are gathered through the recording of participants' verbalizations as they perform a target task (e.g., math problem, puzzle). In recent years, researchers have begun to capitalize on the ability of the computer to model the solving of programming problems. For example, McAllister (1985) was able to record the patterns of children's programming solutions to the Tower of Hanoi disk problem. In a related study, Webb (1984b) merged two data sources to investigate group problem-solving processes—the listings of computer programs, as groups were solving programming problems, with corresponding taped recordings of their verbal interactions. In both instances, insight into children's cognitive processes was gained via the systematic recording of observable behavior during actual problem-solving activity. As with studies that purport the use of ethnographic methods, investigations of children's cognitive processes during programming have also offered anecdotal reports as sole data sources. For example, Papert (1971) includes five brief excerpts from two students' transcripts as evidence that computers teach children how to think. No other analyses were offered or described. The result is that the reader is left with an emotionally charged "Oh, Neat!" but no solid evidence of patterns of thought processes, or consistency of strategies across problems.

Replicability

Another major problem is replicability. As Sheingold et al. (1984) have indicated, "computers per se do not constitute a treatment" (p. 2). Similarly, we would argue that programming per se is not a treatment in the sense that it can be "dropped in" without explanation in an experimental or quasi-experimental design. It is difficult to imagine how one might replicate Dillashaw and Bell's (1985) "treatment":

> The experimental group received ten weeks of instruction in BASIC programming on Apple microcomputers. The group met four days per week (Monday-Thursday) for fifty minutes each morning before school. The *Creative Programming* 1985 materials were used as the basis of the instruction. (p. 6)

More difficult would be to replicate Dalbey and Linn's (1984) treatment involving BASIC "taught in the manner used by the teacher prior to the investigation" (p. 10). If computer programming instruction is to be used as a treatment, researchers are going to have to adopt richer descriptive techniques (e.g., Seidman, 1981), or well-articulated behavioral observation systems (e.g., Kinzer, Littlefield, Delclos, & Bransford, 1985). Clements and Gullo (1984), for example, devote almost a page of their article to a description of their LOGO treatment.

Naturally, the need for more explanation is increased if the programming "treatment" is a discovery one (e.g., Clements & Gullo, 1984; Kinzer et al., 1985; Pea & Kurland, 1984a), since it is difficult to know what has been discovered or how it was discovered (see Doyle, 1983, for a more thorough discussion). One useful device would be to describe what the students know about programming per se before trying to show transfer of some generalized skills (Kinzer et al., 1985). Caution here is necessary, however, because as Kurland and Pea (1985) have shown, it is possible for students to demonstrate an approach (in this case, recursive techniques) without understanding the concept. Such work would indicate that we should be very careful about making statements about transfer unless we are sure that students understand the strategies and processes in question in the specific contexts in which they were taught. The most interesting rationale for not describing what children learned (which also reflected the most unique notion of the conditions necessary for transfer) was provided by Dillashaw and Bell (1985):

> Our interest was not whether this age child can master the programming of a microcomputer in BASIC, but rather whether there are any corollary benefits such as improvement of the child's skill in problem solving and logical thinking. (p. 2)

Comparison Groups

According to traditional research conventions (e.g., Kerlinger, 1973), comparison groups are used to eliminate the effect of a possible influential independent variable on a dependent variable. The researcher "tries systematically to rule out variables that are possible 'causes' of the effects he is studying other than the variables that he has hypothesized to be the 'causes'" (Kerlinger, 1973, p. 4). That is, the purpose of the comparison group is to control extraneous variance due to independent variables that are not relevant to the target study.

In those studies where a comparison group was used, we often found a tendency to arrange the comparison group "treatment" and the subsequent measure of performance on the dependent variable in such a way as to bias the results in favor of the programming group. Clements and Gullo (1984), for example, compared their Logo programming groups to a group which used *drill and practice* CAI for an equivalent amount of time. Thus, the comparison group was not involved in a different approach to learning problem solving, nor was the group simply a comparison group to control for developmental changes; the comparison group may, in fact, have had a more powerful "treatment" than the experimental group. It is perhaps more reasonable to assume that 16 hours of exposure to programs in letter recognition, alphabetization, addition and subtraction drills, etc., would impede such things as fluency, originality, and overall divergent thinking than to assume that 16 hours of Logo discovery would facilitate it. Moreover, it is perhaps also not surprising that drill and practice students showed greater impulsivity (as reflected by smaller latencies on the Matching Familiar Figures Test [Kagan, Rossman, Day, Albert, & Phillips, 1964]) after 16 hours of practicing on software which encouraged them to respond quickly.

A somewhat different problem, then, is the inclusion of a comparison group which is largely ignored. Dalbey and Linn's (1984) work compared students randomly assigned to learn Spider World to students randomly assigned to learn BASIC to students who worked on typing software. Interestingly, although the group which was taught BASIC "learned very little about the BASIC language" (p. 13), they "were not even proficient at identifying syntactically correct BASIC statements" (p. 13) and were subsequently outperformed by the Spider World students on a near transfer test (involving a robot who understood a decidedly spider-like dialect). Also, the Spider World students did not perform appreciably better than the students who trained on drill-and-practice typing software (except in the area of conditionals where even the apparently confused BASIC students outperformed them). Thus, we can be sure that three weeks of BASIC will serve as a reasonably powerful treatment for suppressing performance on a robot test, but we are not too sure whether Spider World produces better results in either problem solving or autonomous learning (not tested, but discussed at some length) than drill-and-practice typing software.

Measurement

Obviously the last discussion touches on one measurement problem that we encountered: transfer of appropriate testing (Morris, Bransford, & Franks, 1977). Others we have mentioned are the problems of measuring what students know about what they learned and coming up with acceptable measures of problem-solving transfer that can be shown to be reliable and valid. However, another facet of measurement—the sensitivity of the measure selected—may be the biggest problem and perhaps the biggest paradox as well. In our reading of Papert's (1980) work, for example, we see a great deal of emphasis on intuitive understanding of concepts such as variables. This does not imply to us that Papert, who is most commonly mentioned in the rationale for such studies, particularly believes that first graders will actually learn the concept of a variable or a particular strategy for planning, debugging, or problem decomposition. Yet all the studies we found that used young children as subjects and Logo as a treatment tested for the presence or absence of such knowledge. The only study we found that might imply such a finding (i.e., intuitive understanding) was Kurland and Pea (1985), who found that subjects could use recursion but could not explain it. One possibility may be to move toward using time saved in learning as a measure rather than testing the presence or absence of a concept or skill in a dichotomous fashion. For example, Kurland and Pea's (1985) finding that students can use, but not understand, the concept of recursion may reflect the beginning of restrictive understanding. If so, then perhaps these children, when confronted with the formal concept at a later time, may learn the formal concept more quickly. That is, the informal use of recursion at an early age may result in a savings in terms of the time it takes to master the concept when it is formally taught at a later time. Higher order knowledge acquisition is not an all-or-none process; it is a continuum of knowledge structures and skills (Norman, 1978). The failure to recognize this fact has caused many researchers to evaluate the impact of programming or problem-solving skills in a manner that is unfairly biased against finding an effect.

A final problem in the selection of dependent measures is captured by Ginther and Williamson (1985) in their discussion of the works of Statz (1973), whose widely cited unpublished dissertation used a word puzzle, a permutation, the Tower of Hanoi, and a horse race task as dependent problem-solving measures and Gorman and Bourne (1983), who used a rule learning task.

> Several of the existing data-based studies have selected as dependent measures tasks that have but the thinnest of rationale for their selections. It appears as if these researchers randomly selected tasks generally regarded as requiring problem-solving abilities but have no direct connection to the activities involved in learning Logo. This lack of logical clarity in the selection of dependent measures can be directly traced to Papert's rather broad and vague assertions regarding the benefits of teaching Logo to children. (p. 76)

Toward a Framework for Programming and Problem-Solving Research

A step in the right direction is Linn's (1985) attempt to establish a chain or taxonomy that could conceivably form the basis of a matrix for specifying near versus remote and specific versus general transfer features. We believe that Linn's examples, however, make her chain of cognitive consequences appear more constrained and limited than her conceptual description or explanation suggests. We further believe that general skills should probably be extracted and learned rather explicitly (see, e.g., Frederiksen, 1984).

As a possible framework we offer the following modification of Linn's (1985) chain of cognitive consequences based on Norman's (1975) phases in complex learning (see Figure 1) and his discussion of transfer potential (see Figure 2). Note that our model attempts to clarify the confound that we find in Linn's (1985) chain between hierarchical skill development and related versus general transfer (see Figure 3).

Three points about the proposed model require emphasis. First, in order to maximize transfer, those elements to be transferred must clearly be articulated. If we may borrow from Logo, the procedure to be "thrown" must be clearly described and presented as a procedure that may have future utility. At the next level it must be "caught" by review and analogy (this approach argues against less explicit techniques such as discovery, although the *process* of discovery could be transferred in this manner [see also, Linn, Sloane, & Clancy, in press].) Secondly, we do not believe that transfer of computer skills from one context to another occurs in an all-or-none manner. We argue that savings should be considered as the most likely measure of transfer. That is, it should take less time to teach procedures, for example, in a new language, but automatic, full-blown usage of general procedures learned in a new context the first few times will likely not be found since the students must learn the new knowledge base (e.g., Norman, 1980), if necessary, and the relevant patterns (e.g., Simon, 1980). Finally, in order to transfer from specific to general, the specific must be firmly in place (Greeno, 1980). It is not realistic or logical to expect knowledge to transfer from specific to general unless the specific knowledge has been learned.

Unfortunately, this implies many hours of practice with feedback (e.g., Anderson, 1982; Glaser, 1979; Newell & Rosenbloom,

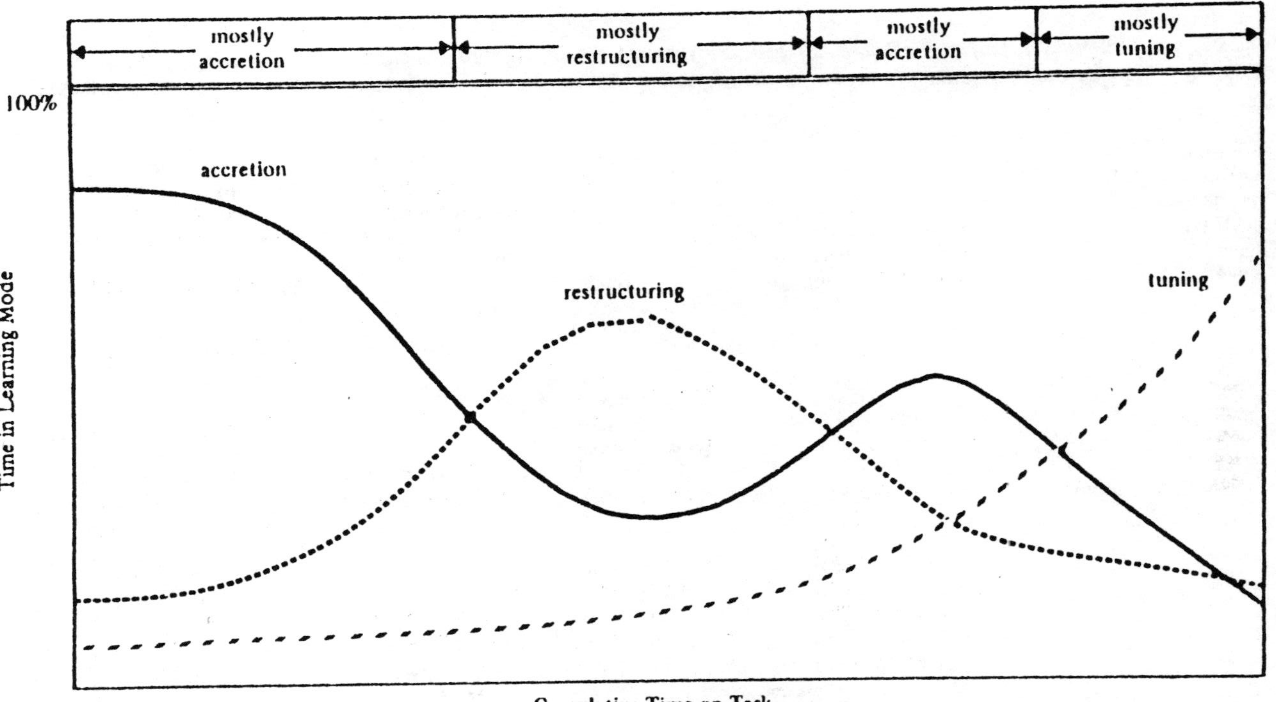

FIGURE 1. Norman's Phases of Complex Learning. From "Notes Toward a Theory of Complex Learning" by D.A. Norman, 1971. In A.M. Lesgold, J.W. Pellegrino, S.D. Fukkema, and R. Glaser (Eds.) *Cognitive Psychology and Instruction*, p. 43. Copyright 1981 by Plenum Press. Reprinted by permission.

Mode	General characteristic	Attributes of the student's knowledge structures	Learning strategy	Testing	Interference from related topics	Transfer to related topics
Accretion	Adding to the amount of knowledge: traditional verbal learning.	Accumulation of knowledge according to existing KMs.	Study, probably using mnemonic systems and good depth of processing.	Factual tests: short answers; multiple choice. Basic recall and recognition tests.	High	Low
Restructuring	Insight. Feeling of understanding material that was previously disorganized. Often accompanied by "oh," or "aha."	New structures for KMs are formed.	Thought, teaching by example, analogy, metaphor. Socratic dialogue.	Conceptual tests. Questions that require inference or problem solving.	Medium	High
Tuning	Making existing KMs more efficient. No new knowledge or structures, but refinement of current skills.	The parameters of KMs are adjusted for maximum efficiency. Special cases are directly encoded.	Practice	Speed, smoothness. Performance under stress or pressure.	Low	Of general knowledge: high Of specific (tuned) knowledge: very low.

FIGURE 2. Transfer Potential by Phases of Complex Learning. From "Notes Toward a Theory of Complex Learning" by D.A. Norman, 19' In A.M. Lesgold, J.W. Pellegrino, S.D. Fukkema, and R. Glaser (Eds.) *Cognitive Psychology and Instruction*, p. 44. Copyright 1981 Plenum Press. Reprinted by permission.

FIGURE 3. Proposed Model of Related and General Transfer Potential as a Function of Developing Programming Expertise

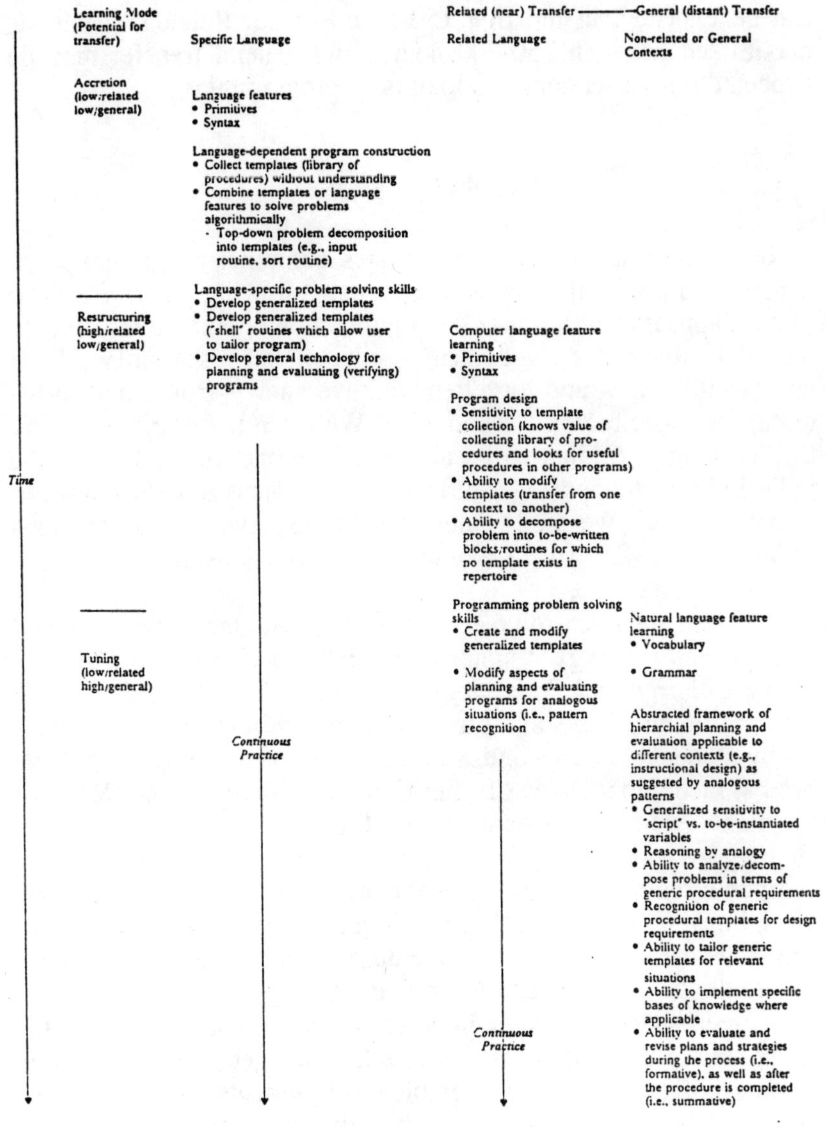

1981). There are no short cuts. As may be seen in Figure 3, even if we use the most conservative estimate for the development of expertise—500 to 600 hours (Linn, 1985)—little transfer of any kind can be expected in the first 150 hours or so. Related transfer is maximized between 250-300 hours, and general transfer may be expected only after some 400 hours of programming.

CONCLUSIONS

Reviewing the literature that relates computer programming to generalized problem solving is not an encouraging enterprise. Too often it appears that because the microcomputer is relatively new to the educational arena and, hence, educational research, we have embraced the new and forgotten what we knew—from relevant literature to basic research techniques. We seem to be driven to find the smoking pistol that will seal our case in one study. As a result, in D. LaMont Johnson's (1985) words, "In answering the question: 'How much do we really know?' I would have to say, precious little, before 1985" (p. 1). We would say, precious little at the time of this writing.

Yet there are at least two encouraging signs. One is the continued interest (and funding) of major research "shops" such as *The Center for Children and Technology* and ACCCEL in the wide ranging study of the processes and products involved in the use of computers by students. The second is in the power of the people that have been attracted to the area of educational cognitive science. Many of the names we have encountered are figures from educational psychology, cognitive psychology, developmental psychology, and computer science who have established records within their own disciplines. Increasingly, they will begin to bring their perspectives and skills to this research milieu. Educational cognitive science will eventually become an interdisciplinary synergy.

A final caveat is perhaps in order, however. The zeal to "sell" computers in the schools as a device to teach generalized problem-solving skills has begun to resemble the arguments for mental discipline that were prevalent in the 19th century—notions grounded in the doctrine of faculty psychology. Consider the brief summary of claims that we presented in our introduction against the following description of a report written in 1828 by a Yale faculty committee (as cited in Kolesnik, 1958):

It recommended, therefore, that those subjects be required and those means of instruction be adopted "which are best calculated to teach the art of fixing the attention, directing the train of thought, analyzing a subject proposed for investigation; following with accurate discrimination the course of argument; balancing nicely the evidence presented to the judgement; awakening, elevating, and controlling the imagination; arranging, with skill, the treasures which memory gathers; rousing and guiding the powers of genius. . . ." Toward this end the Yale faculty insisted upon the value of the study of the classical languages, but maintained that English, mathematics, the physical sciences, logic, philosophy, rhetoric and oratory also had their disciplinary values. (pp. 11-12)

REFERENCES

Afflerbach, P., & Johnston, P. (1984). On the use of verbal reports in reading research. *Journal of Reading Behavior, 16*, 307-322.

Amarel, M. (1983). The classroom: An instructional setting for teachers, students, and the computer. In A.C. Wilkinson (Ed.), *Classroom computers and cognitive science* (pp. 15-28). New York: Academic Press.

Anderson, J.R. (1982). Acquisition of cognitive skill. *Psychological Review, 89*, 369-406.

Barr, R., & Dreeben, R. (1977). Instruction in classrooms. In L. Shulman (Ed.), *Review of Research in Education* (Vol. 5) (pp. 89-162). Itasca, IL: F. E. Peacock.

Bell, D.A. (1978). An empirical study of formal procedure specification. *Contemporary Educational Psychology, 3*, 163-168.

Blitman, E., Jamile, B., & Yee, D. (1984). Computers, children and epistemology. *Educational Perspectives, 22*(4), 16-20.

Brenner, J.E. (1985). The practice of arithmetic in Liberian schools. *Anthropology of Education Quarterly, 16*(3), 177-185.

Brooks, L.D. (1973, June). *Undergraduate students task group approach to complex problem solving employing computer programming.* Paper presented at the Conference on Computers in the Undergraduate Curricula, Claremont, CA.

Brooks, R. (1977). Toward a theory of the cognitive processes in computer programming. *International Journal of Man-Machine Studies, 9*, 737-751.

Canton, J.S., & Spiker, C.C. (1978). The problem-solving strategies of kindergarten and first-grade children during discrimination learning. *Journal of Experimental Child Psychology, 26*, 341-358.

Chase, W.G., & Simon, H.A. (1973). Perception in chess. *Cognitive Psychology, 4*, 55-81.

Chiang, B., Thorpe, H.W., & Lubke, M. (1984). LD students tackle the Logo language: Strategies and implications. *Journal of Learning Disabilities, 17*, 303-304.

Clements, D.H. (1985). Research on Logo in Education: Is the turtle slow but steady or not even in the race? *Computers in the Schools, 2*(2/3), 55-71.

Clements, D.H., & Gullo, D.F. (1984). Effects of computer programming on young children's cognition. *Journal of Educational Psychology, 76*(6), 1051-1058.

Dalby, J., & Linn, M.C. (1985). The demands and requirements of computer programming: A literature review. *Journal of Educational Computing Research, 1*(3), 253-274.

Dalbey, J., & Linn, M.C. (1984, April). *Spider World: A robot language for learning to program. Assessing the cognitive consequences of computer environments for learning*. Paper presented at the annual meeting of the American Educational Research Association, New Orleans, LA.

Darwin, C.T., Turvey, M.T., & Crowder, R.G. (1972). An auditory analogue of the Sperling partial report procedure: Evidence for brief auditory storage. *Cognitive Psychology, 3*, 255-267.

de la Rocha, O. (1985). The reorganization of arithmetic practice in the kitchen. *Anthropology Education Quarterly, 16*(3), 183-198.

Denzin, N. K. (1978). *The research act: A theoretical introduction to sociological methods*. New York: McGraw-Hill.

Dillashaw, F.G., & Bell, S.R. (1985, April). *Learning outcomes of computer programming instruction for middle-grade students: A pilot study*. Paper presented at the annual meeting of the National Association for Research in Science Teaching, French Lick Springs, IN.

Doyle, W. (1987). Paradigms for research on teacher effectiveness. In L. Shulman and G. Sykes (Eds.), *Review of Research in Education* (Vol. 5), (pp. 163-197). Itasca, IL: F. E. Peacock.

Doyle, W. (1983). Academic work. *Review of Educational Research, 53*, 159-199.

Dreyfus, H.L., & Dreyfus, S.E. (1986). *Mind over machine: The power of human intuition and expertise in the era of the computer*. New York: The Free Press.

Egan, D.E., & Schwartz, B.J. (1979). Chunking in recall of symbolic drawings. *Memory & Cognition, 7*(2), 149-158.

Eimas, P.D. (1969). A developmental study of hypothesis behavior and focusing. *Journal of Experimental Child Psychology, 8*, 160-172.

Erickson, F. (1986). Qualitative methods in research on teaching. In M. C. Wittrock (Ed.), *Handbook of research on teaching* (3rd ed.) (pp. 119-161). New York: MacMillan.

Ericsson, K.A., & Simon, H.A. (1984). Verbal reports as data. *Psychological Review, 87*, 215-251.

Evertson, E., Anderson, C., Anderson, L., & Brophy, J. (1980). Relationships between classroom behaviors and student outcomes in junior high mathematics and English classes. *American Educational Research Journal, 17*, 43-60.

Feigenbaum, E.A., & McCorduck, P. (1984). *The fifth generation: Artificial intelligence and Japan's computer challenge to the world*. New York: Signet.

Feurzig, W., Horwitz, P., & Nickerson, R.S. (1981). *Microcomputers in education* (Report No. 4789). Prepared for Department of Health, Education, and Welfare; National Institute of Education; and Ministry for the Development of

Human Intelligence, Republic of Venezuela. Cambridge, MA: Bolt, Beranek & Newman.

Fisher, C., & Mandinach, E. (1985, March). *Individual differences and acquisition of computer programming skill*. Paper presented at the annual meeting of the American Educational Research Association, Chicago.

Frederiksen, N. (1984). Implications of cognitive theory for instruction in problem solving. *Review of Educational Research, 54*(3), 363-407.

Gholson, B. (1980). *The cognitive-developmental basis of human learning: Studies in hypothesis testing*. New York: Academic Press.

Ginther, D.W., & Williamson, J.D. (1985). Learning Logo: What is really learned? *Computers in the Schools, 2*(2/3), 73-78.

Glaser, R. (1979). Trends and research questions in psychological research on learning and schooling. *Educational Researcher, 8*, 6-13.

Gorman, H., Jr., & Bourne, L.E., Jr. (1983). Learning to think by learning Logo: Rule learning in third-grade computer programmers. *Bulletin of the Psychonomic Society, 21*(3), 165-67.

Greeno, J.G. (1980). Some examples of cognitive task analysis with instructional implications. In R.E. Snow, P. Federico, & W.E. Montague (Eds.), *Aptitude, learning and instruction (Vol. 2): Cognitive process analyses of learning and problem solving* (pp. 1-21). Hillsdale, NJ: Erlbaum.

Gross, T.F. (1985). *Cognitive development*. Monterey, CA: Brooks/Cole.

Hawkins, J., Homolsky, M., & Heide, P. (1984, April). *Paired problem solving in a computer context*. Paper presented at the annual meeting of the American Educational Research Association, New Orleans, LA.

Hudgins, B.B. (1977). *Learning and thinking*. Itasca, IL: F.E. Peacock.

Johnson, D.L. (1985). What do we know about Logo? *Computers in the Schools, 2*(2/3), 1-2.

Kagan, J., Rossman, B.L., Day, D., Albert, J., & Phillips, W. (1964). Information processing in the child. Significance of analytic and reflective attitudes. *Psychological Monographs, 78* (1, Serial No. 578).

Kahney, H. (1986). *Problem solving: a cognitive approach*. Philadelphia, Open University Press.

Kerlinger, F. (1973). *Foundations of behavioral research* (2nd ed.). New York: Holt, Rinehart & Winston.

Kinzer, C., Littlefield, J., Delclos, V.R., & Bransford, J.D. (1985). Different Logo learning environments and mastery: Relationships between engagement and learning. *Computers in the Schools, 2*(2/3), 33-44.

Klatsky, R.L. (1980). *Human memory: Structures and processes* (2nd ed.). New York: Freeman.

Kolesnik, W.B. (1958). *Mental discipline in modern education*. Madison: University of Wisconsin Press.

Kounin, J.S. (1970). *Discipline and group management in classrooms*. New York: Holt, Rinehart & Winston.

Kurland, D.M., Mawby, R., & Cahir, N. (1984, April). *The development of programming expertise in adults and children* (Tech. Rep. No. 29). New York: Bank Street College of Education, Center for the Study of Children and Technology.

Kurland, D.M., & Pea, R.D. (1985). Children's mental models of recursive Logo programs. *Journal of Educational Computing Research, 1*(2), 236-243.

Larkin, J.G., McDermott, J., Simon, D.P., & Simon, H.A. (1980). Expert and novice performance in solving physics problems. *Cognitive Psychology, 4*, 55-81.

Lave, J. (1985). Situationally specific practice. *Anthropology and Education Quarterly, 16*(3), 171-176.

Leu, D.J., Jr., & Kinzer, C.K. (1987). *Effective reading instruction in the elementary grades*. Columbus, OH: Merrill.

Linn, M.C. (1985). The cognitive consequences of programming instruction in classrooms. *Educational Researcher, 14*(5), 14-15, 25-29.

Linn, M.C., & Dalbey, J. (1985). Cognitive consequences of programming instruction: Instruction, access and ability. *Educational Psychologist, 20*(4), 191-206.

Linn, M.C., Sloane, K.D., & Clancy, M.J. (in press). Ideal and actual outcomes from precollege Pascal instruction. *Journal of Research in Science Teaching*.

Maddux, C.D. (1985). The need for science versus passion in educational computing. *Computers in the Schools, 2*(2/3), 9-10.

Mayer, R.E. (1975). Different problem-solving competencies established in learning computer programming with and without meaningful models. *Journal of Educational Psychology, 67*(6), 725-734.

Mayer, R.E. (1983). *Thinking, problem solving, cognition*. New York: Freeman.

McAllister, A. (1985). *Problem solving at the threshold of computer programming* (Bulletin No. 13). Toronto: Toronto Board of Education.

McKeithen, K.B., Reitman, J.S., Rueter, H.H., & Hirtle, S.C. (1981). Knowledge organization and skill differences in computer programmers. *Cognitive Psychology, 13*, 307-325.

Miller, G.A. (1956). The magical number seven, plus or minus two: Some limits on our capacity for processing information. *Psychological Review, 63*, 81-97.

Morris, C.D., Bransford, J.D., & Franks, J.J. (1977). Levels of processing versus transfer of appropriate processing. *Journal of Verbal Learning and Verbal Behavior, 16*, 519-533.

Murtaugh, M. (1984). A model of grocery shopping decision process based on verbal protocol data. *Human Organization, 43*(3), 243-251.

Newell, A., & Rosenbloom, P.S. (1981). Mechanisms of skill acquisition and the law of practice. In J.R. Anderson (Ed.), *Cognitive skills and their acquisition* (pp. 1-56). Hillsdale, NJ; Erlbaum.

Newell, A., & Simon, H.A. (1972). *Human problem solving*. Englewood Cliffs, NJ: Prentice-Hall.

Norman, D.A. (1978). Notes toward a theory of complex learning. In A.M. Lesgold, J.W. Pellegrino, S.D. Fokkema, & R. Glaser (Eds.), *Cognitive psychology and instruction* (pp. 39-48). New York: Plenum Press.

Norman, D.A. (1980). Cognitive engineering and education. In D.T. Tuma & F. Reif (Eds.), *Problem solving and education: Issues in teaching and research* (pp. 97-107). Hillsdale, NJ: Erlbaum.

Papert, S. (1980). *Mindstorms: Children, computers, and powerful ideas*. New York: Basic Books.

Papert, S. (1971). *Teaching children thinking* (Artificial Intelligence Memo No. 247). Boston: Massachusetts Institute of Technology, Artificial Intelligence Laboratory.

Patterson, J.H., & Smith, M.S. (1986). The role of computers in higher order thinking. *Yearbook for the National Society for the Study of Education* (Vol. 85:1) (p. 81-108). Chicago: University of Chicago Press.

Pea, R.D. (1983). *Logo programming and problem solving* (Tech. Rep. No. 12). New York: Bank Street College of Education, Center for Children and Technology.

Pea, R.D., & Kurland, D.M. (1984a). *Logo programming and the development of planning skills*. New York: Bank Street College of Education, Center for Children and Technology.

Pea, R.D., & Kurland, D.M. (1984b). *On the cognitive effects of learning computer programming: A critical look* (Tech. Rep. No. 9). New York: Bank Street College of Education.

Pea, R.D., & Kurland, D.M. (1983). *On the cognitive prerequisites of learning computer programming* (Tech. Rep. No. 18). New York: Bank Street College of Education, Center for Children and Technology.

Piaget, J. (1970). *The science of education and the psychology of the child*. New York: Orion Press.

Phillips, S., & Levine, M. (1975). Proving formal hypotheses with adults and children: Blank trails and introacts. *Journal of Experimental Psychology: General, 104*, 327-354.

Pohl, H.L., & Nutter, J.T. (1985). Use of analogy in computer language acquisition. *AEDS Journal, 18* (4), 254-266.

Polya, G. (1957). *How to solve it*. Garden City, NY: Doubleday Anchor.

Polya, G. (1968). *Mathematical discovery. Vol. II: On understanding, learning and teaching problem solving*. New York: Wiley.

Salomon, G., & Gardner, H. (1986). The computer as educator: Lessons from television research. *Educational Researcher, 15*(7), 13-19.

Seidman, R.H. (1981, April). *The effects of learning a computer programming language on the logical reasoning of school children*. Paper presented at the annual meeting of the American Educational Research Association, Los Angeles, CA.

Sheingold, K., Hawkins, J., & Char, C. (1984). *"I'm the thinkist, you're the typist": The interaction of technology and the social life of classrooms* (Tech. Rep. No. 27). New York: Bank Street College of Education, Center for Children and Technology.

Sheingold, K., Kane, J., Endreweist, M., & Billings, K. (1981). *Study of issues related to implementation of computer technology in schools* (Tech. Rep. No. 2). New York: Bank Street College of Education, Center for Children and Technology.

Shulman, L.S. (1981). Disciplines of inquiry in education: An overview. *Educational Researcher, 10*(6), 5-12.

Simon, H.A. (1978). Information processing theory of human problem solving. In W.K. Estes (Ed.), *Handbook of learning and cognitive processes* (Vol. 5), (pp. 248-301). Hillsdale, NJ: Erlbaum.

Simon, H.A. (1980). Problem solving and education. In D.T. Tuma & F. Reif (Eds.), *Problem solving and education: Issues in teaching and research* (pp. 81-96). New York: Erlbaum.

Smith, J.K., & Heshusius, L. (1986). Closing down the conversation: The end of the quantitative-qualitative debate. *Educational Researcher, 15*(7), 4-12.

Soloway, E., Lochhead, J., & Clement, J. (1982). Does computer programming enhance problem-solving ability? Some positive evidence on algebra word problems. In R.J. Seidel, R.E. Anderson, & B. Hunter (Eds.), *Computer literacy: Issues and directions for 1985* (pp. 171-185). New York: Academic Press.

Sperling, G. (1960). The information available in brief visual presentations. *Psychological Monographs, 74*, (Whole No. 498).

Spradley, J.P. (1980). *Participant observation*. New York: Holt, Rinehart & Winston.

Sprigle, J.E., & Schaefer, L. (1984). Age, gender, and spacial knowledge influences on preschoolers' computer programming ability. *Early Childhood Development and Care, 14*, 243-250.

Statz, J.A. (1973). *The development of computer programming concepts and problem-solving abilities among ten-year-olds learning Logo*. Unpublished doctoral dissertation: Syracuse University, NY.

Tulving, E., & Thomson, D.M. (1973). Encoding specificity and retrieval processes in episodic memory. *Psychological Review, 80*, 352-373.

Webb, N.M. (1984a). Microcomputer learning in small groups: Cognitive requirements and group processes. *Journal of Educational Psychology, 76*(6), 1076-1088.

Webb, N.M. (1984b, April). *Problem-solving strategies and group processes in small groups learning computer programming*. Paper presented at the annual meeting of the American Educational Research Association, New Orleans.

Wilkinson, A.C., & Patterson, J. (1983). Issues at the interface of theory and practice. In A.C. Wilkinson (Ed.), *Classroom computers and cognitive science* (pp. 3-12). New York: Academic Press.

W. Michael Reed
David B. Palumbo

The Effect of the BASIC Programming Language on Problem-Solving Skills and Computer Anxiety

RATIONALE

Researchers indicate that, in problem-solving/programming language studies, research design problems may contribute to the lack of support for the speculated link between learning programming languages and problem-solving skills (e.g., Burton & Magliaro, this issue). Such factors include length of treatment (developing problem-solving skills takes time and, thus, the treatment may not be long enough), type of treatment (whether a programming language is in fact taught), and dependent measures (whether they measure problem-solving skills).

Other factors may pose problems in this line of inquiry. For example, if a person is anxious toward computers, that anxiety may easily interfere with the learning of the programming language purported to develop problem-solving skills. Possibly, relatively high degrees of computer anxiety may impede the learning of a programming language, lessening a person's competence with the language and thus affecting peripheral kinds of skills such as the ability to problem solve. This reasoning has been evident in the area of writing apprehension; writers with relatively high degrees of writing apprehension perform more poorly on writing tasks and have poorer writing skills than do writers of relatively low apprehension (e.g.,

---

W. MICHAEL REED is Assistant Professor of Computer Education and English Education, West Virginia University, Morgantown, WV 26506.
DAVID B. PALUMBO is a doctoral candidate, Educational Psychology, West Virginia University, Morgantown, WV 26506.

Daly & Miller, 1975; Daly & Wilson, 1983; Reed, Burton, & Vandett, in press; Reed, Vandett, & Burton, 1984).

Another factor is that much of the research related to problem solving and programming languages generally ends with problem-solving gains (a pretest design) or group differences (experimental group-control group comparison; Dillashaw & Bell, 1985; Soloway, Lochhead, & Clement, 1982). Because of speculation that learning a programming language promotes the development of problem-solving skills (Burton & Magliaro, this issue; McCoy & Orey, this issue; Reed, 1986), programming language competence needs to be considered in such studies. For example, if someone has not mastered the language as well as another, it may be that the development of such peripheral skills as problem solving may likewise not be comparable (e.g., Cantor & Spiker, 1978; McCoy & Orey, this issue; Palumbo & Vargas, this issue; Sherman, this issue). Programming and debugging exercises may help determine whether the treatment has resulted in an ability to work with a language. Certainly, unless the person is able to work with the language at a more sophisticated level, the development of more complex and peripheral kinds of skills such as problem solving may not occur.

The traditional question—what is the effect of the BASIC programming language instruction on problem-solving skills?—was asked. Additionally, novel questions also were asked: What is the effect of BASIC programming language instruction on computer anxiety? What is the relationship between problem solving and computer anxiety? What is the relationship between problem solving and debugging? And, what is the relationship between problem solving and programming?

Because computer anxiety may affect not only problem-solving skills but also competence at debugging and programming, additional questions were asked: What is the relationship between computer anxiety and debugging? And, what is the relationship between computer anxiety and programming? Because prior experience with the BASIC language might affect programming language mastery and attitudes toward computers, four final questions were asked: What is the relationship between problem solving and prior experience? What is the relationship between computer anxiety and prior experience? What is the relationship between debugging and prior experience? And what is the relationship between programming and prior experience?

DESIGN OF THE STUDY

Sample

Twenty-three students enrolled in three computer courses participated in this study. The courses were a graduate course on the BASIC programming language ($n = 7$), an undergraduate/graduate course on microcomputer uses in the English classroom ($n = 5$), and an undergraduate course on microcomputer uses in Family Resources ($n = 11$). Four of the 7 students in the programming course reported prior experience with the BASIC programming language; 2 of the 5 in the English course reported prior experience; and, 4 of the 11 in the Family Resource class reported prior experience, for a total of 10 out of 23 participants having had prior experience with the BASIC programming language.

Instruments and Other Measures

Instruments. Problem-solving skills were measured by responses to the Analysis of Relevant and Irrelevant Information and Analysis of Attributes sections of the Ross Test of Higher Cognitive Processes and the Deduction and Interpretation sections of the *Watson-Glaser Critical Thinking Appraisal*. These four sections contained a total of 61 test items and were chosen because of their similarity to the kinds of skills needed in order to debug and to program efficiently and effectively. *Computer anxiety* was measured by responses to an adaptation of Spielberger's Self-Evaluation Questionnaire, a 20-item, Likert-scale (four-point) instrument that requires the participants to respond to statements about how they feel. Each item was reworded so that the "feeling" clearly related to computers; for example, the statement "I feel tense" was restated "I feel tense when I work with a computer."

Other Measures. Debugging competence was measured by scores on a debugging segment of the BASIC programming language test (see Appendix A). *Programming performance* was measured by scores on an at-the-computer programming assignment also as part of the BASIC programming language test (see Appendix B). *Prior experience* was self-reported by the participants when they responded to the pretest participant profile sheet.

Procedures

During the first class meeting, all participants responded to the pretest, which included the participant profile sheet, the problem-solving instrument, and the computer anxiety instrument. Each class received identical instruction delivered by the weekly programming assignments designed by the same instructor; the students also used the same BASIC programming instructional text developed by the instructor. Instruction took place for eight weeks (see Appendix C for a detailed explanation of the instruction and weekly programming assignments). During the meeting of the eighth week, all classes took the same test on the BASIC programming language. And, during the class meeting of the ninth week, they responded to the posttest, which included the computer anxiety and problem-solving instruments. Because the posttest contained the identical items given nine weeks earlier, several participants were randomly selected and were interviewed on whether they had been able to recall the exact answers they had given previously. All answered that they could not recall any of them and had to "rework" the instrument items.

Analysis of the Data

To determine the effect of BASIC programming language instruction on problem-solving skill and computer anxiety, two dependent *t*-tests were conducted. In the first one, the pretest scores on the problem-solving instrument were compared to the posttest scores. In the second one, the pretest scores on the computer anxiety instrument were compared to the posttest scores. To determine the relationships among problem-solving skills, computer anxiety, prior experience, debugging, and programming performance, four simple linear regressions were conducted, regressing problem solving on the four independent variables. To determine the relationships between computer anxiety and programming performance and debugging, two simple linear regressions were run, regressing these latter variables on computer anxiety. To determine the relationship between prior BASIC experience and computer anxiety, debugging, and programming performance, each of these latter variables was regressed on prior experience. Because such scores as debugging and programming performance emerged as part of the testing which occurred at the end of the treatment, computer anxiety and problem-solving posttest scores, rather than pretest scores, were used in these regressions.

RESULTS

In answer to the questions concerning whether there were pretest-posttest differences in problem-solving skills and computer anxiety, two dependent *t*-tests were conducted. Scores on the problem-solving instruments increased significantly over the course of the BASIC programming treatment: $t(22) = -2.282$, $p = .0326$. Inversely, computer anxiety scores decreased significantly: $t(22) = 2.328$, $p = .0296$. A statistically significant, negative relationship existed between problem solving and computer anxiety: $F(1,21) = 5.034$, $SEb = .154$, R(squared) $= .19$, $p < .05$; in other words, as computer anxiety decreased, the ability to solve problems increased (see Table 1 for means, standard deviations, and ranges).

There were also statistically significant positive relationships between problem solving and (a) debugging: $F(1,21) = 16.981$, $SEb = .246$, R(squared) $= .44$, $p < .01$; (b) programming: $F(1,21) = 5.157$, $SEb = .079$, R(squared) $= 20$, $p < .05$; and (c) prior BASIC experience: $F(1,21) = 8.078$, $SEb = 2.831$, R(squared) $= .28$, $p < .01$ (see Table 1 for means, standard deviations, and ranges). Those people who scored higher on the debugging component of the test also scored higher on the problem-solving instrument. Likewise, those who scored higher on the programming component of the test scored higher on the problem-solving instrument; and, those who had had prior experience with the BASIC language also scored higher on the problem-solving instrument.

There were statistically significant, negative relationships between computer anxiety and (a) debugging: $F(1,21) = 4.757$, $SEb = .102$, R(squared) $= 18$, $p < .05$; and (b) Prior BASIC experience: $F(1,21) = 8.071$, $SEb = 3.598$, R(squared) $= 28$, $p < .01$. At the .06 level, there was also a negative relationship between computer anxiety and programming: $F(1,21) = 4.028$, $SEb = .065$, R(squared) $= .16$ (see Table 1 for means, standard deviations, and ranges). Based on these results, people who were less apprehensive toward computers scored higher on the debugging component of the test. Also, those people with prior experience were less apprehensive. Accepting the .06 level of significance, we can also claim that those people who were less apprehensive per-

Table 1

Means, Standard Deviations, Instrument Ranges, and Study Instrument Ranges of Measures

Measure	Mean	*SD*	Range	Study Range
problem solving--pretest	44.00	8.22	0-61	28-55
problem solving--posttest	45.65	7.74	0-61	34-59
computer anxiety--pretest	38.22	9.37	20-80	22-58
computer anxiety--posttest	35.48	9.83	20-80	20-60
prior experience	.43	.51	0-1	0-1
programming	31.26	3.14	0-35	24-35
debugging	18.91	5.10	0-30	12-27

formed better on the programming component of the test. There was also a statistically significant, positive relationship between prior BASIC experience and programming performance: $F(1,21) = 10.813$, $SEb = 1.097$, R(squared) $= .34$, $p < .01$. However, there was not a statistically significant relationship between prior experience and debugging: $F(1,21) = 3.647$, $p > .05$.

DISCUSSION

Features of Design

A wealth of studies have reported nonsignificant relationships between problem-solving skills and learning programming languages or nonsignificant effects of learning programming languages on problem-solving skills. We, however, found a significant gain in problem-solving skills and significant relationships between problem-solving skills and prior experience with the treatment language, the ability to debug, and programming competence. Such findings may be due to our problem-solving dependent measures. We chose sections of highly valid and reliable instruments that parallel the kinds of problem-solving skills involved when people program; these sections again were Analysis of Relevant and Irrelevant Information, Analysis of Attributes, Deduction, and Interpretation. Although these problem-solving subskills represent only part of what occurs when people solve problems, they are more in line with programming-like problem-solving skills. As Burton and Magliaro (this issue) point out, the dependent measures are crucial when trying to determine effects or relationships. If researchers are looking for gains or relationships but use problem-solving measures that are not representative of the kinds of problem-solving skill the participants engage in when programming, part of their design is faulty.

An often-overlooked variable in the research is computer anxiety. Common sense tells us that anxiety toward a kind of skill such as writing or math or toward an instructional device such as a computer will have some impact on how effectively that skill or device is used (Price, 1985). The results of this study indicate that a relationship between computer anxiety and problem-solving ability does exist. In terms of design-construction, researchers should take such a factor into account. Because it does have a negative relationship with problem-solving skill-development, researchers should either build in computer anxiety as a classification variable or relate problem solving and computer anxiety as a follow-up test of some sort in order to help explain problem-solving results of significance or nonsignificance.

The Issue of Prior Experience

According to this study, there was a positive relationship between prior experience and (a) problem solving and (b) programming performance. As Burton and Magliaro (this issue) contend, both prior experience and length of treatment have certain research implications. Because we included a prior-experience variable, the design of our study was cross-sectional and, perhaps loosely, can be considered to have had a longer or extended treatment. Since some of the participants were already competent with the programming language, they were able to focus on the finer aspects of the language and what could be done with it. If students have had prior experience with the language, they obviously enter the experimental situation with more knowledge. This entry-level competence should allow them to move beyond those who enter with none. People with longer exposure to a language who are receiving the same instruction as those who have had no prior experience may develop different degrees of problem-solving skills, simply because they have interacted with the language longer. Because they have reached a higher degree of language competence, they should be able to use it more effectively, efficiently, and perhaps more creatively than those with lower language competence.

Instructional Implications

In addition to the research design considerations discussed previously, there are instructional implications suggested by these findings. In this study, computer anxiety had negative relationships with problem solving, prior experience, debugging, and programming (at the .06 level). Those with greater anxiety had less success at debugging and programming, in addition to not developing as effective problem-solving skills. Until anxiety is overcome, desired learning related to computers will be delayed. Because there exist different degrees of anxiety for people of varying programming backgrounds, separate courses should be designed based on programming language entry-level. Those new at computers and/or at programming should be instructed on general uses of the microcomputer and brief, fairly simple programs, rather than being enrolled in a course that focuses only on a programming language; such an approach may help to alleviate computer anxiety, and would force us to separate instruction whose purpose is to reduce anxiety from instruction whose purpose is to teach a programming language.

That BASIC was used in this study is one of the study's strongest implications because BASIC is less procedurally oriented than either Logo or Pascal. Its syntax does not require breaking a task into components and forcing the student to program in parts operations that more closely parallel general problem-solving strategies. It is highly likely that the effective learning of languages such as Logo and Pascal, which are extremely procedurally oriented, will result in comparable and perhaps even better results. As Reed (1986) purports, the teaching of programming languages should dominate existing curricula because they develop problem-solving skills. Galanter (1984) feels that programming languages may be the language of "operational logic" (p. 31), an area that is often overlooked in schooling. If a primary goal of education is to help students develop problem-solving skills, programming language instruction should be at the curricular forefront.

REFERENCES

Bowles, K.L., Franklin, S.D.,& Volper, D.J. (1982). *Problem solving using UCSD Pascal*. New York: Springer-Verlag.

Cantor, J.S., & Spiker, C.C. (1978). The problem-solving strategies of kindergarten and first-grade children during discrimination learning. *Journal of Experimental Child Psychology, 26*, 341-358.

Clements, D.H. (1985). Research on Logo in education: Is the turtle slow but steady, or not even in the race?" *Computers in the Schools, 2*(2,3), 55-72.

Daly, J.A., & Miller, M.D. (1975). The empirical development of an instrument to measure writing apprehension. *Research in the Teaching of English, 9*(4), 272-289.

Daly, J.A., & Wilson, D.A. (1983). Writing apprehension, self-esteem, and personality. *Research in the Teaching of English, 17*(4), 327-342.

Dillashaw, F.G., & Bell, S.R. (1985). Learning outcomes of computer programming instruction for middle-grade students: A pilot study. Presented at the annual conference of the National Association for Research in Science Teaching, French Lick Springs, IN.

Galanter, E. (1984, September). Homing in on computers. *Psychology Today*, 30-33.

Ginther, D.W., & Williamson, J.D. (1985). Learning Logo: What is really learned? *Computers in the School, 2*(2,3), 73-78.

Hassett, J. (1984, September). Computers in the Classroom. *Psychology Today*, 22-28.

Maddux, C.D. (1985). The need for science versus passion in educational computing. *Computers in the Schools, 2*(2,3), 9-10.

Papert, S. (1980). *Mindstorms: Children, computers and powerful ideas*. New York: Basic Books.

Price, W.L. (1985). *The effects of in-service workshops on computer anxiety in elementary teachers*. Unpublished doctoral dissertation, Virginia Polytechnic Institute and State University, Blacksburg, VA.

Reed, W.M. (1986). Teachers' attitudes toward educational computing: Instructional uses, misuses, and needed improvements. *Computers in the Schools, 3*(1), 73-80.

Reed, W.M., Burton, J.K., & Vandett, N.M. (in press). Daly and Miller's Writing Apprehension Test and Hunt's T-unit analysis: Two measurement precautions in writing research. *Journal of Research and Development in Education*.

Reed, W.M., Vandett, N.M., & Burton, J.K. (1984). The effects of writing skills, sex, and preparation on writing apprehension. *FORUM in Reading and Language Education, 1*(1), 45-60.

Soloway, E., Lochhead, J., & Clement, J. (1982). Does computer programming enhance problem-solving ability? Some positive evidence on algebra word problems. In R.J. Seidel, R.E. Anderson, & B. Hunter (Eds.), *Computer literacy: Issues and directions for 1985* (pp. 171-185). New York: Academic Press.

APPENDIX A: DEBUGGING EXERCISE

There are 10 programming errors in the following *hi-res graphics* program. The errors range from incorrect sequence of commands to incorrect commands for a given mode to absent commands to unnecessary commands. Any of these problems will keep the program from being executed properly.

You need to do the following three steps by using page 5 as an answer sheet:

1. Identify the error.
2. Explain what would happen or not happen if the error were executed.
3. Make the changes needed to correct the error.

You may tear off the answer sheet to facilitate your taking this part of this test. However, be sure that it is stapled with the rest of the test when you turn it in.

```
10 HOME
20 GR25 REM ******** BACKGROUND *******
30 HCOLOR = 1
40 FOR A = 0 TO 159
50 HPLOT 0, B to 279, B
60 NEXT A
70 HCOLOR = 3
75 REM ******** ANIMATION *******
80 FOR PLANE = 0 TO 200 STEP -2
90 GOTO 1000
100 HCOLOR = 1
110 GOSUB 2000
120 HCOLOR = 0
```

```
130 GOSUB 1000
140 GOSUB 2000
150 NEXT PLAIN
1000 REM ********* FIRST PART OF OBJECT ************
1010 HPLOT PL, 0 TO PL + 20, 0 TO PL + 50, 10 TO PL + 20,
    20 TO PL, 20 TO PL, 0
2000 REM ******** SECOND PART OF OBJECT *********
2010 HLIN PL, 21 TO PL + 80, 21 TO PL + 80, 31 TO PL, 31
    TO PL, 21
2020 RETURN
```

APPENDIX B: PROGRAMMING ASSIGNMENT

1. You have the remaining time to construct a program in BASIC so that the following program is run.
2. I suggest that you conceptualize and write the program on paper before you enter the program into the computer. Basically, what is each component of the overall program and what is the sequence of commands needed to have the computer perform each part?
3. When you are ready to enter the program, get a test disk from me and boot it up.
4. After you have finished the program, save it under *your name* (no spaces between the first and last name), for example, JOHN DOE.

This part of the test will be evaluated on the following criteria: (a) how closely it matches the assignment; (b) whether the program runs; (c) how logically and efficiently the program has been written; (d) internal documentation (REM's); and (e) how aesthetically the information is presented on the screen (you should use all TEXT commands – VTAB, HTAB, SPEED = , etc.).

ASSIGNMENT

Write a program that asks the user for two numbers and then asks him/her which mathematical operation (addition, subtraction, division, or multiplication) he/she would like to perform on those two numbers. Once the user has given the numbers and the choice of mathematical operation, you should then have the computer display the "result" of the operation; for example, if the *user has given* the *two numbers 5 and 7 and multiplication*, then the computer should display *35*.

Important information: the command for addition is +; for subtraction, −; for multiplication, *; and, for division, /. You should also accommodate the *division by zero error* by including a conditional *in the division section* that if the user chooses 0 as the second number, he should pick another number.

****

Once you have finished this assignment, you need to turn this sheet in and any papers on which you constructed this program. Make sure your name is on this sheet and all other papers.

****

APPENDIX C: DETAILED EXPLANATION OF INSTRUCTION AND ASSIGNMENTS*

(*Generally the instruction for each class beginning with the second class was broken down into two or three segments with each segment dealing specifically with each of the assignments for the next week; class time was allowed for the students to begin a particular assignment to identify early potential problems and to provide assistance for these problems; after the second class, each class meeting started out with a review of the previous week's commands and running the programs that the students had created.)

Meeting 1: overview of course, familiarization with computers via familiarization software program, lecture on computer architecture, responding to study instruments.

Meeting 2: instruction on DOS (SAVE, LOAD, CATALOG, RUN) versus Applesoft BASIC lo-res graphics commands (GR, COLOR =, PLOT, HLIN, and VLIN) and immediate execution mode versus delayed execution mode (primarily the reasons for using program line numbers—to delay the execution of commands and the sequencing of the execution of commands); assignments were to write (a) a program that displayed the programmer's three initials on the screen and (b) a program that displayed a scene of some sort (a beach scene, a city scene, etc.)—class time was set aside to get started on the programs, but they were due the next week.

Meeting 3: instruction on creating a background color, diagonal lines, and animation in lo-res (the use of numeric variables, FOR/NEXT loops, GOSUB/RETURN); assignments were (a) to create a program that displayed a flag with a background, a border along all four sides, diagonal lines crisscrossing, and an emblem and (b) a program that moved a fairly simple, one-colored object from left to right.

Meeting 4: instruction on animating an object of more than one color (each part of a different color requires a different subroutine since colors cannot be included in subroutines except in a few cases), moving an object from right to left and from bottom to top (the use of the STEP—command in the FOR line), and hi-res graphics; assignments were to write (a) a program that moved a lo-res object of more than one color from left to right, (b) a program that moved a lo-res object from left to right and then from the bottom to the top, and (c) a program that moved a hi-res object diagonally (including the variable for both the X and Y values).

Meeting 5: instruction on animating a multi-colored hi-res object, embedded DOS commands, and displaying text (PRINT, SPEED =, INVERSE, FLASH, HTAB, VTAB); assignments were to write (a) a program that would move a multi-colored hi-res object, (b) a program that would give a listing of the programs on the disk (an embedded CATALOG command), and (c) a program that displayed text on the screen (using various text commands such as SPEED = and FLASH) that was related to one of the earlier graphics programs that had been created and would have the computer run the graphics program after the text had been displayed (the embedded RUN command).

Meeting 6: instruction on presenting questions and having the computer "remember" the responses as values of string variables (INPUT) and presenting questions that would have the computer display certain messages based on the answers (GET, IF/

THEN); the assignments were to write (a) a program that asked the user five questions about himself or herself and then at the end integrated the five responses in a paragraph (for example, "Where do you live?"/INPUT PLACE$ and then later PLACE$ "is a nice place to live.") and (b) a program that presented fives test questions with choices (for example, "Where did *Hamlet* take place?"/"A. Hohenschwangau/B. Elsinore/C. Neuschwanstein"/GET A$) and then had the computer inform the student whether the answer was right or wrong (IF A$ = "A" OR A$ = "C" THEN GOSUB 1000 [the wrong answer subroutine]; IF A$ = "B" THEN GOSUB 2000 [the right answer subroutine]).

Meeting 7: review for test; in-class problems highlighting numeric versus string variables and conditionals.

Meeting 8: test on the BASIC programming language; all students had an assignment due several weeks later to develop an instructional unit that would present information with graphics illustrations and then test the user on the information—this was similar to developing a piece of software requiring the student to continue working with the language.

Meeting 9: responding to study instruments.

W. Michael Reed
David B. Palumbo
Aletha L. Stolar

The Comparative Effects of BASIC and Logo Instruction on Problem-Solving Skills

Since the advent of microcomputers in educational settings during the last decade, three primary instructional uses of computers have emerged: (a) Computer-Assisted Instruction (CAI); (b) Computer-Managed Instruction (CMI); and (c) the teaching/learning of programming languages. Much research related to the effect of CAI on learning has been conducted, and impressive findings have been reported. Such findings include (a) CAI can accommodate individual needs; (b) it often allows for student-determined pace of instruction; (c) it generally forces more interaction between student (computer user) and content (CAI program); and (d) it often results in greater motivation for learning (e.g., Chambers & Sprecher, 1980; Feurzeig, Horwitz, & Nickerson, 1981; Kulik, Bangert, & Williams, 1983; Kulik, Kulik, & Cohen, 1980).

Little research on the effects of CMI has been conducted since the primary basis for its use is to facilitate the teacher's job. Although such use lends itself to research, essentially the benefit of CMI is based on the degree of facilitation which is often evident without research. Computer-Managed Instruction includes such uses as customizing data base and spreadsheet programs to reflect a

W. MICHAEL REED is Assistant Professor of Computer Education and English Education, West Virginia University, Morgantown, WV 26506.
DAVID B. PALUMBO is a doctoral candidate, Educational Psychology, West Virginia University, Morgantown, WV 26506.
ALETHA L. STOLAR is a Master's degree student, Home Economics, West Virginia University, Morgantown, WV 26506.

specific teacher need, using word-processing packages for correspondence purposes, and using specially designed software such as grade-keeping and test-generating programs. A strong sentiment, which perhaps has prevented any research on CMI uses, is that, once teachers learn a particular kind of CMI package well, they will use it effectively and it will in fact facilitate some of their often complex and time-consuming teaching tasks.

The teaching/learning of programming languages, on the other hand, is one of the most intensely researched topics in educational computing to date. Several years ago, computer educators felt that programming should be taught to prepare students for the future job market (Reed, 1986). As more computers enter the educational setting and as computers are also becoming more user-friendly—essentially, people need to know less about them due to improved software and machinery. Thus, what people will need to know about computers to perform jobs involving the use of computers will continue to be less and probably can be handled via on-the-job training. Certainly a background in programming will be limited to the relatively few systems design positions, the training for which will be provided by computer science departments and short-term computer training schools.

Although most computer educators agree that teaching programming languages cannot be based on the future job market, they still believe that programming should be taught. Their line of reasoning is that formal schooling often ignores problem-solving skills as an instructional emphasis. Some feel that programming languages may be the language of operational logic (Galanter, 1984). If formal schooling involves little practice at solving problems and programming languages are the linguistic basis for solving problems, the teaching/learning of programming languages may have a place in formal schooling.

With the issue of programming languages and development of problem-solving skills, an important question arises: Which programming language should be taught? Of the three predominantly taught languages in educational settings—BASIC, Logo, and Pascal—Logo appears to have greater support, especially when compared to BASIC (e.g., Clements, 1985; Ginther & Williamson, 1985; Papert, 1980; Taylor, 1985). According to Lockard (1985/86), however, the instruction, regardless of language, should focus on (a) top-down design, (b) modularity, and (c) limited logical constructs. Bennett and Walling (1985) feel that the emphasis should not be on the language, but rather on how structured the instruction is; the more emphasis on structure, the better it promotes sound problem-solving activities.

Given the inherently procedural nature of Logo and Pascal, devising a structured approach to teaching either language is certainly easier as compared to BASIC. Essentially for these two languages, a successful procedure is based on how procedurally compatible and syntactically correct the language is with the inflexible, inherent structure necessary for producing the desired product. Although programming in BASIC does not require a tightly structured approach, it can be taught in a structured way to promote better problem-solving skills and more efficient program design.

According to Lockard (1985/1986), *top-down design* requires that the programmer devise "a program by identifying the primary tasks to be performed, then the subtasks essential to the achievement of each primary task, and so on, until a minimal level of complexity is reached" (p. 107). Taught to approach a programming task top-down, any student, regardless of the language, can solve the programming problem in this manner. *Modularity* involves controlling the program via a "driver module . . . [under which] . . . each identifiable function becomes a module of its own" (Lockard, pp. 108-109). In Logo, the requirement of modularity is met via procedures and subprocedures; in Pascal, subprograms of a larger program; and in BASIC, subroutines. *Limited logical constructs* refer to the use of conditionals and presence of iteration capability, both of which are features of all three languages.

Although a consensus among possibly all computer educators is that the inherent structure of Logo and Pascal might better ensure the inclusion of all three elements of top-down design, an interesting point to consider is whether a structured approach to BASIC might have a more lasting effect than Logo or Pascal, since the inherent structure is absent in BASIC. Or, because there has to be greater intent, and thus greater awareness of a structured approach, for programming in BASIC in a structured manner, a possible effect may be a more lasting sense of structured programming. A theoretical basis for this point may be the notion of *metacognition*, a stage when learners become increasingly aware of appropriate and effective strategies they employ for a particular task (Flavell, 1979).

The other programming language/problem-solving debate has centered on the question, Does learning a programming language improve problem-solving skills? Many researchers have attempted to answer that question and have produced a plethora of studies that do not support such a claim. Rather than claim that such a relationship between problem-solving skills and programming languages does not exist, research reviewers have critiqued existing studies. For example, Burton & Magliaro (this issue) have identified several faulty design features. Such features include (a) inadequate length of treatment; (b) lack of ideationally rigorous treatment; (c) whether, in fact, a language was even taught; (d) the use of insufficiently sensitive and/or inappropriate dependent measures; (c) the lack of a theoretical, problem-solving basis for conducting the studies; and, (f) developmental aspects of the research participants (whether the research participants are too young or developmentally incapable to understand the complex commands, combinations of commands, and/or concepts involved when learning a programming language that might affect problem-solving skills).

Given the two debates—which language better lends itself to being taught and learned in a structured manner? and, does a programming language in fact promote problem-solving skills?—we posed the following research question: What are the comparative effects of BASIC and Logo instruction on problem-solving skills? We chose to compare Logo and BASIC because Logo has been the focal language of the majority of programming language/problem-solving research to date and because BASIC has been highly criticized as an inappropriate language to be taught for promoting problem-solving skills.

DESIGN OF THE STUDY

Using Burton and Magliaro's (this issue) potentially faulty design features and a prior study (Reed & Palumbo, this issue) in which the teaching/learning of the BASIC programming language proved to positively affect problem-solving skills, we constructed a research design that took into account solutions to such potential problems and effective features; how we accommodated the Burton and Magliaro guidelines are explained within each design element.

Sample

Twenty-one students enrolled in formal computer courses at a mid-Atlantic, land-grant university participated in this study. Thirteen of the 21 participants were enrolled in two classes that contained eight weeks of identical instruction on the BASIC language. The other eight participants were enrolled in a Logo class. Burton and Magliaro (this issue) have criticized the choice of participants in previous related research because the samples have been young children who are either at the concrete operations stage or close to the formal operations stage and thus possibly incapable of learning any language beyond rote memorization and fairly simplistic command combinations. Since our sample was comprised of undergraduate and graduate students, such a concern was accommodated.

Treatment

Because Reed and Palumbo's study (this issue) resulted in positive pretest-posttest problem-solving gains, we decided to continue with the nine-week treatment (see Appendix C in Reed & Palumbo, this issue, for the BASIC curriculum and the appendix, this article, for the Logo curriculum). Essentially this treatment involved 27 in-class hours, plus at least another 54 hours of out-of-class programming assignments for a minimum total of 81 hours. Although Burton and Magliaro (this issue) refer to Norman's (1978) notion that development of expertise in a complex area is estimated to require between 5,000 and 10,000 hours of practice with feedback, we felt the nine-week, or approximately 81 hours, might be adequate given the findings of the Reed and Palumbo study. Despite the fact that the Norman-Simon lengths of time cannot be easily, or even realistically, accommodated in a research study, we felt that such times are optimal estimates and that, at certain points of developing from novice to expert, effects can be measured since such development is based on a continuum. A person does not have to first reach expert level in order for competence of a complex task, or other skills peripherally related to it, to become evident and thus measurable.

We accommodated not only Burton and Magliaro's (this issue) contention that a language must be taught but also that the instruction must be rigorous. As the curricula for both languages indicate, both languages were taught and were always the instructional focus of in-class and out-of-class activities. The ideational rigor of the instruction is perhaps best determined by the degree to which instruction of either language parallels the three characteristics of structured programming, as explained by Lockard (1985/86): (a) top-down design, (b) modularity, and (c) limited logical constructs. The instruction for both closely paralleled these characteristics.

Cognitive psychologists (e.g., Frederiksen, 1984; Glaser, 1979) have suggested certain instructional elements for promoting problem-solving skills. Students should be taught to segment the problem in a systematic fashion. They should be given systematic guidance and frequent opportunities to practice and to ask questions so that ambiguities are minimized and redundant information is identified. They should also be taught how to recognize patterns, often through appropriate models. In both treatments, commands were taught within the context of specific programming problems; the participants then used the commands and clusters of related commands for solving other problems. Often attempts were made to speculate what would happen if inappropriate commands or an incorrect sequence of commands were used in a particular sample program; attempts to tie in novel problems with previously learned problems were also made.

Appropriate Dependent Measures

When constructing the design for their study on the effect of BASIC on problem-solving skills, Reed and Palumbo (this issue) reviewed well-established problem-solving instruments and chose two sections from the *Ross Test of Higher Cognitive Processes* (Analysis of Relevant and Irrelevant Information and Analysis of Attributes) and two sections from the *Watson-Glaser Critical Thinking Appraisal* (Deduction and Interpretation). It was felt that these four sections related to some of the kinds of problem-solving activities involved when people specifically learn to program. As Burton and Magliaro (this issue) contend, much of the problem-solving/programming language research that has provided nonsignificant results has not been grounded in problem-solving theory and, thus, has not been devised so that changes in problem-solving skills might be measured.

According to Frederiksen (1984), there are specific elements of problem-solving theory: (a) *problem representation* (task environment—"structure of facts, concepts, and their interrelationships that make up the problem" [p. 367]; and problem space—"problem-solver's mental representation of the task environment" [p. 367]); (b) *means-ends analysis* (the difference between where the problem-solver is now and where he or she wants to be? And what can be done to reduce that difference?); and, (c) *pattern recognition* ("recognize at a glance patterns [or chunks] of related pieces . . . and to use such patterns in processing information" [p. 369]). Given the problem-solving approach of the curricula, we felt that such processes would be employed. As importantly, we felt that the instrument sections Analysis of Relevant and Irrelevant Information, Analysis of Attributes, Deduction, and Interpretation appropriately reflect some of the elements of problem-solving theory. As such, these instruments should measure any changes in programming-related, problem-solving skills.

Procedures

All 21 participants responded to the problem-solving instrument which was comprised of Analysis of Relevant and Irrelevant Information, Analysis of Attributes, Deduction, and Interpretation comments during the first class meeting. For seven weeks thereafter participants received instruction on either Logo or BASIC. Then, during the eighth week, they responded to the same problem-solving instrument.

Analysis of the Data

A dependent t-test was conducted to measure pretest-posttest differences of the Logo participants in order to determine if there were statistically significant gains in problem-solving scores. Likewise, another dependent t-test was conducted to measure pretest-posttest differences for the BASIC participants to determine if there were statistically significant gains in problem-solving scores. The results of the two t-tests would indicate whether problem-solving skills improved due to the instruction of either or both of the programming languages. Finally, an analysis of covariance (ANCOVA) was conducted, with pretest scores as the covariate, to determine if the gains in the problem-solving scores of the Logo group differed significantly from the problem-solving scores of the BASIC group. Such a procedure would indicate if one language promoted a greater increase in problem-solving skills than the other, providing guidelines for using one language in preference to the other for more effectively and efficiently promoting problem-solving skills.

RESULTS

Both the Logo instruction ($t(7) = -3.08, p < .05$) and the BASIC instruction ($t(12) = -3.22, p < .05$) resulted in statistically significant gains in problem-solving skills. The Logo pretest scores had a mean of 43.75 ($SD = 9.74$), and the posttest scores had a mean of 46.63 ($SD = 10.25$). The BASIC pretest scores had a mean of 45.08 ($SD = 6.13$), and the posttest scores had a mean of 47.15 ($SD = 5.39$). However, there was not a statistically significant difference between the gains in the Logo and BASIC groups: $F(1,19) = 5.32, p > .05$. The adjusted posttest mean for the Logo instruction was 44.06, and the adjusted posttest mean for the BASIC instruction was 44.88. These findings indicate that, although both languages effect an increase in problem-solving skills, neither promotes such a development over the other.

DISCUSSION

The Issue of Which Language

Contrary to acclamations for teaching Logo instead of BASIC for promoting problem-solving skills, the results of this study support the teaching of either, with no clear indication for teaching one over the other. This finding is not surprising since computer educators have established the following criteria for selecting programming languages to affect problem-solving skills: The language should (a) allow a top-down approach for solving problems, and its command structure (b) should promote modularity and (c) have limited logical constructs. Although Logo's procedural nature more automatically accommodates the criteria, the teaching of BASIC can also have a top-down design; the language does have modularity via subroutines and has limited logical constructs. Perhaps the major difference is that BASIC might be taught and/or learned in a haphazard manner and the programs may still work, although they are poorly structured and consequently less efficient. Ignoring such factors as top-down design and modularity when teaching and/or learning Logo will often result in poorly constructed programs that will not run. Logo seems to force these criteria more than does BASIC.

But the issue essentially is how a particular language is taught, which is more of an issue with the teacher and how he or she structures the teaching than with the language.

The Issue of Treatment

Based on the results of this study, the programming language/ problem-solving issue centers on not which language to teach but rather on the method of instruction. As indicated by the curriculum for each language, the instruction—or treatment—was highly structured and cyclical. The student-participants were taught not only commands but also sequencing of related commands and segmenting components of a particular programming task. In addition, they were given the opportunities to ask questions to minimize ambiguities and identify redundancies. They were then given programming problems that related to the commands and their relationships with one another; such tasks related to previously learned commands an their sequential relationships. Cognitive psychologists, such as Frederiksen (1984) and Glaser (1979), have stated that such instructional characteristics are needed for promoting problem-solving skills. With such a tightly constructed treatment, the major elements of problem solving—problem representation, means-ends analysis, and pattern recognition—were accommodated.

As explained earlier, successful problem recognition involves the task environment and problem space (Frederiksen, 1984). Designing the instruction so that problem recognition is successful requires a systematic introduction and explanation of commands so that the interrelationships of facts and concepts are clearly understood. Once a sophisticated understanding of commands and their interrelationships are in place, the problem solver's problem-space can be more easily defined.

Such instruction also promotes a means-ends analysis. With a solid basis in a given language, programmers can more easily identify what they presently know or can do and where they need to be so that the presently know or can do and where they need to be so that the programming task is done properly. Once the entry skills and exit skills are identified, they can begin to plan the steps needed to reduce that difference. Such factual awareness leads to the strategic awareness of recognizing patterns and knowing how to manipulate those patterns at increasing degrees of refinement and automaticity (Norman, 1978).

A Matter of Cost and Ease

Although teachers may choose Logo over BASIC for the forced accommodation of the programming language/problem-solving criteria, they should keep in mind that other issues such as cost and ease of language might be important considerations. If BASIC is taught, it is not necessary to purchase additional language software since BASIC comes with most computers; Logo software is fairly expensive, especially when a classroom of 15 computers would require the purchasing of 15 Logo program language disks.

Although Logo has often been considered the language for young children, ease of use is still a debatable point. There are perhaps different levels of complexity of the Logo language; the easier levels can be somewhat quickly learned by young children. But, as they master the easier levels, they also quickly reach more complex levels—probably too complex for them without relying heavily on teacher assistance. If moment-by-moment assistance is needed, one could easily challenge whether the children are learning the language sufficiently so that such skills as problem solving are effectively engaged and developed. Certainly the research by such people as Pea (1983) and Horner and Maddux (1985) suggests that either the language is not being learned or complex, peripheral skills such as those associated with solving problems are not being affected.

Burton and Magliaro (this issue) point out that the children-participants in many studies may not have the cognitive abilities required for a complex task. If that is the case, the simple notion of attempting to promote such skills may be unsupported. And, if young children are developmentally incapable of improving their problem-solving capabilities via a programming language, we come to the point of older learners. Since Logo has typically been chosen for its appropriateness for young children, we have reached a debatable point: Which language is more appropriate? If we agree that young children cannot learn the more sophisticated aspects of a language that might promote problem-solving skills and Logo has been selected for its appropriateness for young children, the real issue, then, is based on other points such as top-down design, modularity, limited logical constructs, and cost. Coupled with these points is the question, is Logo or BASIC more appropriate for older learners? The results of this study indicate that for older learners both languages are equally effective. With that case in point, the real issue may be the simple one: cost. Now, we have reached a point that is not debatable.

CONCLUSIONS

The strengths of this study lie in its accommodation of the six potentially faulty features of existing programming language/problem-solving studies, as identified by Burton and Magliaro (this issue): (a) inadequate length of treatment, (b) lack of ideationally rigorous treatment, (c) whether, in fact, a language was even taught, (d) the use of insufficiently sensitive and/or inappropriate dependent measures, (e) the lack of a theoretical, problem-solving basis for conducting the studies, and (f) the lack of developmental or cognitive capabilities of the research participants.

The fact that problem-solving gains occurred indicates that the length of treatment was adequate; the curricula reflect the criteria for language-selection and a problem-solving approach for delivering the instruction. And clearly, mastery of the programming languages was the primary focus of the instruction. We chose dependent measures that were sufficiently sensitive for measuring certain changes in problem-solving skills associated with learning a programming language. Our sample was comprised of older learners, people with sufficient cognitive capabilities to learn commands and sequential command structures, both of which parallel the two major characteristics of "expert" problem solvers: having (a) a good command of the "linguistic" basis needed for solving a problem and (b) effective strategies for employing that basis so that a problem is solved. If the learner is incapable of obtaining a strong linguistic base, the effective strategies will not be possible simply because there is not a factual or conceptual foundation to be employed (Hayes, 1981).

We feel our findings provide a clearer direction for designing programming language/problem-solving instruction—or treatment—in addition to locating a group of learners for whom developing problem-solving skills via a programming language is possible. A sufficient number of studies have identified which instructional approaches and/or samples are inappropriate for teaching programming languages for the purpose of promoting problem-solving skills. Perhaps additional, better-designed studies need to be conducted. Our findings certainly support the need to look at post-adolescents as ones capable of benefitting from instruction in programming languages for problem-solving skill development. Additionally, appropriate instruction can be designed for pre-adolescents, specifically elementary level students, to provide them with the linguistic base for future acquisition and development of problem-solving skills. Such programming instruction would focus on beginning skill development in the basics of any programming language. These basics may include simple graphics problems, use of text features, and other universal commands common to programming languages.

The acquisition and development of problem-solving skills occurs throughout the lifespan. Better designed instruction and better designed studies are needed to support our claims that learning programming languages can facilitate and enhance problem-solving skills development.

REFERENCES

Bennett, H., & Walling, D. (1985). Once again, structured programming: Is it necessary? *Computers in the Schools, 2*(2/3), 171-178.

Burton, J. K., & Magliaro, S. (1988). Computer programming and generalized problem-solving skills: In search of direction. *Computers in the Schools* (this issue), *4*(3/4).

Chambers, J. A., & Sprecher, J. W. (1980). Computer-assisted instruction: Current trends and critical issues. *Association for Computing Machinery Communications, 23*, 332-342.

Clements, D. H. (1985). Research on Logo in education: Is the turtle slow but steady, or not even in the race? *Computers in the Schools, 2*(2/3), 55-72.

Feurzeig, W., Horwitz, P., & Nickerson, R. S. (1981). *Microcomputers in education*. Cambridge, MA: Bolt, Beranek, & Newman. (ERIC Document Reproduction Service No. ED 208 901)

Flavell, J. H. (1979). Metacognition and cognitive monitoring. *American Psychologist, 34*, 906-911.

Frederiksen, N. (1984). Implications of cognitive theory for instruction in problem solving. *Review of Educational Research, 54*(3), 363-407.

Galanter, E. (1984). Homing in on computers. *Psychology Today*, 30-33.

Ginther, D. W., & Williamson, J. D. (1985). Learning Logo: What is really learned? *Computers in the Schools, 2*(2/3), 73-78.

Glaser, R. (1979). Trends and research questions in psychological research on learning and schooling. *Educational Researcher, 8*, 6-13.

Hayes, J. R. (1981). *The complete problem solver*. Philadelphia: Franklin Institute Press.

Horner, C. M., & Maddux, C. D. (1985). The effect of Logo on attributions toward success. *Computers in the Schools, 2*(2/3), 45-54.

Kulik, J. A., Bangert, R. L., & Williams, G. W. (1983). Effects of computer-based teaching on secondary school students. *Journal of Educational Psychology, 75*(1), 19-26.

Kulik, J. A., Kulik, L. C., & Cohen, P. A. (1980). Effectiveness of computer-based college teaching: A meta-analysis of findings. *Review of Educational Research, 50*, 525-544.
Lockard, J. (1985/1986). Computer programming in the schools: What should be taught? *Computers in the Schools, 2*(4), 105-114.
Norman, D. A. (1978). Notes toward a theory of complex learning. In A. M. Lesgold, J. W. Pellegrino, S. D. Fokkema, & R. Glaser (eds.), *Cognitive psychology and instruction* (pp. 39-48). New York: Plenum Press.
Papert, S. (1980). *Mindstorms: Children, computers, and powerful ideas*. New York: Basic Books.
Pea, R. D. (1983). *Logo programming and problem solving* (Tech. Rep. No. 12). New York: Bank Street College of Education, Center for Children and Technology.
Reed, W. M., & Palumbo, D. B. (1988). The effect of the BASIC programming language on problem-solving skills and computer anxiety. *Computers in the Schools* (this issue), *4*(3/4).
Reed, W. M. (1986). Teachers' attitudes toward educational computing: Instructional uses, misuses, and needed improvements. *Computers in the Schools, 3*(2), 73-80.
Taylor, R. W. W. (1985). Breaking away from BASIC. *Computers in the Schools, 2*(2/3), 165-170.

APPENDIX: LOGO CURRICULUM AND ASSIGNMENTS*

(*The instruction for each class was generally broken down into one or two student-led instructional units. Each of these instructional units dealt with a related set of Logo commands; class time was allowed for the students to begin working with the new commands and integrating them into functional Logo programs; after the second class meeting, each class meeting began with a review of the previous week's commands and demonstrations of the programs that the students had created. In addition to the in-class assignments, each student was to develop a piece of instructional software using the Logo programming language, and thus an ongoing assignment was to use the various Logo commands to develop this software.)

Meeting 1: overview of the course, in class activity on Piaget's stages of development, videotape of the use of Logo in educational settings, responding to study instruments.

Meeting 2: introduction to turtle graphics in the immediate execution mode, examples of the CLEARSCREEN, PENUP, PENDOWN, SETBG, SETPC, REPEAT, FORWARD, BACK,

HOME, LEFT, AND RIGHT commands; the assignment was to generate a program on paper that when typed in would produce a picture of a multi-colored object on the screen.

Meeting 3: instruction on the definition and use of procedures in Logo; the assignment was to create a group of procedures that when executed would draw a complex picture on the screen.

Meeting 4: instruction on the Logo editor and management of the Logo workspace and saving and loading files to and from disk; the assignment was to create a program using a driver procedure that called the program procedures, and once successfully completed, to save the program to disk.

Meeting 5: instruction on commands to manage the screen output (WRAP, WINDOW, FENCE, SETHEADING, SETPOS, SETX, AND SETY commands); the assignment was to use these commands to create a setting with multiple objects.

Meeting 6: instruction on the use of variables and arithmetic operations in Logo; the assignment was to write a program that used both variables and at least one defined arithmetic operation.

Meeting 7: instruction on the use of conditionals in Logo and the concept of conditional recursion; the assignment was to generate a program that used a recursive conditional to perform an operation a fixed number of times.

Meeting 8: instruction on the use of text in Logo programming; the assignment was to generate a program that used both text and graphics commands.

Meeting 9: instruction on getting user input via the keyboard (KEYP, READCHAR, READLIST, READWORD commands) and to output information to the printer or screen (PRINT, SHOW, TYPE commands) and also the generation of sound using the TOOT commands; the assignment was to make a previously written program more interactive by allowing for user input and also adding a music procedure; responding to the study instruments.

David B. Palumbo
W. Michael Reed

Intensity of Treatment and Its Relationship to Programming Problem Solving

Computer technology has entered our educational system. The microcomputer revolution has made computers available to even the smallest school district. "To compute or not to compute" is no longer the question facing educators. Instead we are faced with the question of "how" and "to what end" to use microcomputers. With this rapidly developing technology has come a division in both the "how" and the "to what end" answers to these questions. Should we use a currently limited resource to teach our students programming languages or should we spend even more money to purchase instructional software to teach specific content-area skills via computer-assisted instruction (CAI)? Papert's (1980) powerful ideas concept emphasizes the use of programming languages that will allow students the opportunity to teach themselves these powerful ideas. Kulik, Bangert, and Williams (1983), on the other hand, cite the effectiveness to which microcomputers can be used in computer-based teaching. Unfortunately, there is a finite number of computers and funds to support microcomputer uses in education; therefore, educators are being forced to make a decision as to the uses of the available hardware and software resources.

Research indicates that superior and quicker gains in content-area learning can be achieved when using CAI over more traditional methods of instruction (e.g., Burns & Bozeman, 1981; Chambers & Sprecher, 1980; Vinsonhaler & Bass, 1972). Those who support the teaching of programming languages are equally adept at provid-

DAVID B. PALUMBO is a doctoral candidate, Educational Psychology, West Virginia University, Morgantown, WV 26506.
W. MICHAEL REED is Assistant Professor of Computer Education and English Education, West Virginia University, Morgantown, WV 26506.

ing impressive prospects for the gains related to problem-solving skills to be achieved through learning to program (McCoy & Orey, this issue; Reed, 1986). Yet while the data affirm claims made by CAI supporters, Burton and Magliaro (this issue) point out that such claims do not exist for programming language research. This absence of findings for teaching programming languages has led some to question the speculated link between learning programming languages and higher level thinking skills (Hassett, 1984; Maddux, 1985).

Because of the lack of support for teaching programming languages as a means of developing problem-solving skills, the more diligent of the programming language supporters have begun to look for possible design flaws in the research that has resulted in these less than impressive findings (Burton & Magliaro, this issue; Reed & Palumbo, this issue). As Burton and Magliaro point out, researchers have employed faulty components of research design such as insufficient length of treatment, superficial instruction in the programming language, and inappropriate dependent measures and, in doing so, have produced findings that support the opposition's point of view.

RATIONALE

As Sheingold, Hawkins, and Char (1984) have pointed out, "Computers per se do not constitute a treatment." One can similarly argue that lengthier treatments do not necessarily lead to more impressive gains. As an example, Pea (1983) showed that after a year of exposure to a programming language (in this case Logo), there was not any more improvement in planning skills by the experimental group than of the control group. Based on this result, he expressed doubts about the benefits of teaching programming languages. However, Brown and Rood (1984) reported a slight significant relationship between programming and problem-solving skills in gifted students after 12 hours of intervention. Gorman and Bourne (1983) have found that students exposed to one hour per week of programming performed significantly better than those with only 30 minutes exposure per week. The major distinction in the findings of these three studies centers on "intensity of treatment": the amount of time students are exposed to the programming language—*not in terms of weeks* extended over long periods of time but rather *in terms of hours or minutes* that are in close proximity to one another.

To focus on treatment, we have used the term *intensity of treatment*, which is comprised of three major components: (a) amount of hands-on computer time; (b) rigor of the information presented; and (c) proximity of instructional or treatment sessions to each other. Our research question is, What is the effect of intensity of treatment on problem-solving skills?

DESIGN OF THE STUDY

Sample

Fourteen teacher education undergraduate students enrolled in an introductory computer course at a mid-Atlantic, land-grant university participated in this study.

Materials, Measurements, and Procedures

Problem-solving skills were measured by responses to the Analysis of Relevant and Irrelevant Information and the Analysis of Attributes sections of the *Ross Test of Higher Cognitive Processes* and the Deduction and Interpretation sections of the *Watson-Glaser Critical Thinking Appraisal*; these four sections contained a total of 61 items. A modified version of Spielberger's *Self-Evaluation Questionnaire*, a 20-item, Likert-scale (four-point) instrument was also administered to measure computer anxiety. Each item of the Spielberger instrument was reworked so that the "feeling" measured clearly related to computers; for example, the statement "I feel tense" was changed to "I feel tense when I work with computers."

Prior to receiving instruction in the BASIC programming language, the participants responded to the problem-solving and computer anxiety instruments. After four weeks of BASIC instruction (the midpoint of the treatment), they responded to the instruments again. Then, after the eighth week of instruction, students responded to the instruments a third time.

The participants met for three hours once a week for classroom instruction and computer work. They were also given outside programming assignments designed to take another six to eight hours per week to complete.

Analysis of the Data

To determine the effect of BASIC instruction on problem-solving skills and computer anxiety, six dependent *t*-tests were conducted to determine differences between (a) problem-solving pre- and posttest scores, (b) computer anxiety pre- and posttest scores, (c) problem-solving pre- and midtest scores, (d) problem-solving mid- and posttest scores, (e) computer anxiety pre- and midtest scores, and (f) computer anxiety mid- and posttest scores.

RESULTS

Two dependent *t*-tests were conducted to determine whether problem-solving scores significantly increased and computer anxiety decreased from pretest to posttest. Problem-solving scores showed a significant increase: $t(13) = -3.073, p = .009$. Computer anxiety scores showed a significant decrease from pretest to posttesting: $t(13) = 3.788, p = .002$. Through the course of the eight-week treatment, problem-solving scores significantly increased and computer anxiety significantly decreased.

In answer to the question concerning whether problem-solving skills would increase and computer anxiety decrease after four weeks (the midpoint) of treatment, two dependent *t*-tests were conducted. Scores on the problem-solving instrument did not increase significantly over the course of the first four weeks of BASIC treatment: $t(13) = -.329, p = .746$. Computer anxiety scores, however, did show a significant decrease from pretest to the midpoint of the treatment: $t(13) = 2.575, p = .023$. In essence, the initial four weeks of treatment were not sufficient for increasing problem-solving skills but were sufficient for decreasing computer anxiety.

Two dependent *t*-tests were also conducted to determine whether problem-solving skills increased and computer anxiety decreased between the fourth (the midpoint) and the eighth week (the posttest) of the treatment. Scores on the problem-solving instrument did show a significant increase (at the .06 level): $t(13) = -2.059, p = .06$. Computer anxiety scores did not show a significant decrease between the midtest and the posttest: $t(13) = 1.583, p = .137$. Once the language base was constructed and computer anxiety decreased (during the first four weeks of the treatment), problem-solving skills began to increase.

DISCUSSION

Educators have based the inclusion of programming languages in the curriculum on the speculated link between learning such languages and development of problem-solving skills. Much research (i.e., Pea, 1983; Seidman, 1981) investigating such a link has been conducted, and little support for this link has surfaced. As Burton and Magliaro (this issue) point out, however, much of this research has been lacking in sound design considerations. The findings of our study address some of the concerns that Burton and Magliaro have raised: (a) length and (b) rigor of treatment. We have added another dimension to the treatment-factor: proximity of treatment, or essentially how much time passes between treatment sessions.

In two other of our studies (Reed & Palumbo, this issue: Reed, Palumbo, & Stolar, this issue), problem-solving gains resulted after eight weeks and approximately 81 hours of treatment. Although our studies, including this one, appear to be shorter in weeks than others (i.e., Pea, 1983), length of treatment in terms of weeks is very deceptive—especially when the actual minute or hour "unit" per week is low. For example, 40 weeks at 30 minutes per week may easily be weaker than eight weeks at 150 minutes, although the time in minutes is the same. An additional confounding factor in the 40-week treatment is that, even if gains in problem-solving skills occur, there is no guarantee that the treatment caused such a gain (unless there is a control group). Whereas, with eight weeks of treatment, it is more likely that problem-solving gains were due to the treatment, since problem-solving skills are quite complex and much time is probably needed to cause some measurable change when such change is not intended.

In this study and the two previously mentioned ones, approximately 4,860 minutes were spent dealing with the BASIC programming language over an eight-week period. In all three studies, statistically significant problem-solving gains resulted.

In our first study (Reed & Palumbo, this issue), we investigated the effect of BASIC on problem-solving skills. In our second study (Reed, Palumbo, & Stolar, this issue), we investigated the comparative effects of BASIC and Logo on problem-solving skills; this second study served two purposes: (a) to replicate the first study and (b) to determine if one language—BASIC or Logo—had a greater effect than the other.

In this study, we were interested in determining certain points at which problem-solving skills might be initially affected. We chose the treatment midpoint because of the two-stage interpretation of problem-solving theory; essentially, good problem solvers are those people who have a "great deal of knowledge and a large repertory of powerful strategies to use in attacking their problems" (Flower, 1980, p. 3). We considered that the first half of the treatment (four weeks at approximately 2,430 minutes) would be spent mostly learning the language; given that the treatment was developmental so that subsequent instruction was based on what was previously learned, such an assumption makes sense. Although new commands would be learned during the second half, the students' linguistic (or knowledge) base would be well developed by that point; they could be assigned more difficult problems to solve which would be more dependent on strategies than during the first half. We were working with the assumption that, even after 2,430 minutes of treatment over a four-week period, problem-solving skills would not yet be affected since this period would be primarily spent building the linguistic base.

Because anxiety toward a specific task or device has been proved to affect performance at that task or with that device, we also felt that anxiety toward computers would need to be addressed. In other research we have conducted (Reed & Palumbo, 1987), computer anxiety decreases as people have more computer experiences with increasing degrees of engagement. We worked with the assumption that the students would need to overcome their anxiety toward computers before they could begin to employ effective strategies; we felt that such reduction in anxiety would occur during the first half of the treatment and that additional reduction may or may not occur from midpoint to end-point.

Changes in Computer Anxiety

Based on our findings, computer anxiety decreased significantly from the onset to the midpoint (or the four-week mark). Such a finding supports our assumption that one of the first concerns the students would deal with is the anxiety they felt toward computers, not to mention the need for building the linguistic base. Researchers, expecting change in something as complex and almost peripheral at the beginning stages of content-acquisition as problem-solving skills, are ignoring crucial considerations when designing research, especially when during this period people are concentrating much on survival factors such as dealing with anxiety. Evidently, time for overcoming certain other factors must be built in the design.

That computer anxiety scores did not significantly decrease from midpoint to end-point seems to support this interpretation even more. Sometime during the first four weeks, they had resolved the potentially debilitating effects of anxiety, along with establishing a BASIC linguistic base. After the midpoint, they were then able to focus more on additional commands, more sophisticated combinations of commands, and effective strategies for using these commands or combinations. This insight seems to be supported by the continuum of problem-solving skill development, as indicated by the problem-solving results.

Gains in Problem-Solving Skills

Based on the findings in this study, problem-solving skills did not significantly improve from the onset to the midpoint. Two explanations are offered. First, because there was such a significant decrease in computer anxiety, much effort was spent alleviating this anxiety; the pretest anxiety mean was 48.296, and the midpoint mean was 40.29. Second, effort was also spent learning the commands themselves to establish a linguistic base. As Flower (1980), states, good problem solvers have both a great deal of knowledge and powerful strategies for using that knowledge in a variety of ways. The knowledge logically precedes the strategies. This insight seems especially applicable to a wide range of tasks requiring complex skills—for example, good chess players and good writers. Good chess players must first invest much time learning the different "pieces" and what they each can do before playing chess strategically. Good writers likewise must first discover language and its rules before they can strategically solve a rhetorical problem.

This two-stage approach to developing problem-solving skills is further supported by the fact that problem-solving skills did significantly increase from midpoint to end-point (at the .06 level of significance). It should be noted also that computer anxiety did not decrease from midpoint to end-point, indicating that anxiety had been sufficiently overcome. The period from onset to midpoint resulted in a significant decrease in anxiety and a sufficient acquisition of the language. But, this acquisition was without a significant increase in problem-solving skills. We might easily infer that, once the students had overcome their anxiety and had acquired a certain level of language acquisition, they were then able to think of the language as a vehicle for solving problems. Such later engagement with the language then allows for affecting such peripheral kinds of skills as those associated with solving problems. The findings of this study strongly support this interpretation.

RESEARCH IMPLICATIONS

Given the promising findings of the two previous studies (Reed & Palumbo, this issue; Reed, Palumbo, & Stolar, this issue), we wanted to determine whether or not problem-solving skills might be significantly affected much earlier in the eight-week treatment. Based on the two-stage approach of problem solving (first knowledge has to be acquired before the knowledge can be used strategically), we chose the midpoint, assuming the first half would be needed for acquiring the knowledge. A preliminary, yet strong inference, is that most likely problem-solving skills will not be affected until after the linguistic base is formed; based on our study this effect will not occur soon and not even before the students have worked the language for almost 2,500 minutes, or approximately 40 hours, within a four-week period. Although we have not determined exactly when such development becomes measurable, we can speculate that it occurs sometime during the fourth to eighth week and between 2,500 and 4,860 minutes. Such a finding gives other researchers, especially those who have conducted studies involving more brief exposures of the language, some direction in how lengthy the treatment should be, in addition to the proximity of treatment sessions. Proximity also appears to be a critical issue; the closer the sessions are to one another, the less likely students will need extensive time to recall the information they already received. Certainly studies in which students receive treatment once a week for one hour without accompanying assignments seem to violate the notion of proximity so that much of the next treatment session must be spent reacquainting them with the information previously learned, but evidently not learned well or practiced sufficiently. A question unanswered in this study is how close should the sessions be to one another? Or, how much time do people need in between sessions to assimilate and accommodate the information they have learned? And, might sessions too close to one another be comparable to mass learning, an approach that might not be conducive for affecting complex skills? Certainly, additional questions need to be posed and empirically tested. The findings of this study provide some much-needed direction in designing treatments for programming language/problem-solving research.

REFERENCES

Brown, S. W., & Rood, M. K. (1984, April). *Training gifted students in Logo and BASIC: What is the difference*? Paper presented at the annual meeting of the American Educational Research Association, New Orleans.

Burns, P. K., & Bozeman, W. C. (1981). Computer-assisted instruction and mathematics achievement: Is there a relationship? *Educational Technology, 21*(10), 32-40.

Burton, J. K., & Magliaro, S. (1988). Computer programming and generalized problem-solving skills: In search of direction. *Computers in the Schools* (this issue), *4*(3/4).

Chambers, J. A., & Sprecher, J. W. (1980). Computer-assisted instruction: Reports from a national survey. *Newsletter issue no. 4*. Baltimore: The Johns Hopkins University.

Flower, L. (1980). *Problem-solving strategies for writing*. New York: Harcourt Brace Jovanovich.

Gorman, H., & Bourne, L. E. (1983). Learning to think by learning Logo: Rule learning in third-grade computer programmers. *Bulletin of Psychonomic Society, 21*, 165-167.

Hassett, J. (1984, September). Computers in the classroom, *Psychology Today*, pp. 22-38.

Kulik, J. A., Bangert, R. L., & Williams, G. W. (1983). Effects of computer-based teaching on secondary school students. *Journal of Educational Psychology, 75*(1), 19-26.

McCoy, L. P., & Orey, M. A., III (1988). Computer programming and general problem solving by secondary students. *Computers in the Schools* (this issue), *4*(3/4).

Maddux, C. D. (1985). The need for science versus passion in educational computing. *Computers in the Schools, 2*(2/3), 9-10.

Papert, S. (1980). *Mindstorms: Children, computers, and powerful ideas*. New York: Viking Press.

Pea, R. D. (1983). *Logo programming and problem-solving* (Technical Report Number 12). New York: Bank Street College of Education, Center for Children and Technology.

Reed, W. M. (1986). Teachers' attitudes toward educational computing: Instructional uses, misuses, and needed improvements. *Computers in the Schools, 3*(2), 73-80.

Reed, W. M., & Palumbo, D. B. (1987, March). *Computer anxiety: Its relationship with computer experience and locus of control*. Paper presented at the Annual Meeting of the Eastern Educational Research Association, Boston.

Reed, W. M., & Palumbo, D. B. (1988). The effect of the BASIC programming language on problem-solving skills and computer anxiety. *Computers in the Schools* (this issue), *4*(3/4).

Reed, W. M., Palumbo, D. B., & Stolar, A. L. (1988). The comparative effects of BASIC and Logo instruction on problem-solving skills. *Computers in the Schools* (this issue), *4*(3/4).

Seidman, R. H. (1981, April). *The effects of learning a computer programming language on the logical reasoning of school children*. Paper presented at the annual meeting of the American Educational Research Association, Los Angeles.

Sheingold, K., Hawkins, J., & Char, C. (1984). *"I'm the thinkist, you're the typist": The interaction of technology and the social life of classrooms* (Tech. Rep. No. 27). New York: Bank Street College of Education, Center for Children and Technology.

Vinsonhaler, J. F., & Bass, R. K. (1972). A summary of ten major studies on drill and practice. *Educational Technology, 12*, 29-32.

Susan Magliaro
John K. Burton

Adolescents' Chunking of Computer Programs

In the last decade, much has been made of the cognitive benefits of computer programming for children (e.g., Papert, 1980). Students have been taught such programming languages as BASIC and Logo with the goals of increasing their planning abilities, problem-solving skills, and metacognitive awareness of the problem-solving process itself. However, research to date has produced contradictory results concerning the effects of learning to program on the development of children's complex cognitive skills (Pea & Kurland, 1984). At this point in time, it seems logical to focus research efforts on more basic questions. Specifically, what do children learn about the programming process? And, how do they organize that knowledge in memory?

Researchers of the psychology of computer programming have employed an information-processing perspective in their attempts to uncover knowledge about the cognitive processes of programming (e.g., Brooks, 1977; Mayer, 1981). Specifically, problem-solving theories have served as a theoretical framework for the investigation of the cognitive processes required to construct workable computer programs (e.g., Newell & Simon, 1972).

In focusing on computer programming, recent studies using adult subjects suggest that expert programmers have a "plan library" of

---

SUE MAGLIARO is a doctoral candidate, Educational Psychology, Center for Reading Diagnosis, Evaluation, and Remediation, Virginia Tech, Blacksburg, VA 24061.
JOHN K. BURTON is Associate Professor, Educational Psychology, Education Microcomputer Lab, Virginia Tech, Blacksburg, VA 24061.

The authors wish to thank Norman Dodl, Director of the Virginia Tech Computer Camp, the staff members who assisted in the data collection, and the campers who graciously participated.

basic computer programming "schemas," or recurrent functional chunks of programming code that are often used (Pea & Kurland, 1983). In an investigation of the knowledge structures of programmers with varying levels of expertise, McKeithen, Reitman, Reuter, and Hirtle (1981) found that experts could recall more program lines and procedural chunks across trials than either intermediate or novice programmers. Further, experts were able to recall larger and more highly organized chunks of a coherent program (using the ALGOL W programming language) than were intermediate or novice programmers. However, when students were given a scrambled version of the program, no differences were found across the groups. These results suggest that coherent programs were more meaningful for the experts, thus allowing them to apply what they knew about programming to the recall task.

The information derived from the recall protocols of novices indicated that these individuals focused on surface structures of the program. That is, they used mnemonic techniques based on orthography to enhance recall. The intermediates recalled small chunks of programming code, typically those expressed in natural language terms (i.e., IF-THEN-ELSE and FOR-STEP-WHILE-DO). Expert programmers demonstrated a great deal of clustering of the ALGOL W commands. These clusters were based on the function of the commands and the flow of control processes in the program. These results suggest that the experts' knowledge structures were richer and more complex than the structures of the intermediate or novice programmers.

In a related study, Adelson (1981) found differences in memory capacity and the nature of the knowledge structures of expert and novice programmers. When asked to recall programs in the Polymorphic Programming Language (PPL) code, experts were able to recall more of the program than novices. Further, the findings suggest that while both groups of programmers had conceptual categories for the elements of PPL, the expert programmers seemed to have a more complex conceptualization of the code. That is, the novice programmers' recalls were in the form of a syntax-based organization, while the expert programmers' recalls assumed a semantic, hierarchical organization based on principles of command functions.

Research on the changes in children's conceptual structures after instruction in a computer programming environment has begun to emerge. For example, Pea and Kurland (1983) examined children's learning of programming syntax and comprehension of frequently used subroutines. Their findings indicate that child programmers learn the basic syntax of the language and can construct simple, workable programs. However, they are not able to understand their own program's flow-of-control or more advanced concepts of recursion, conditionals, and variables.

In an effort to investigate what children do learn in a programming environment, the purpose of this study was to examine how students of varying programming abilities recall and organize programming concepts. Specifically, this study focused on the recall of advanced, intermediate, and beginning adolescents for coherent and scrambled computer programs. The specific research questions were:

1. What is the relationship between level of programming expertise and the number of program lines and chunks recalled from coherent versus scrambled programs?
2. What is the relationship between level of programming expertise and the nature of the line and chunk recall in coherent versus scrambled programs?

DESIGN OF THE STUDY

Setting

The study was conducted during the second session of the Virginia Tech Computer Camp which took place the third and fourth weeks of July 1985.

Treatment

On the first day of the 12-day camp, all campers took a test on programming skills to facilitate placement in appropriate instructional groups: beginning, intermediate, and advanced. Beginning programmers were taught to program in Applesoft BASIC. Intermediate programmers were taught advanced concepts in Applesoft BASIC (e.g., text files). Advanced programmers had a background in BASIC and were taught PASCAL, a more structured, procedurally organized language than BASIC. At all levels, instruction involved the learning of programming syntax and debugging. In addition, the instruction emphasized structured programming skills which included thoughtful planning before beginning on-line programming and the use of top-down programming structure. A typical daily schedule included approximately five hours of instruction, four of which were spent in planning programs or on-line programming.

Participants

From a pool of 50 campers, ages 10 to 18, 5 advanced programmers, 7 intermediate programmers, and 4 beginning programmers agreed to participate in the study. Four of the 16 participants were girls, 12 were boys. This ratio of girls to boys was approximately the same for the camp as a whole. Participants ranged in age from 12 to 17.

Materials

Two coherent and two scrambled versions of computer programs were constructed by the researchers and pilot tested during the first session of the camp (i.e., first two weeks of July). These programs reflected the concepts that were taught in the beginning classes and reinforced in the intermediate and advanced classes. All programs were 16 to 18 lines long and written in the Applesoft BASIC programming language. Coherent programs were arranged in a structured, top-down programming style, which inherently organizes the program into procedural chunks. Scrambled programs were constructed from programs consisting of the same concepts as the coherent programs with the program lines rearranged to separate program lines that formed coherent procedural chunks.

Data Collection

Data were collected on the tenth day of the two-week session. All participants were gathered in one classroom and given a packet containing the four programs, four pieces of loose-leaf paper, and a pencil. The presentation of the to-be-remembered programs was randomly ordered for each participant. Participants were instructed that they would have two minutes to read the program and try to remember it as best they could. At the end of two minutes, they were asked to close the program packet and write on a clean piece of paper as much of the program as they could remember. The recall period lasted four minutes, which appeared to be ample time for recall since all students completed their recall protocols, for scrambled and coherent programs, before the end of the four-minute time period. Between each trial the recall sheets were collected and the participants engaged in a brief distractor task.

Analysis of the Data

The recall sheets were scored for number of correct programming lines. A program line was considered correct if the command was spelled correctly and subsequent syntax allowed the gist of the command line to be executed. For example, a recalled line would be counted correct if the original program line read, PRINT "Hi, I'm glad to meet you," and the participant wrote, PRINT "Hi, nice to meet you." Also, if the participant changed the variable letters in a loop (e.g., FOR I = 1 to 5; to FOR S = 1 to 5), the program line was counted correct if all subsequent lines using the variable had assumed the correct variable assignment. The recall sheets were also scored for the number of procedural chunks recalled by the participants. Descriptive statistics were calculated for number of correct program lines and number of procedural chunks recalled. Two separate 3 × 2 × 2 split plot analyses of variance were conducted to assess group differences in line and chunk recall for each version of the coherent and scrambled programs. Tukey tests were used to further investigate main effects within specific cells. Finally, protocols were qualitatively analyzed to examine the nature of the line and chunk recall.

RESULTS AND DISCUSSION

Table 1 reports the mean number of program lines and procedural chunks recalled across program conditions and groups. The raw data indicated that there was a difference in line and chunk recall according to program type (coherent versus scrambled). All three groups of programmers recalled more program lines and chunks from the coherent programs than from the scrambled programs. From the graphs of the raw data (see Figures 1 and 2), this difference was found to be especially apparent for the intermediate programmers. This finding may be due to the curricular emphasis at the computer camp, as well as the programmers' experience level. The advanced group, although familiar with the BASIC language, had been programming in PASCAL during their time at computer camp. These campers may not have been as able as the intermediate group to spontaneously apply schemata or templates for coherent models of BASIC programs. While both the intermediate and beginning programmers had been programming in BASIC, the intermediate group, with their increased level of experience and greater knowledge about what makes programs work, might have been more sensitive to the programs' level of coherence.

The results of the two analyses of variance confirmed these findings. There was a significant main effect for program version (coherent versus scrambled), for both line recall [$F(1,13) = 7.22, p < .017$] and chunk recall [$F(1,13 = 19.477, p < .001$]. While not reaching an acceptable level of significance (i.e., $p < .05$) in either the line [$F(2,13) = .497, p = NS$] or chunk [$F(2,13) = 3.50, p < .066$] recall analysis, an interaction between level of experience and program type can be seen in the graphs of the mean scores (see Figures 1 and 2). Contrary to the findings of Adelson (1981) and McKeithen et al. (1981), the advanced programmers did not recall the most program lines or chunks in the coherent condition. When compared with the advanced or beginning programmers, the intermediate programmers recalled more lines and chunks in the coherent condition, but not in the scrambled program condition. In the scrambled condition, the advanced programmers recalled more than the intermediates, who, in turn, recalled more than the beginners.

This interaction may be explained in terms of the development of a specific versus general knowledge of programming. That is, the primary and, for the most part, sole programming language of the intermediate programmers was the BASIC language. During their 10 days at camp, their expressed tasks had been to construct coher-

TABLE 1. Mean number of program lines and procedural chunks recalled across conditions and groups.

	Beginning		Intermediate		Advanced	
	Lines	Chunks	Lines	Chunks	Lines	Chunks
Coherent	7.38	0.63	9.93	2.36	8.90	1.40
SD	2.20	0.74	4.25	1.78	3.78	1.43
Scrambled	5.75	0.00	7.21	0.14	7.80	0.60
SD	1.28	0.00	2.42	0.36	1.93	0.84

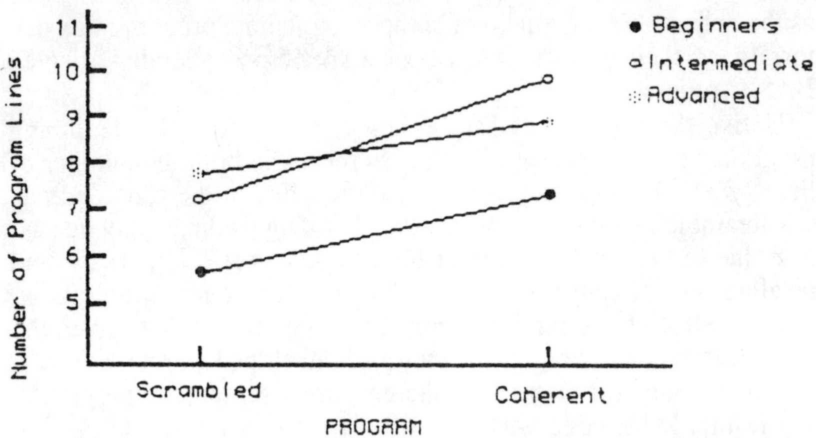

FIGURE 1. Mean number of lines recalled across groups and conditions.

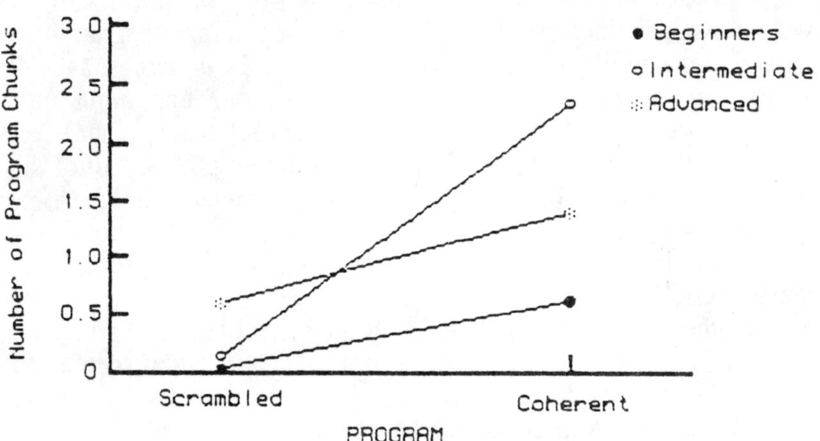

FIGURE 2. Mean number of chunks recalled across groups and conditions.

ent programs that were procedurally organized, resulting in a specific knowledge of a programming language. The advanced group, on the other hand, had a working knowledge of BASIC and were expanding their knowledge of programming to another environment – PASCAL. Thus, the advanced programmers were developing a broader, more general knowledge of programming. As a result, the advanced programmers were able to use this general knowledge to organize procedural chunks in the scrambled, as well as the coherent, programs, while the intermediate programmers had to rely on their specific knowledge base of procedurally oriented BASIC programs.

Unlike the findings of McKeithen et al. (1981), the beginning programmers showed significant differences in both the number of lines ($p < .05$) and chunks ($p < .01$) recalled in the coherent versus scrambled conditions. While the chunking findings may be suspect due to the narrow range of the raw scores (i.e., the beginners recalled only two procedural chunks from the coherent programs, and none from the scrambled programs), it appeared that, given the mean difference in line recall, they had developed a level of expertise that could differentiate coherent from scrambled programs. While this knowledge was not sufficient to enable the beginning programmers to recall as many lines or chunks as the more experienced programmers, they were able to demonstrate some degree of knowledge of the domain.

Closer examination of the nature of the program line recall revealed two distinct patterns. First, the beginning programmers tended to group like commands together from the coherent, as well as the scrambled, programs. For example, one beginning programmer wrote all of the lines that called subroutines together (i.e., GOSUB 70, GOSUB 70, GOSUB 200). Another grouped all of the code that controlled the colors of the programmed graphic (i.e., COLOR = 7, COLOR = 2, COLOR = 0). Thus, while not forming chunks related to procedures, the beginners did organize their recall according to syntactic features. The advanced programmers, on the other hand, attempted to recall the scrambled, as well as the coherent, programs in a procedural order. That is, they seemed to try to make "sense" out of the scrambled programs by reordering some of the lines to produce workable procedural chunks.

The second response pattern paralleled the serial position effect reported by Rundus (1971) in his research on verbal rehearsal and word list recall. His findings indicated that the probability of recalling a word depended upon its position in a list. Typically, words appearing in the beginning or at the end of the list were recalled more often than words in the middle of the list. Words at the beginning of the list were rehearsed more often than the other words, giving them a higher probability of being retrieved from long-term memory. Words at the end of the lists were most recently seen, thus having them accessible in short-term memory. This same serial position effect was seen in beginning programmers' recall of coherent programs and all programmers' recall of scrambled programs. These patterns of recall support the notion that the beginning programmers relied on a rote recall based on syntactic or physical features for coherent and scrambled programs, while the more experienced programmers reverted to this method only when they could not extract some meaning from the programs.

These findings suggest that as adolescents gain expertise in programming, they develop specific schemata for often-used chunks of programming procedures. Even the beginning programmers, who had only 10 days of programming, demonstrated a rudimentary knowledge of the BASIC language and procedures. The findings from the intermediate group indicated that their proficiency as programmers was advanced enough to be successful when the program made sense, but fragile enough to falter when the program was incoherent. The advanced programmers seemed to be able to take a program, either coherent or scrambled, and order the lines into meaningful procedural chunks that would allow the program to run successfully. Similar results were reported by McKeithen et al. (1981) with adult programmers, and Egan and Schwartz (1979) with electronics experts. In the McKeithen et al. study, the adult expert programmers added specific lines to the scrambled program in order to produce coherent nested loops and output sequences. In the Egan and Schwartz study, the electronics experts attempted to recall symbols systematically when the symbols of the electronics diagram were inappropriately positioned.

Differences between advanced and intermediate programmers also became evident in their comments about the recall task. Only advanced programmers remarked about the incoherence of the scrambled programs and stated that those programs were more difficult to remember because "they didn't make any sense." Thus, the difference between intermediate and advanced programmers was seen in their desire to make the program "make sense" as well as in their confidence in declaring that something was wrong with the scrambled program.

CONCLUSIONS

The results of this preliminary investigation indicate that adolescents do learn and organize meaningful knowledge about computer programming much the same way that adults do. That is, those adolescents with more experience and practice develop a level of expertise that allows them to recall programs in terms of semantically related procedures rather than syntactic or physical features. In terms of this study, even those participants who were not programming in BASIC on a day-to-day basis were still able to recall their prior experience with BASIC and the procedures that produce certain programmed results.

While the generalizability of this study is restricted to this sample and setting, it is encouraging to see evidence that adolescents can acquire some levels of expertise in the area of programming. Continued study in this area will be able to reveal individuals' conceptual organization of this programming knowledge. Further investigation into the types of instructional environments and individual differences that are related to the acquisition of programming knowledge is also warranted. By assessing what children are learning in programming environments, we will be better able to ascertain the cognitive benefits of learning to program.

REFERENCES

Adelson, B. (1981). Problem solving and the development of abstract categories in programming languages. *Memory and Cognition*, *9*, 422-433.

Brooks, R. E. (1977). Toward a theory of the cognitive processes in computer programming. *International Journal of Man-Machine Studies, 9*, 737-751.

Egan, D. E., & Schwartz, B. J. (1979). Chunking in recall of symbolic drawings. *Memory and Cognition, 7*, 149-158.

Mayer, R. E. (1981). The psychology of how novices learn computer programming. *Computing Surveys, 13*, 121-141.

McKeithen, K. B., Reitman, J. S., Reuter, H. H., & Hirtle, S. C. (1981). Knowledge organization and skill differences in computer programmers. *Cognitive Psychology, 13*, 307-325.

Newell, A., & Simon, H. A. (1972). *Human problem solving*. Englewood Cliffs, NJ: Prentice-Hall.

Papert, S. (1980). *Mindstorms: Children, computers, and powerful ideas*. New York: Basic Books.

Pea, R. D., & Kurland, D. M. (1984). *On the cognitive effects of learning computer programming: A critical look* (Tech. Rep. No. 9). New York: Bank Street College of Education.

Pea, R. D., & Kurland, D. M. (1983). *On the cognitive prerequisites of learning computer programming* (Tech. Rep. No. 18). New York: Bank Street College of Education.

Rundus, D. (1971). Analysis of rehearsal processes in free recall. *Journal of Experimental Psychology, 89*, 63-77.

Michael A. Orey, III
David P. Miller

Diagnostic Computer Systems for Arithmetic

DIAGNOSTIC SYSTEMS

The computer's potential to diagnose students' misconceptions in their learning processes has far-reaching implications for the field of education. Brown and Burton (1978) developed a program called *Debuggy* that would diagnose student errors in subtraction. Ohlsson and Langley (1985) also developed a general diagnostic system called *DPF* that was supplied with the subtraction "problem space" and was then compared to *Debuggy*. Johnson (1985) constructed a program called *PROUST* that could detect and isolate certain types of semantic bugs in students' Pascal programs. This paper looks at the strengths and weaknesses of these programs, compares them, and suggests an alternative approach to arithmetic diagnosis using a computer. A preliminary case study will be presented as evidence for the need of this new system.

The theoretical basis for *Debuggy* is that "students are remarkably competent procedure followers, but that they often follow the wrong procedures" (Brown & Burton, 1978, p. 157). The theoretical basis for DPF is that "subjects/students (a) change their procedures in 'midflight,' replacing one buggy procedure with another in the midst of solving a problem, (b) learn while doing, and (c) make a fair number of random mistakes" (Ohlsson & Langley, 1985, p. 43). *PROUST* operates on the theory that students are often able to come up with the correct plans for each piece of a problem but are

---

MICHAEL A. OREY, III, is a doctoral student, Division of Curriculum and Instruction, Education Microcomputer Lab, Virginia Tech, Blacksburg, VA.
DAVID P. MILLER is an Assistant Professor of Computer Science, Virginia Tech, Blacksburg, VA 24061.

not always able to combine those plans correctly into a coherent strategy. Clearly, these programs take completely different approaches.

DEBUGGY

The *Debuggy* program makes use of an extensive bug library (20 compound bugs and 110 primitive bugs). It takes a set of problems and their solutions as input and attempts to match the solutions with one or a combination of the bugs that are in the data base. It, of course, takes correct procedures into account. The process of determining which bug fits best is performed by eliminating possibilities and ranking the remaining ones. When the analysis is complete, *Debuggy* will have a subset of possible bugs that represent the solutions that were supplied. It then reports the ranked bugs in their ranked order of viability. It must again be emphasized that the resulting diagnosis is based on *all* of the solutions.

Debuggy was applied to 1,325 student responses to a 15-item subtraction test. According to the analysis by *Debuggy*, 460 students exhibited some inconsistency in their solutions, and 207 appeared to be random in their solutions (Brown & Burton, 1978). The number of students who were diagnosed, at least partially, was 505. The remaining students in this analysis were completely correct in their solutions or missed only one or two problems. Therefore, there were 1,172 buggy test papers, and *Debuggy* was capable of only diagnosing 505 or 43%. This analysis cannot be directly compared to *DPF*, because *DPF* was run with mostly generated bugs. By generated bugs, it is meant that a few of the more common subtraction bugs were selected and solutions were generated by following these faulty algorithms. The above result, 43%, does however, cast some doubt as to the practicability of *Debuggy* as a tool in the schools. In fact, the approach that Brown and Burton selected for their *Debuggy* program, that students tend to follow the same procedure throughout a task, might also be questioned.

DPF

The most significant difference between *DPF* and *Debuggy* is that *DPF* is a general diagnostic system, similar in many respects to Newell and Simon's GPS program (cited in Ernst & Newell, 1969).

The way in which the *DPF* system becomes domain specific is with its inputs. One of the inputs to the system is the problem space. "A problem space is defined through (a) a notation which encodes those properties of the task that the problem solver takes into account, (b) a list of basic cognitive operators which the problem solver uses to process the task, and (c) a termination criterion which the problem solver uses to decide that he has finished the task" (Ohlsson & Langley, 1985, p. 4). The problem space that Ohlsson and Langley used for their test of *DPF* on subtraction will not be reproduced here, but let it suffice to say that the system hinges on the quality of the problem space that is supplied to the system.

The remaining three inputs to the system are the specific tests to be run. First, *DPF* needs the problems to be tested. Second, it needs the correct solution paths for those problems. The correct solution paths need to be in terms of the problem space operators. Finally, the system accepts the buggy solutions that are to be analyzed.

It should be noted here that in the analysis of this system, the program was not supplied with those solutions which were correct. The reason for this is that the system would output the given "correct" solution path that it had received as input. The problem with this is that a student quite often gets the correct answer to a problem, but arrives at that answer using their faulty algorithm. Therefore, the "correct" solution path is not the solution path that the student followed.

In order to assess *DPF* as a diagnostic system, Ohlsson and Langley (1985) selected subtraction because this domain already had been traversed. Essentially, they used bugs that had been found and published by VanLehn (1982) and compared the results of *DPF* with these expected bugs.

The test run consisted of selecting five of the most frequent bugs from VanLehn's (1982) bug library and calculated the result of 17 problems for each of the five bugs. That is a total of 85 buggy answers. *DPF* found the expected bug in 57 of the 85 problems, or 67%. It must be noted that these were perfect bugs and not empirical data. *DPF* was then applied to three sets of solutions done by three different students. These data were also applied to the *Debuggy* program, and the results were then compared. It was determined that *DPF* had difficulty in diagnosing the systematic child. However, *DPF* found an interesting diagnosis for one of the faulty answers given by a student that had been classified as unsystematic by *Debuggy*. In other words, *DPF* found a diagnosis that did not exist in the bug library.

The actual process for *DPF* is that it produces every combination of operators on a given place value to get the value that the student produced. It keeps all of these possible solutions in a list and then reduces this list by comparing those solutions in the list to the possible solution paths for the next place value, keeping those that are in common. It also uses a rating function that uses current psychological research to determine the best solution path. In essence, it uses a best-first search in combination with solution matching.

PROUST

There is a third bug creation theory which has not been thoroughly explored in arithmetic, but has been well documented in analyzing novice computer programmers. Many programming bugs are believed to result when the programmer correctly uses the correct algorithms for solving the problem, but interfaces them incorrectly. When the interface between algorithms is not carefully considered, there is a possibility of a side-effect, from one algorithm, grievously interacting with other parts of the same program.

Semantic program bugs of this sort were able to be detected and analyzed by the *PROUST* program (Johnson, 1985). *PROUST* operates by intention-based diagnosis. In other words, in order to find a bug it is first necessary to know what it is the program is supposed to do. The condition is critical for *PROUST* because the bugs it is trying to detect do not necessarily involve an error in any of the program steps, but rather an error in the way in which those steps are combined.

Unlike an arithmetic problem, a program represents the method for deriving a solution, rather than the solution itself. *PROUST* could conceivably find fault with a program that produced the correct answer, but went about it in a faulty way.

PROUST's general algorithm is to break the program down into a set of relatively independent plans. It can then compare the plans to its interpretation of the problem statement. *PROUST* assigns code from the program it is examining to the plans for which that code serves. By referencing library implementations of each of the plans, the system is able to determine whether each of the necessary plans has been correctly implemented. By examining the program statements that serve more than one plan, *PROUST* can determine if the plans have been assembled correctly. Once all of the plans are identified and the appropriate code is associated with each plan, it is possible for *PROUST* to examine the code and make sure that each step in each plan can be executed without interference.

COMMENTS

It seems that *DPF*, *Debuggy*, and *PROUST* have taken opposing theoretical frameworks for their systems. *Debuggy* takes the approach that people are good procedural thinkers, but sometimes follow faulty procedures. *DPF* takes the approach that people are continually learning by doing and therefore are constantly modifying their procedures. *PROUST* argues that people are good procedural thinkers but are not always able to combine procedures into a coherent whole.

DPF's strategy of examining each problem independently raises some questions about the quality of its diagnosis. While it is undeniably true that people learn by doing, people must be made aware that they have made a mistake before they can correctly modify their behavior. In a subtraction test, where no feedback is given until the test is completed, it is unlikely that a student would intentionally change his or her behavior from problem to problem. Since *DPF* examines each buggy problem independent of those that have preceded it, it can sometimes diagnose a problem in one way that is clearly different than a plausible alternative that would have been chosen had the subject's earlier behavior been taken into account.

The *PROUST* program has never been applied to the analysis of arithmetic. It would not be possible to apply *PROUST* in the same way that *Debuggy* or *DPF* have been used. A Pascal program can be looked upon as a protocol by students of how they are going about solving a problem, while the answer to an arithmetic problem is just that—an answer with no explicit information about how the answer was derived. What the *PROUST* system indicates is that knowing something about the plans used to solve a problem can provide important information for debugging faulty behavior. This is as applicable in the arithmetic domain as it is in debugging programs.

Both *Debuggy* and *DPF* use the way people do subtraction problems in order to diagnose buggy algorithms. Neither of these systems takes into account the process that teachers use to determine buggy student algorithms. Rather, both programs neglect the possibility that the bug discovery process is separate from the algorithm following process. It would appear that research in the area of diagnostic processes needs to be investigated.

It is hypothesized that an approach that would look for systematic errors in subtraction problems could be modified to take into consideration a student who has changed procedures midstream in a test. That is, if the student is classified as unsystematic, the program could then look to see if the student was systematic over some subset of the problems. This is a combination of the strategies used by *DPF* and *Debuggy*. Such a system could be verified and aided through the use of protocols, in addition to the solutions to the test problems.

This approach seems logical in two respects. First, *DPF* does not make use of knowledge that we already have. It must reinvent the wheel on each run of the diagnostic system. Second, the theoretical perspective of *DPF* (i.e., the search through the possible solution paths) has merits. *Debuggy* fails to account for this variety of possibilities. *Debuggy* could be revised to look to see if the student has changed midstream in the task and therefore make itself more powerful.

CASE STUDY

In order to gain a greater understanding of the process of developing such a diagnostic system and the student modelling that goes along with it, a case study was done. The following is the description of a think-aloud protocol that was conducted with a second-grade student named "Bonnie." Here is a sample of Bonnie's results:

$$\begin{array}{r}78\\+41\\\hline 119\end{array}\qquad\begin{array}{r}798\\+\ 37\\\hline 71215\end{array}\qquad\begin{array}{r}398\\+783\\\hline 101{,}711\end{array}$$

Bonnie was consistent throughout the problem set of 24 addition problems.

The problem set was developed to encompass all facets of the addition process. The range of problem types was from 2-digit plus 1-digit numbers to 3-digit plus 3-digit numbers (see Table 1 for the complete listing of problems used). It was designed to have carries in some places, but not in others or carries across all places or no

Table 1.
A case study: **Bonnie.**

	Problem	Correct Solution	Bonnie	Computer
1.	13 + 4	17	17	17
2.	48 + 5	53	53	53
3.	27 + 12	39	39	39
4.	35 + 16	51	410	411
5.	78 + 41	119	119	119
6.	64 + 37	101	911	911
7.	145 + 52	197	197	197
8.	473 + 18	491	4,810	4,811
9.	593 + 34	627	5,127	5,127
10.	798 + 37	835	71,215	71,215
11.	346 + 57	403	3,912	3,913
12.	318 + 471	789	789	789
13.	745 + 137	882	8,712	8,712
14.	713 + 194	907	8,107	8,107
15.	395 + 529	924	81,114	81,114
16.	187 + 418	605	5,915	5,915
17.	704 + 368	1072	10,612	10,612
18.	506 + 295	801	7,911	7,911
19.	346 + 831	1,177	1,177	1,177
20.	639 + 361	1,000	9,910	9,910
21.	456 + 583	1,039	9,139	9,139
22.	329 + 972	1,301	12,911	12,911
23.	398 + 783	1,181	101,711	101,711
24.	923 + 798	1,721	161,111	161,111

carries at all. There were enough digits in the problem set to test most addition facts.

Bonnie's procedure for addition was simply to treat each place value as a separate addition problem. For example, problem 23 (398 + 783) would be calculated by first adding the *ones* digits 8 + 3 and writing the 11 in the *ones* place. (This was determined by Bonnie saying, "8 + 3 is 11" and then observing her write the solution in the *ones* place.) She would then calculate 9 + 8 and write 17 in the *tens* place. Finally, she would calculate 3 + 7 and write the 10 in the *hundreds* place. The result was 101,711, which was cramped into the answer space by writing two digit numbers where a single digit was expected.

It was determined from the discussion following the protocol that Bonnie had never been taught how to carry in her second-grade class. She attempted to accommodate these slightly different types of addition problems into her present procedure and came out with a consistent procedure across the entire problem set. Also, it was determined that Bonnie did not have addition facts for digits whose sum was greater than 10. This was determined by noticing that when she was working on a sum that was greater than 10, she would use her fingers. This addition production system accounted for the fact that there were three addition errors, following her process, out of the 24 addition problems.

These fact errors also had some consistency, but not enough to generalize over her entire addition procedure. For example, in problem eight:

$$\begin{array}{r} 473 \\ +18 \\ \hline 4,810 \end{array}$$

Bonnie continued to follow her procedure, but in her digit sum production system she produced 3 + 8 is 10. The consistency that she exhibited in these three-fact production errors (problems 4, 8, and 11) was that it took place in the unit's place, the actual sum was greater than 10, and her result was always one less than the correct fact.

However, the reason that this bug could not be generalized over her entire procedure was that she was not consistently wrong across all the problems. In fact, in problem 20 (923 + 798) the unit's place digits are the same and in the same order as problem 8, and Bonnie responded with the correct fact, 11, in problem 20 and the incorrect fact, 10, in problem 8. This discrepancy will be discussed further in the section on the diagnostic protocol.

There is one more quirk to Bonnie's procedure that needs to be mentioned. That is, she could produce the correct answer to a carry problem that consisted of 2-digit plus a 1-digit number. For example, problem 2 (48 + 5) was solved to be the correct answer, 53.

By analyzing the protocol, it was determined that she used her fact production system to produce this answer. That is, she started with 48 and counted 49, 50, etc., until she had five fingers extended, and the result was 53.

A simple LISP program was created which modeled Bonnie's behavior, as described above. It was quite exciting to have the computer produce all but the three-fact errored solutions that Bonnie had produced. It was also interesting to see how little code was necessary to produce this output. The entire program is well under one page.

DIAGNOSTIC PROTOCOL

The next logical step in this study was to produce two separate worksheets—one with Bonnie's solutions and one with the computer's solutions. These two forms were then presented to a math education professor in a protocol environment for her to diagnose the buggy procedure in each.

An interesting thing happened during the beginning moments of this protocol. It may have been that the subject was in an experimental environment, but she was initially stumped by the bug. The reason for this was that she looked at each of Bonnie's results one at a time and tried to determine some definite patter between each. Here is the top row of the problem set:

$$\begin{array}{r} 13 \\ +4 \\ \hline 17 \end{array} \qquad \begin{array}{r} 48 \\ +5 \\ \hline 53 \end{array} \qquad \begin{array}{r} 27 \\ +12 \\ \hline 39 \end{array} \qquad \begin{array}{r} 35 \\ +16 \\ \hline 410 \end{array}$$

Obviously, the first three answers are correct. However, problem four is completely wrong. By completely wrong it is meant that the expected result is much smaller than the actual result. To complicate things further, this initial exhibition of Bonnie's faulty behavior is compounded by the fact error in the unit's place. The dialogue that follows is taken from this period of the protocol.

J: 17, so that one's right	(Problem #1)
J: And that one's right	(Problem #2)
J: Is that an 8?	(8 in problem #2)
R: Yeah	

J: OK
J: That one's right (Problem #3)
J: What in the world? (Problem #4)
J: All right, 11 (Unit's digits)
J: I don't have a clue
J: 3 + 1 (Ten's digits)
J: 35 + 16, Why would they write 410?
J: 119, OK (Problem #5)
J: 911, All right (Problem #6)

At this point she had figured out the pattern and made the comment that this is one of the more common addition bugs that exist. She continued to go through the problems to verify that the pattern was consistent throughout the remainder of the problem set.

When "Jane" got to problem eight (473 + 18 is 4,810), she realized that Bonnie had made a few addition errors in her buggy procedure, but essentially followed the procedure consistently on each of the problems in the problem set. In addition, she found that problem 2 (48 + 5 = 53) was done correctly by counting from 48 until she used 5 fingers.

It was then stated that, if the fact errors were not in the problems (i.e., the computer's results), it would be very easy to determine the error pattern that was exhibited by Bonnie. In fact, Jane was prompted by being told that anyone who was competent in addition could probably recognize the pattern. Why would this be so? Her response was, "Maybe our perception is that you know what 8 and 7 are [In reference to problem twelve (798 + 37 = 71,215)]. It's 15, and she's not put down the five. [Also], you pick out that 15, you pick out that 15 [in the unit's place] as an entity and the 12 [in the ten's place] here. Why is that so easy to pick out? I guess that's because you see the number that you know is the answer [to the sum of that particular place value]." Jane analyzes the problem set using her diagnostic methodology. This might imply that her methodology is reflected in the aforementioned dialogue. It would seem that her methodology goes something like this. Look at the problem: (a) If it seems correct, do the calculation to make sure; otherwise, (b) immediately begin checking for a bug by going through the solution process and check for possible buggy solution paths. In the case of problem 12, she knew something was wrong because Bonnie's solution was so large. Therefore, she began to find the solution to the problem, and she recognized the "entity of 15" located in the area of the unit's digit. Furthermore, this hypothesis was immediately reinforced when she checked the *tens* place.

In the case of writing a diagnostic system to follow Jane's process, the search and pattern matching might be constrained by looking at the solution and determining if the solution were correct. If it were not, then determine if the solution is within some close range of the correct answer, say plus or minus 5. Finally, it could be determined if the correct answer has about the same number of digits as the given solution. This could constrain the solution path to looking for fact errors for numbers that are close to the correct answer. If protocol information is provided, it should be possible to make some analysis of whether the subject is using the correct procedures for solving the problem. In Bonnie's case it would become clear very quickly that she was totally missing a necessary procedure.

REFERENCES

Brown, J. S., & Burton, R. R. (1978). Diagnostic models for procedural bugs in basic mathematical skills. *Cognitive Science, 2*, 155-192.

Ernst, G., & Newell, A. (1969). *GPS: A case study in generality and problem solving*. New York: Academic Press.

Johnson, W. L. (1985). *Intention-based diagnosis of errors in novice programmers*. New Haven, CT: Department of Computer Science, Yale University (YALEU/CSD/RR #395).

Ohlsson, S., & Langley, P. (1985). *Identifying solution paths in cognitive diagnosis*. Pittsburgh, PA: The Robotics Institute, Carnegie Mellon University (CMURI-TR-85-2).

VanLehn, K. (1982). Bugs are not enough: Empirical studies of bugs, impasses, and repairs in procedural skills. *Journal of Mathematical Behavior, 3*, 3-72.

Leah P. McCoy
Michael A. Orey, III

Computer Programming and General Problem Solving by Secondary Students

INTRODUCTION

The microcomputer is fast becoming a standard fixture in secondary schools. Some schools stress basic literacy and computer-assisted instruction, but many are offering programming instruction at elementary, middle, and high school levels. Some proponents of programming instruction claim that improved problem-solving ability is a natural outcome of programming instruction (e.g., Papert, 1980). Significant relationships have been found between achievement of college students in introductory programming classes and (a) ability to solve algebra word problems (Soloway, Lochhead, & Clement, 1982), and (b) general problem-solving ability (Nowaczyk, 1984). While there is some tentative evidence of gains in problem-solving ability as a result of instruction in computer programming, these studies are not conclusive.

Research studies have identified a number of significant predictors for programming achievement. Such variables in undergraduate computer science courses have been problem-solving ability (Nowaczyk, 1984), grade-point average, general ability, verbal ability, numerical ability (Peterson & Howe, 1979), verbal SAT score, mathematics SAT score, and high school rank (Leeper & Silver, 1982). With secondary students, Webb (1985) found that mathematics skill and spatial ability were significant predictors of

---

LEAH P. McCOY is Assistant Professor, Mathematics Education and Computer Education, Indiana University, South Bend, IN 46615.
MICHAEL A. OREY, III, is a doctoral student, Division of Curriculum and Instruction, Education Microcomputer Lab, Virginia Tech, Blacksburg, VA 24061.

programming ability in both group and individual settings. Linn (1985) found that general ability was significantly related to programming achievement in typical middle schools.

The purpose of this study was to determine cognitive prerequisites for, and outcomes of, computer programming achievement in secondary schools. Specifically, it examined (a) the effect of computer programming on problem-solving ability, and (b) the relationship of ability and problem-solving scores with computer programming achievement.

DESIGN OF THE STUDY

Sample

Participants in this study were novice computer programming students in public middle and high schools in a rural school district. All students enrolled in introductory BASIC programming classes in two middle schools ($n = 73$) and one high school ($n = 47$) were included in the study.

Many of the students enrolled in the programming classes at all three schools were placed in the class by the school on the basis of previous high school achievement, though no particular test score was the criterion. Other students, especially at the high school level, chose the class as a free elective.

Instruments

Programming achievement was measured by the BASIC Programming Achievement Test. This 40-item test was developed for this study in consultation with a panel of computer educators. Items were designed on the basis of generally accepted topics in beginning BASIC, with no knowledge of the exact curriculum of the schools in the sample. Subtests include Knowledge, Comprehension, Composition, and Debugging. This partitioning of programming skill was suggested by Schneiderman (1976). An estimate of internal consistency (using Cronbach's Alpha) was .85.

General problem-solving ability was measured by the General Problem Solving Test, adapted from Nowaczyk (1984). This test includes seven items dealing with logical operations, algebraic solutions, transformations, and identification of relationships. Test-retest reliability was .49.

The Science Research Associates Achievement Battery (SRA, 1978) was used to assess general ability for the middle school students. This test has a reported internal consistency reliability (KR-20) of .90. The publisher also claims high content validity based on selection of items by a panel of experts. Scores selected for inclusion in this study were Verbal Educational Ability and Nonverbal Educational Ability. Raw scores were used in the analyses.

The Differential Aptitude Tests (DAT, 1973) were used to obtain measures of general ability for the high school students. The subtests of this test, have reported Spearman-Brown split-half reliability estimates from .88 to .96. Scores included in this study were Verbal Reasoning and Numerical Ability. Raw scores again were used in the analyses.

Procedures

At the beginning of the semester, students were pretested on the BASIC Programming Achievement Test and General Problem-Solving Test. Aptitude scores were obtained from school files.

Students then received one semester of daily instruction in BASIC programming. Briefly, the courses were standard beginning BASIC, including graphics and text with iteration and conditionals. At the end of the semester, students were posttested on programming achievement and general problem solving.

RESULTS

Means and standard deviations were calculated for each variable for each group (middle and high school; see Table 1). The group means for posttest scores in Programming Achievement were significantly higher than pretest scores in both groups: middle school (t (72) = 12.20; $p < .0005$) and high school ($t(46) = 18.67$; $p < .00005$).

Examination of General Problem-Solving scores revealed a significant difference between pre- and posttests for middle school ($t(72) = 4.68$; $p < .0005$) and high school ($t(46) = 3.44$; $p < .0001$).

Pearson Product-Moment Correlation Coefficients were calculated to determine relationships. In the middle school, the only variable significantly related to Programming Achievement was Problem-Solving Ability (pretest; Table 2).

Table 1.

Means and Standard Deviations of Variables

		Scores			
		Middle School[a]		High School[b]	
Measures		**Pretest**	**Posttest**	**Pretest**	**Posttest**
Programming achievement	*M*	4.16	18.52	5.81	29.04
	SD	(2.87)	(7.91)	(3.15)	(8.72)
Problem solving	*M*	2.55	3.32	4.28	4.98
	SD	(1.46)	(1.36)	(1.41)	(1.24)
Verbal ability	*M*	20.33			
	SD	(3.87)			
Nonverbal ability	*M*	17.85			
	SD	(5.10)			
Verbal reasoning	*M*			31.53	
	SD			(8.10)	
Numerical ability	*M*			30.92	
	SD			(5.17)	

[a]$n = 73$, [b]$n = 47$

Table 2.

Correlation Matrix for Middle School Sample

	Programming achievement	Problem solving	Verbal ability	NonVerbal ability
Programming achievement	----	.271*	.185	-.049
Problem solving	.271*	----	.318**	.166
Verbal ability	-.185	.318**	----	-.019
Nonverbal ability	-.049	.166	-.019	----

$n = 73$
*$p < .05$, **$p < .01$

In the high school, Programming Achievement was significantly related to both Problem-Solving Ability (pretest) and Verbal Reasoning Ability (see Table 3).

Further analysis involved using Stepwise Multiple Regression to construct a prediction model for Total Programming Achievement. For both groups, the prediction equation contained only one significant predictor variable, General Problem-Solving Ability (pretest; see Table 4).

DISCUSSION

Based on the differences in pretest and posttest programming achievement scores, it is apparent that the middle and high school students learned BASIC programming. Since the two levels were not compared directly, there is no evidence that one or the other group learned more or better. Further research might examine the relative gains, but the conclusion of this study is that both groups learned BASIC programming.

Perhaps the most important result of this study is the gain in problem-solving ability after one semester of programming instruction for both middle school and high school students. Many computer educators intuitively believe that programming trains the mind and improves general problem solving. Even though this study did not include a control group, these results constitute preliminary evidence of improved problem solving as a result of programming instruction.

Table 3.

Correlation Matrix for High School Sample

	Programming achievement	Problem solving	Verbal ability	NonVerbal ability
Programming achievement	----	.470**	.303*	-.015
Problem solving	.470**	----	.370*	.102
Verbal reasoning	.303*	.370*	----	.384**
Nonverbal ability	-.015	.102	.384**	----

$n = 47$
$^*p < .05$, $^{**}p < .01$

Table 4.

Stepwise Multiple Regression Analysis

Criterion = Programming Achievement		High School (n = 47)
PREDICTOR	**BETA WEIGHT**	**F OF BETA WEIGHT**
General problem solving (Pretest)	.470	12.73*
	ADJUSTED R^2 = .203	

Criterion = Programming Achievement		Middle School (n = 73)
PREDICTOR	**BETA WEIGHT**	**F OF BETA WEIGHT**
General problem solving (Pretest)	.271	5.644**
	ADJUSTED R^2 = 203	

*$p < .001$, **$p < .05$

Similar to the results of Nowaczyk (1984), this study found evidence of a relationship between general problem-solving ability and programming achievement. In addition to evidence of a gain in general problem-solving ability as a result of programming instruction, a relationship between pretest problem-solving ability and programming achievement was detected. In both the middle and high school samples, the pretest score for general problem-solving ability had a positive relationship with Programming Achievement scores. In both samples, General Problem-Solving Ability was the only significant predictor in the Multiple Regression Equation. Again, this is tentative but important information.

Based on the results of this study, one can conclude that there is a relationship between computer programming and problem-solving ability. It appears that general problem-solving ability is the best available predictor of programming achievement. It also appears that programming instruction has a positive effect on problem-solving ability and therefore is a worthwhile subject for study by secondary students.

REFERENCES

Differential aptitude test. (1973). New York: Psychological Corporation.

Leeper, R. R., & Silver, J. L. (1982). Predicting success in a first programming course. *SIGGSE Bulletin, 14* (1), 147-150.

Linn, M. C. (1985, May). The cognitive consequences of programming instruction in classrooms. *Educational Researcher*, pp. 14-29.

Nawaczyk, R. H. (1984). The relationship of problem-solving and course performance among novice programmers. *International Journal of Man-Machine Studies, 21*, 149-160.

Papert, S. (1980). *Mindstorms: Children, computers, and powerful ideas*. New York: Basic Books.

Peterson, C. G., & Howe, T. G. (1979). Predicting academic success in introduction to computers. *AEDS Journal, 12*, 182-191.

Schneiderman, B. (1976). Exploratory experiments in programmer behavior. *International Journal of Computer and Information Science, 5*, 123-143.

Science research associates achievement series. (1978). Chicago: Science Research Associates.

Soloway, E., Lochhead, J., & Clement, J. (1982). Does computer programming enhance problem-solving ability? Some positive evidence on algebra word problems. In R.J. Seidel, R.E. Anderson, & B. Hunter (Eds.), *Computer Literacy: Issues and Directions for 1985* (pp. 171-185). New York: Academic Press.

Webb, N.M. (1985). Cognitive requirements of learning computer programming in group and individual settings. *AEDS Journal, 18*, 183-193.

Leah P. McCoy
John K. Burton

The Relationship of Computer Programming and Mathematics in Secondary Students

INTRODUCTION

There is currently little evidence as to the cognitive prerequisites for computer programming instruction with children. As computer courses become increasingly common in elementary and secondary schools, it is important that this area be investigated.

Mathematics is an area that intuitively seems related to computer programming. Pea and Kurland (1983) state that general mathematics ability is a possible prerequisite to success in computer programming. Studies have found significant relationships between mathematics-related variables and programming achievement in college students (Mayer, 1975; Nowaczyk, 1984). In a study with children age 11 to 14, Webb (1985) found a significant relationship between general mathematics ability and computer programming achievement. Soloway, Lochhead, and Clement (1982) found a positive relationship between knowledge of mathematical variables and computer programming, again with college-age subjects. Thus, there is some evidence of a relationship between mathematics and computer programming, but very little research has been done with elementary and secondary age children.

Other variables have also been discussed as possible predictors of computer programming achievement. Pea and Kurland (1983) present the problem of how old, or at what Piagetian developmental

LEAH P. McCOY is Assistant Professor of Mathematics Education and Computer Education, Indiana University, South Bend, IN 46615.
JOHN K. BURTON is Associate Professor, Educational Psychology, Education Microcomputer Lab, Virginia Tech, Blacksburg, VA 24061.

level, children must be to benefit from computer programming experience. Webb (1985) found a nonsignificant correlation between age and computer programming ability with a constrained sample. Little research is available that relates Piagetian developmental level to programming achievement (c.f., Clements & Gullo, 1984).

A final possible predictor of programming achievement is gender of student. Since there is a possible close relationship between mathematics and computer programming, the ever-present topic of gender differences must be considered. The one available study that considered gender as a variable (Linn, 1985) found a nonsignificant relationship with programming achievement.

This study examined the relationships of six variables (gender, age, developmental level, mathematics background, ability to use mathematical variables, and mathematical problem-solving ability) with computer programming achievement in children.

METHODS AND PROCEDURES

Sample

Participants in this study were novice computer programming students, age 10 to 17, in an introductory BASIC programming class at a summer computer camp. All 21 students who completed the course during a two-week session were included in the sample. While the students were all motivated to learn programming as evidenced by their enrollment in the computer camp, there were no entrance requirements. Students came from various educational backgrounds and achievement levels.

Instrumentation

Age, Gender, and Number of Higher Mathematics Courses Successfully Completed (Algebra I and above) were determined from a *Personal Data Questionnaire*. Developmental Level was assessed by the *Inventory of Piaget's Developmental Tasks* (Furth, 1970). The score on this 36-item pencil and paper test is interpreted as reflecting a child's degree of formal operativity. Patterson and Milakofsky (1980) have studied this measure extensively. They report a test-retest reliability of .84 to .86 for ninth-grade students taking this test. Based on individual tests and interviews, they conclude that this measure has concurrent and construct validity.

Ability to Use Mathematical Variables and Mathematical Problem-Solving Ability were determined from subtest scores on the *Algebra Readiness Test* (Lueck, 1947). Split-half reliability, corrected by the Spearman-Brown formula, is reported to be .96.

Computer Programming Achievement was determined from a departmental test used in beginning computer courses in a large university. Four scores were obtained from this test: Knowledge of Programming Terminology and Commands, Debugging, Program Construction, and Composite Computer Achievement (the sum of the three subtest scores).

Procedure

A test battery was administered to all students on the first day of camp. It included the Personal Data Questionnaire, Inventory of Piaget's Developmental Tasks, the two subtests of the Algebra Readiness Test, and the Computer Programming Achievement Test.

The students then received 10 days of intensive instruction in BASIC programming on Apple IIe microcomputers. A typical day included two hours of lecture, four hours of supervised practice, and three hours of optional practice.

Briefly, the beginning BASIC curriculum consisted of the following key components.

1. Use of a concrete computer model to illustrate machine functions
2. Use of graphics (static and animated) to concretize key concepts
3. Top-down structured programming using subroutines
4. Text formatting
5. Arithmetic operators
6. Input/output
7. Graphics using peripherals (Koala Pad, etc.)
8. Conditionals using IF..THEN.. statements
9. Introduction to word processing
10. History and architecture of the microcomputer
11. Maximum individual hands-on experience
12. Group projects

Participants were posttested the last day of camp on the Computer Programming Achievement Test and the two subtests of the Algebra Readiness Test.

RESULTS

The difference between the means of the pre- (4.43) and post- (29.71) Composite Computer Achievement scores were statistically significant ($t(20) = 11.350$; $p < .0005$) as were the differences between pre- (7.42) and post- (9.71) mean scores for Mathematical Problem Solving ($t(20) = 4.200$; $p < .0005$) and the pre- (7.33) and post- (8.29) mean scores for Ability to Use Mathematical Variables ($t(20) = 2.020$; $p < .05$). (See Table 1.)

Examination of the intercorrelation matrix of simple Pearson product moment correlations (see Table 2) revealed several significant relationships. The Composite Computer Programming Achievement gain score was significantly related to Age ($r = .53$; $p < .05$), Higher Mathematics Courses Completed ($r = .59$; $p < .01$), Mathematical Problem Solving Ability ($r = .52$; $p < .05$) and Ability to Use Mathematical Variables ($r = .66$; $p < .01$). Results were similar for achievement subscores for Knowledge and Programming. Debugging Achievement, however, showed no significant relationship with any of the predictor variables. Other nonsignificant relationships were Developmental Level and Gender with all achievement scores.

DISCUSSION

The results of this study indicate a relationship between mathematics and computer programming achievement. All three mathematics variables (Higher Mathematics Courses, Mathematical Problem-Solving Ability, and Ability to Use Mathematical Variables) were related to programming achievement.

These results, agreeing with those of Mayer (1975) and Webb (1985), suggest that mathematical variable is an important concept for beginning programmers. This concept is traditionally taught in secondary school Algebra I classes. It appears that mathematics courses in elementary and middle school should emphasize the concept of variable. In addition to being related to Programming Achievement, Ability to Use Mathematical Variables is also related

Table 1.

Means and Standard Deviations for Pre and Post Measures

	Pretest		Posttest	
Variable	*M*	*SD*	*M*	*SD*
Age	13.333	1.932		
Gender	.429	.507		
Developmental level	22.762	5.898		
Higher math courses	.952	1.322		
Math problem solving	7.429	3.458	9.710	3.410
Math variables	7.333	5.825	8.290	6.460
Achievement knowledge	3.429	4.864	16.810	7.884
Achievement debugging	1.000	1.304	6.048	1.564
Achievement construction	0.000	0.000	6.860	5.280
Achievement composite	4.430	5.410	29.710	12.930

to Number of Higher Mathematics Courses Completed and to Mathematical Problem Solving. It is possible that an improvement in the understanding of mathematical variables would result in an increase in both general mathematics achievement and in mathematical problem-solving ability, as well as programming achievement.

The results of this study indicate that age is significantly related to programming achievement. Webb (1985) did not find an age difference, but the subjects in her study were of a more restricted age range than this study. Similarly, the present study found no significant relationship between Developmental Level and Programming Achievement. This is also possibly due to a restricted range of participants. Even though the standard deviation of Devel-

Table 2

Correlation Matrix

	Developmental Level	Age	Higher Math Courses	Math Problem Solving	Math Variables	Gender	Achievement Composite	Achievement Knowledge	Achievement Debugging
Age	.61**								
Higher Math Courses	.40	.83**							
Math Problem Solving	.59**	.66**	.43						
Math Variables	.37	.70**	.65**	.76**					
Gender	-.06	.00	.03	-.05	.15				
Achievement Composite	.41	.53*	.59**	.52*	.66**	.26			
Achievement Knowledge	.43	.53**	.50*	.48*	.64**	.19	.91**		
Achievement Debugging	-.19	.09	.19	-.12	-.02	-.03	.13	.05	
Achievement Construction	.35	.40	.52*	.49*	.55**	.30	.86**	.62**	-.10

* $(p < .05)$, ** $(p < .01)$

opmental Level scores was 5.898, it is possible that all participants were close to the same Piagetian stage (probably early Formal), because the test measures degree of formality rather than its presence or absence. Further study should concentrate on the relationships between age and Developmental Level with beginning programming achievement.

Another important result of this study is the non-significant relationship of Gender with Programming Achievement. This replicates the results of Linn (1985) and suggests that male and female students are equally capable of learning computer programming.

Debugging Achievement was not related to any of the predictor variables, indicating that it is a distinct skill. Other studies have described the difficulties of students in learning to debug programs (Kurland, Pea, Clement, & Mawbry, 1986). This study agrees with other studies that have identified debugging skill as an integral part of the programming process (Dalbey & Linn, 1985; Pea & Kurland, 1983). Further research in this area is recommended.

After programming instruction, both Ability to Use Mathematical Variables and Mathematical Problem-Solving Ability scores were significantly improved. This has far-reaching implications for secondary school curricula. If further research confirms that computer programming does have a significant positive effect on areas of mathematics achievement, computer programming should become a requirement for each secondary student.

REFERENCES

Clements, D. H., & Gullo, D. F. (1984). Effects of computer programming on young children's cognition. *Journal of Educational Psychology, 76*(6), 1051-1058.

Dalbey, J., & Linn, M. C. (1985). The demands and requirements of computer programming: A literature review. *Journal of Educational Computing Research, 1*(3), 253-274.

Furth, H. (1970). *An inventory of Piaget's developmental tasks*. Washington, DC: Catholic University.

Kurland, D.M., Pea, R.D., Clement, C., & Mawbry, R. (1986). A study of the development of programming ability and thinking skills in high school students. *Journal of Educational Computing Research, 2*(4), 429-458.

Linn, M. C. (1985, May). The cognitive consequences of programming instruction in classrooms. *Educational Researcher*, 14-29.

Lueck, W. R. (1947). *The algebra readiness test*. Indianapolis: Bobbs-Merrill.

Mayer, R. E. (1975). Different problem-solving competencies established in learning computer programming with and without meaningful models. *Journal of Educational Psychology, 67*, 725-734.

Nowaczyk, R. H. (1984). The relationship of problem solving and course performance among novice programmers. *International Journal of Man-Machine Studies, 21*, 149-160.

Patterson, H. O., & Milakofsky, L. (1980). A paper-and-pencil inventory for the assessment of Piaget's tasks. *Applied Psychological Measurement, 4*(3), 341-353.

Pea, R. D., & Kurland, D. M. (1983). *On the cognitive prerequisites of learning computer programming* (Tech. Rep. No. 18). New York: Center for Children and Technology, Bank Street College.

Soloway, E., Lochhead, J., & Clement, J. (1982). Does computer programming enhance problem-solving ability? Some positive evidence on algebra word problems. In R. J. Seidel, R. E. Anderson, & B. Hunter (Eds.), *Computer literacy: Issues and directions for 1985* (pp. 171-185). New York: Academic Press.

Webb, N. M. (1985). Cognitive requirements of learning computer programming in group and individual settings. *AEDS Journal, 18*, 183-193.

PROBLEM-SOLVING SOFTWARE

One of the most enlightening and important developments in educational computing has been the recent improvement of instructional software—and specifically those programs that enhance problem-solving skills. This section opens with Kay Gore's review of general problem-solving software. She effectively addresses how such software may help answer, "What knowledge is most worth having?" Her rhetorical framework for discussing problem-solving software centers on (a) software that specifically addresses the teaching and reinforcement of generic problem-solving skills; (b) software that is specifically designed to teach and enhance problem-solving skills within the content areas; and, (c) software that is not designed to teach and strengthen such skills but which teachers use successfully to do so.

Following Kay Gore's article is one by W. Michael Reed who addresses the use of composing process software in the context of writing theory and problem-solving theory. He begins with a brief review of writing theory followed by an explanation of problem-solving processes associated with writing, as identified by Linda Flower. According to Reed, good solvers of rhetorical problems must have (a) a great deal of knowledge and (b) a large repertory of powerful strategies to use in attacking their problems. Because success at writing is related to writing ability, poor and perhaps even average writers will minimally not have effective strategies "to use in attacking their problems." Composing process software segments the writing task into specific stages and guides writers through activities related to each stage while allowing them to access an activity or stage at any point. He applies the problem-solving theory and writing theory to *Writer's Helper*, one of several composing process programs.

Next is Don Cook and Tom Teates's article on science-related problem-solving software. They begin their discussion with an overview of the concern for the lack of a problem-solving focus in the science curriculum. They state that "the science taught in schools remains basically a collection of facts with students expected to display their knowledge-level command of these facts on school tests and standardized national exams." Clearly the science curriculum is not the only culprit that is employing the "holding-students-accountable-primarily-for-factual-information" syndrome; all content areas need to extend students beyond the rote level. They divide problem solving and science into four categories: (a) science simulations, (b) microcomputer-based labs, (c) general problem solving, and (d) multimedia combinations.

Suzanne Bazak and Ben Bazak provide an overview of mathematics problem-solving software. They claim that through effective problem-solving software, the computer is capable of (a) "making the learning of mathematics the investigative journey that it was meant to be"; (b) "making the mathematics learned more relevant"; (c) "providing a new approach to teaching problem-solving skills"; and, (d) "freeing the math student form the burden of mastery of manipulative skills and providing more time for students to develop higher order thinking skills."

This section ends with Wayne Nelson's article on problem solving and software design. He discusses the problem-solving activities associated with making decisions as people design software. Effectively placing the software design process in the context of novice and experienced programmers, he states "that novice and expert designers differ not only in the amount of knowledge about programming but also in their ability to recognize and control the design process." This particular point extends to a higher level the notion of problem solving beyond acquiring a working knowledge of a programming language and employing strategies that are used when manipulating the language: What is the most effective way to present information, via a programming language, for the intended user?

The intent of this section has been to extend the link between problem solving and computers from the misconception that problem-solving skills can be developed only via programming languages. One strong qualifier, however, is that educators need to realize that problem-solving skills are complex and require much time and practice to develop. Enhancing problem-solving skills via problem-solving software will require, like attempting to improve problem-solving skills through programming languages, much interaction between student and software. An occasional pass with problem-solving software will probably have no more of an effect than will an occasional exposure to a programming language. Certainly research needs to be conducted to verify the points made by the authors in this section.

Kay Gore

Problem-Solving Software to Implement Curriculum Goals

What knowledge is most worth having?

Certainly not much of what we attempt to fill kids' heads with while they are in school! I remember a few years ago being horrified at the methods of a movement called curriculum mapping. As I understand the process, teachers were to keep an honest record of what they covered in their classes and the time allotted each activity and then districts were to construct their curricular objectives based on what the teachers were actually teaching. The goal was to ensure high district-wide competency test scores because the districts would be testing students on what the teachers were actually teaching rather than testing them on the mandated objectives that are often neglected. In this system the knowledge most worth having seems to be the answers to questions on a paper-and-pencil test!

We don't hear much about curriculum mapping these days, probably because the districts that attempted the process discovered that mapping simply didn't work. Either their teachers were chicken-livered liars who claimed to be teaching the mandated objectives, fearing reprisals should they tell the truth – no need to map. Or the teachers had no real need of employment, told the truth, and demonstrated that no teachers of the same subject were teaching anything for the same amount of time or, for that matter, were even teaching the same content and objectives – no way to map.

I mention this brief flash in the educational literature because of its fundamental folly: It fails to address the question asked at the outset of this article – What knowledge is most worth having?

In an Information Age, the knowledge most worth having is probably intellectual self-confidence, the knowledge that we can

---

KAY GORE is a doctoral candidate, Arizona State University, Tempe, AZ 85281.

make sense of things without requiring someone else to interpret those things for us. Someone who is intellectually self-confident, for example, has a greater tolerance for ambiguity, feels more comfortable with change, and has a greater need to know . . . everything. Such people do not view themselves as victims of their present circumstances but as authors of their fate – self-directed, interested in the world that surrounds them, seeking to collaborate. The intellectually self-confident person is a successful problem solver, *the* essential characteristic.

How can schools develop and implement curricula that help students become intellectually self-confident? A major tool for realizing such a curriculum is the computer. The computer demands that the student be an active maker of meaning rather than a passive recipient of information. Computers are uniquely suited to developing environments that encourage problem-solving skills and strategies.

But a serious obstacle to wide acceptance of the need to incorporate problem solving exists: the lack of a universally accepted definition of problem solving. One popular definition is the solving of word or story problems in math. However, a careful reading of such guidelines as *Computers in Education: Goals and Content* derives another definition, one that is more compatible with a wide range of subject areas. Problem solving, in these guidelines and in much of the recent literature, is defined as skills in critical thinking and/or logic. Moursund (1985) offers a nontechnical definition of the term; a problem has three parts:

1. How something actually is (initial state).
2. How you would like the thing to be (goal state).
3. What you can do about the situation (allowable types of actions to move from the initial state to the goal state). (p. 3)

In order to solve a problem, according to Moursund, a person has to have a desire to solve the problem, a broad base of knowledge and experience, a "feeling of power – a repertoire of possible actions" (p. 3), and the ability to take action and assess those actions. While this is a clear, direct explanation of problem solving and problem-solving behaviors, it fails to include the actual mental processes and strategies that underlie the behaviors.

A recent study (Gore & Martin, 1986) examining software that can be used to teach and enhance problem-solving skills discovered three classifications for problem-solving software: (a) software designed to teach and reinforce generic problem-solving skills, (b) software designed to teach and enhance problem-solving skills within the content areas, and (c) software not designed to teach and strengthen such skills but which teachers use successfully to do so.

Two software publishers best known for developing software whose explicit objective is to teach and provide practice in problem-solving skills are Sunburst Communications (39 Washington Avenue, Pleasantville, NY 10570-9971) and The Learning Company (545 Middlefield Road, Suite 170, Menlo Park, CA 94025). *The Super Factory* ($59.00) by Sunburst extends problem solving into three dimensions by having students work with cubes. The program offers three activities: research, design, and challenge. The research section provides students with the opportunity to become familiar with the program by experimenting with a cube, selecting pictures, and placing them on the cube. In placing the pictures, students must learn how to rotate the cube using the arrow keys.

In the design section, students design a cube but must create the design two-dimensionally by developing a plan that consists of selecting pictures and directing the turns. When the plan is complete, the program translates the design onto a three-dimensional cube. Students have the option to edit their design by inserting or deleting pictures or rotations of the cube. Students can also go through their plan, one step at a time, pressing RETURN to see each step executed.

In the challenge section, students choose from five levels of difficulty. The goal is to duplicate the design of the challenge cube. The difficulty levels range from easy, where only two to three pictures must be placed on the cube correctly, to super, where the same picture may be used several times. Students plan as they did in the design activity, but here they can select one of three help options: to rotate the challenge cube, rotate both cubes at the same time, or see the plan for the challenge. Once they think they have duplicated the challenge cube, students can try the plan out and then return to the planning stage for revisions, step through the plan one step at a time, or check the plan against the challenge cube.

Students must (a) analyze the challenge cube, (b) plan their steps, (c) try their plan, and (d) check to see if they have successfully matched the challenge cube. In so doing, they have completed the four steps in problem solving: analyze, plan, try, and check. Students can exit the program at any time, and they can save a design or challenge situation to return to for later use.

Robot Odyssey I ($64.95 for the Addison Wesley school version) by The Learning Company also helps students develop and practice problem-solving skills, but here the context is a five-level adventure game where the students escape from Robotropolis by working their way up from the lowest of the five levels with the help of robots they construct. The robots enable the players to overcome obstacles that would otherwise defeat them. Each obstacle presents a logic puzzle that the players solve through the attributes they select to build into their robots.

One interesting aspect of the construction process is that the program offers the capability of constructing prototype chips in the Innovation Lab. These chips can be designed to perform discrete functions so that they can be burned into small chips that in turn can be used as sections in solving a larger problem. Thus, the program encourages students to break a problem down into smaller steps in order to arrive at a solution—an important concept in problem solving.

The advantage of software that teaches and reinforces problem-solving skills that are not embedded in any one subject area is that teachers can discuss the strategies and processes being employed as strategies and processes that are basic to problem solving in all areas. Students and the teacher together can then explore methods for incorporating the skills into solving subject-area problem situations. But through such programs, students come to understand that problem solving is not the domain of any one subject.

CONTENT AREA PROBLEM-SOLVING SKILLS SOFTWARE

Software that enhances problem-solving skills through a content area then builds upon the knowledge gained in such programs as *The Super Factory* and *Robot Odyssey I*. One assumption of content-specific programs is that people need a knowledge base before they can be successful problem solvers. These programs can help students become aware of the necessity to draw from past experiences and previously acquired information.

Some exciting programs in this category use reading instruction as a vehicle for practicing problem-solving strategies. *Alice in Wonderland* ($49.00) by HRM (175 Tompkins Avenue, Pleasantville,

NY 10570) is designed for second through seventh grades. The program uses an adventure program format to create a context that demands the application of sequencing, predicting, inferencing, trial and error, memory skills, and logic.

The program is based on the Lewis Carroll classic, *Alice in Wonderland*. Students assume the role of Alice. As the adventure progresses, they are confronted with options that direct the structure of the story so that the Carroll premise is present—Alice becomes bored reading a book, falls asleep, encounters a strange rabbit that leads her down the rabbit hole into a wondrous land—but the details along the way, as well as the ending, depend on the reader's choices.

Mystery Mazes ($49.95 per disk or $89.00 for the two-disk program) by Educational Activities, Inc. (P.O. Box 392, Freeport, NY 11520), is another reading program that provides practice in problem-solving strategies. The program employs the context of a detective adventure and offers two cases that can be purchased together or separately. Students read a police report of a crime and follow the clues that are presented to decide which of the suspects is the actual criminal. The program encourages students to take notes as they progress through the adventure.

The *Social Studies Explorer Series* by Mindscape (3444 Dundee Road, Northbrook, IL 60062) are social studies programs that make history and geography come alive while they also provide students with the opportunity to apply problem-solving skills. Structured in the format of adventure programs, *Revolution and Constitution, Discovery and Exploration, Westward Expansion, Civil War and Reconstruction, Central United States*, and *Western Europe* ($39.95 each) have students make choices that determine what information they will uncover about the event or location being presented. Once they have identified the historical event or the geographical location, they must then identify which clues lead them to the answer. Students must make inferences and scan for clues while drawing upon the knowledge of history or of geography. The *Explorer Series* programs give teachers an excellent opportunity to help students understand the importance of using problem solving and critical thinking to make sense of history and geography.

Where in the World Is Carmen San Diego? ($49.95) by Broderbund (1948 Fourth Street, San Rafael, CA 94901) is another program that enhances problem-solving skills in the format of a geography lesson embedded in another detective adventure. The program presents a crime that has just been committed, and the students must determine the identity of the criminal and track the culprit down. In each city that the criminal visits, the program offers three options: Students can search for clues to the criminal's identity and the city he or she fled to next, identify characteristics of the culprit uncovered in the search and thereby eliminate suspects, or see what cities the planes fly to from a particular location. To aid in determining cities, the program comes with an almanac.

SOFTWARE NOT DESIGNED TO TEACH AND REINFORCE PROBLEM SOLVING

The last category of software is used successfully to teach and reinforce problem-solving skills but does not claim to do so. Electronic Arts (2755 Campus Drive, San Mateo, CA 94403) has many excellent programs designed primarily for the entertainment market but which are powerful resources and tools for teaching problem solving. *Heart of Africa*, a sound geography program despite its development for the home market, illustrates this point. In the tradition of *Seven Cities of Gold*, marketed to the schools by Mindscape but developed by Electronic Arts, *Heart of Africa* is a game of exploration that challenges the user to explore Africa in search of an ancient Egyptian emperor's gold-encrusted tomb. The computer becomes the map to this treasure, but it is a historically and geographically correct map where the students must apply map reading skills and search strategies in order to be successful.

Car Builder ($39.95) by Weekly Reader Family Software (245 Long Hill Road, Middletown, CT 06457) is a scientific simulation program that enables users to experience the process of car design. Students begin by designing the mechanical guts of the car, selecting chassis length, engine, transmission, and fuel tank. They then choose the suspension options and the tires and brakes. Once this process is complete, they design the body of the car. The program even allows the user to customize the body of the car.

Each of these programs can contribute to students' intellectual self-confidence by making them aware of a repertoire of skills and strategies that they can apply when faced with a problem. They begin to understand that problem solving is a process in which there is rarely one right solution. They should then consciously follow the process and select the most appropriate skills and strategies to apply to the situation. Such an approach can make the problem a stimulating adventure rather than a frustrating nightmare.

And, for teachers who feel uncomfortable teaching problem solving or feel there is no room for it as a separate topic in the curriculum, computer software offers an effective vehicle for teaching these skills as well as for making them part of the existing curriculum.

What knowledge is most worth having? Knowledge of how to continue to gain knowledge throughout one's entire life. Such knowledge derives from intellectual self-confidence, the self-confidence that working through problem situations can be a rich source of intellectual growth.

REFERENCES

Gore, K., & Martin, N. (1986). Four methods for using the computer to integrate problem solving into the curriculum. *Proceedings of the sixth annual microcomputers in education conference: Ethics and excellence in computer education: Choice or mandate*. Rockville, MD: Computer Science Press.

Moursund, D. (1985). Problem solving: A computer educator's perspective. *Computing Teacher*, 2-5.

W. Michael Reed

Problem-Solving, Writing Theory, and Composing Process Software

PROBLEM-SOLVING THEORY AND WRITING THEORY

Much from cognitive psychology's theory of problem solving has been applied to the composing process. One of the foremost researchers/theorists in the area of writing as a problem-solving process is Linda Flower who, through her writing text entitled *Problem-Solving Strategies for Writing* (1985), segments writing stages into problem-solving processes. Flower's approach to viewing writing as an attempt to solve a rhetorical problem is an extension of the three-stage approach to attempting and completing a writing task. To put Flower's interpretation in its historical context, a look at the theory preceding hers may be helpful.

Rohman (1965), one of the modern pioneers in writing process theory, identified three basic stages that writers undergo when writing. The first stage, called *prewriting*, essentially includes strategies writers employ to generate potential ideas for the essay. Prewriting is followed by what is called the *writing* stage, or the acts of elaborating the selected ideas generated during the prewriting stage, finalizing sentence structure, attending to audience and grammatical accuracy, and establishing paragraph flow. During the final stage, called *rewriting* or, perhaps more specifically, revising, the writer attempts to finalize the text for the reader. Given that solving a problem is best approached as a top-down process (first "identifying the primary tasks to be performed, then the subtasks essential to the achievement of each primary task, and so on until a minimal level of complexity is reached," [Lockard, 1985/1986]), the three-

W. MICHAEL REED is Assistant Professor of Computer Education and English Education, West Virginia University, Morgantown, WV 26506.

stage approach increases the likelihood of attempting a writing task in a problem-solving like manner.

Rohman's (1965) model has proved to be a valid framework for understanding writing behaviors. Later researchers (i.e., Emig, 1971; Flower, 1979; Perl, 1979; Sommers, 1979, 1980; Stallard, 1974) have modified Rohman's interpretation of writing processes. First, they have found that the three-stage approach is not strictly linear—that, in fact, writers may easily employ prewriting strategies during the rewriting stage when they sense a particular idea needs further development. As Perl (1980) states: "[R]ecursiveness in writing implies that there is a forward-moving action that exists by virtue of a backward-moving action" (p. 364). A reason for this kind of activity may be due to what Perl terms *retrospective structuring* and *projective structuring*:

> The former relies on the ability to . . . attend to what is there, . . . and then to assess if those words adequately capture one's meaning. The latter relies on the ability to assess how the words on the page will affect someone other than the writer, the reader. (p. 369)

Perl is referring to the notion of ability and how it may affect the extent to which a writer may employ the necessary steps in producing effective prose. Researchers have found that writing ability affects how one approaches a writing task: Poor writers typically do not prewrite or rewrite, essentially believing their first draft is also their final draft.

Rohman's model and its subsequent modifications have certain implications for viewing writing as a problem-solving process. Flower states that "[g]ood problem solvers . . . typically have a great deal of knowledge and a large repertory of powerful strategies to use in attacking their problems" (1980, p. 3). Coupling insights into writing as a three-stage process, its modifications, and the requisite knowledge and skills of good problem solvers poses a few essential questions. If poor writers do not prewrite or rewrite, they probably do not have the strategies to generate content or revise the prose they produce. What kinds of instructional activities might be used to help them overcome these deficiencies? What are some of the more specific processes involved when people prewrite or rewrite? More specifically, if prewriting is generating ideas, what specific strategies are needed to generate ideas? If rewriting is polishing up the written product for the reader, what kinds of strategies are needed for the writer to succeed?

Writing-schema researchers (i.e., Daiute, 1984; Reed, Burton, & Kelly, 1985; Reed & Sherman, in press) have likewise found some discrepancies based on writing ability. Reed, Burton, and Kelly have found that writers of low ability have poorly developed schemata (organized bodies of information stored in permanent memory) related to descriptive and persuasive writing, yet well-developed schemata related to narrative writing. Average writers and very good writers likewise have well-developed schemata related to narrative writing but also have better developed schemata related to descriptive and persuasive writing. Very good writers' descriptive-related schemata are extremely well developed, almost to the point of automatic use. Reed and Sherman (in press) have found that poor writers produce their best text when not employing an imposed idea-generation strategy and not writing potential ideas down on paper for later reference; whereas, very good writers produce their best text when they do employ both strategies. Daiute (1984) has found that writers "store a variety of complex sentence structures . . . [which] . . . serve as patterns that guide the production of novel sentences" (p. 210); however, the relative stability of sentence-structure patterns is affected by writing ability, indicating that poor writers do not have at their disposal some of the more complex sentence-structures for use as they write and revise their essay. Whether needed writing-related schemata are present, and even if they are not, to what extent they have been developed may play an important role in how effectively certain writers may be able to solve problems. The content of the essay may be there, but the strategic frameworks may not be.

Such discrepancies can be useful in predicting how successful a writer may be in solving a rhetorical problem. If good problem solvers have both "a great deal of knowledge and a large repertory of powerful strategies," (p. 3) as Flower (1980) claims, we can immediately speculate that poor writers—and probably average writers, too—will not be good solvers of rhetorical problems. Although they may have adequate knowledge, assuming that this knowledge is the potential content of an essay, they most likely do not have the strategies needed to retrieve this information from permanent memory (Reed & Sherman, in press), put it in its correct modal framework (Reed, Burton, & Kelly, 1985), and present it in a variety of sentence structures (Daiute, 1984).

Problem-solving theorists (i.e., Frederiksen, 1984) have identified specific elements of problem solving: (a) problem representation, (b) means-end analysis, and (c) pattern recognition. *Problem representation* includes both the task environment ("structure of facts, concepts, and their interrelationships that make up the problem" [p. 367]) and problem space (the "problem-solver's mental representation of the task environment" [p. 367]). *Means-end analysis* centers on the difference "between where I am now and where I want to be?" and "what can I do to reduce that difference?" (p. 368). And, *pattern recognition* refers to the ability to "recognize at a glance patterns of related pieces and to use such patterns in processing information" (p. 369).

The elements of problem solving can be easily applied to writing. The *task environment* is made up of the topic itself, the information related to the topic that the writer may have, and the strategies involved in manipulating that information. The *problem space* is the writer's mental representation of the writing task. The *means-end analysis* would be the process of constantly checking the evolving text with the imagined final-product and employing strategies to obtain the goal. And, *pattern recognition* refers to the modal frameworks and the complex sentence structures at the writing stage of the process and to the rules that govern language during the rewriting stages. Based on earlier points, the success of solving a rhetorical problem is highly related to the knowledge and strategies the problem solver has at his or her disposal. The recursive nature (or not solving a problem in a strictly linear fashion) certainly parallels the findings by those researchers who have modified Rohman's model.

One of the greatest contributions Flower has given to writing research is isolating more specific mental processes writers must ideally engage in when they compose (1985). She has broken the prewriting stage into (a) exploring the rhetorical problem ("testing the writer's image of the problem" [p. 63] and having the writer "explain the assignment" [p. 63] to himself or herself), (b) making a plan (making "a plan to do and a plan to say" [p. 63] and operationalizing the goals), and (c) generating new ideas ("turning off the editor and brainstorm," "talking to the reader," "systematically exploring the topic," and "resting and incubating" [p. 79]).

The writing stage is segmented into (a) organizing ideas ("expanding code words" and "building an issue tree" [p. 89]), (b) knowing the needs of the audience ("analyzing the audience," "anticipating the reader's response," and "organizing for a creative reader" [p. 129]), and (c) transforming writer-based prose into reader-based prose ("setting up a shared goal between writer and reader," "developing a reader-based structure," and "giving your reader cues" [p. 159]). The subprocesses of the rewriting stage are (a) reviewing the paper and its purpose ("compare the paper to the plan" and "simulate the reader's response to the paper" [p. 185]), (b) testing and editing the writing ("editing for economy and forceful style" [p. 185]), and (c) editing for connections and coherence ("transforming listlike sentences" and "revealing the inner logic of the paragraphs" [p. 201]). All of these strategies may be easily placed under the problem-solving umbrella, are dependent upon the competence of the writer at having, accessing, and employing these strategies, and will not be activated in a strictly linear manner.

WRITER'S HELPER: ITS RELATIONSHIP WITH PROBLEM-SOLVING THEORY

The process of writing quite clearly is a very complex and time-consuming activity. If writing is to be taught well and correctly, a writing instructor needs to attend to the three-stage approach in conjunction with the subprocesses identified by Flower (1985). Faced with large numbers of student writers and the need to teach with sound pedagogy in mind, instructors have a very demanding job ahead of them. Perhaps one way of assisting the teacher is the use of what is called *composing-process software*, computer programs that allow the writer to engage in programmed prewriting activities and analysis of the final-written product for certain grammatical features. Computer researchers (i.e., Vinsonhaler & Bass, 1972) have found that computers are very effective when used as instructional supplements and often are more effective than traditional methods alone. Given the discrepancies in writing-related skills between writers of different abilities, the effectiveness of computers as an instructional supplement, the computer as motivator and its accommodation of such individualized factors as student-determined pace and immediate feedback, and the finding that students of low ability seem to benefit most from computer-assisted instruction, computer use for developing effective writing strategies may be justified.

Writer's Helper (Wresch, 1984a) is one of numerous available composing-process software programs (see Wresch [1984b] for a collection of articles on different software). It is divided into three programming parts: (a) prewriting, (b) writing, and (c) rewriting.

The prewriting component is broken into three areas: (a) finding a subject, (b) exploring a subject, and (c) organizing information. For writers not sure of what they would like to write about, the finding-a-subject option allows them three possible ways to locate a subject: (a) Brainstorming (the writer is to begin writing on anything for a specified number of screen lines and then, after stopping, is to read what has been produced and decide if a topic has emerged); (b) Lists (the writer is to list a number of topics that interest him or her and then later choose one of the topics to write on); and (c) The Questioner (asks the writer a series of questions, such as "Who is the strangest person you know?" After all questions have been either answered or skipped over, the writer is to choose one of the answers as a topic).

For those who have a subject in mind, the explore-a-subject is most appropriate. It has two options for exploration: (a) Crazy Contrasts and (b) Three Ways of Seeing. Crazy Contrasts has the writer compare and contrast the topic with unusual things such as comparing the student-selected topic with a ski lift, an abandoned building, and an old calendar. Through such a process the writer should acquire a better understanding of the topic. Three Ways of Seeing prompts the writer to view the topic in isolation, within a larger context, and as a process of change. The explore-a-subject section also has Teacher's Questions, allowing the instructor to add heuristics of his or her own choosing; such invention strategies as Burke's pentad or Aristotle's Common Topics could easily be included as an option for this section.

The organizing-information option provides four choices: (a) Trees, (b) Debating an Issue, (c) Comparing and Contrasting, and (d) the Five-Paragraph Theme. Trees has the writers cluster generated information into categories to help them organize related information for inclusion in specific paragraphs. Debating an Issue has the writers state an opinion and then lists points in support of and points against the opinion. If the points against the opinion outnumber supporting points, the writers are asked if they would like to take the opposite stand. The program then presents the points of their stand and has them choose the three best; it performs the same display for those against and then generates an outline. Comparing and Contrasting asks the writers to name their topic and then a similar one that might be more familiar to the reader. Then, the writers are to list three most important similarities and three most important differences; the six key points are then displayed in outline form. The Five-Paragraph Theme has the writer choose a purpose for the essay (compare, contrast, etc.) and has the writer address how the audience might feel about the topic. The writer then provides three statements related to the topic which serve as topic sentences for paragraphs. The program produces an introduction, displays the three paragraphs created by the writer, and then produces a concluding paragraph. The purpose of this choice is to require the writer to pay attention to purpose, accommodate the audience, and provide information about the topic.

Unlike some other composing process software, *Writer's Helper* does not have a word-processing component, meaning that the writer leaves *Writer's Helper* and, via a word-processing program in the computer, loads the work generated during the earlier prewriting activities. One benefit of this option is that the writers can use dictionary, spell check, and thesaurus programs compatible with the word-processing program they are using, after elaborating the text during the writing stage.

The rewriting or revision features of *Writer's Helper* will do a series of final-product analyses. The messages displayed as part of this analysis only suggest that the writer change something and explain why such a change may be needed. The writer still must perform the changes. Three features center on presentation of text for the writer's review. One feature is an outline of the first sentences of each paragraph so that the writer can attend to topic sentences (this, of course, is based on the assumption that the first sentence is the topic sentence). Another features is a word frequency count, which lists all words in the paper and the number of times each words occurs; this gives the writer some idea of redundant use of words and possibly vague words. And a third feature is listing the document by sentences, which isolates each sentence so that the writer can focus on its structure separately from the rest of the paragraph.

Three analyses of the product include (a) number of words per paragraph, (b) number of words per sentence, and (c) readability level. The revision component will produce a graph of words per paragraph and another of words per sentence and inform the writer if the essay has too many or too few words per paragraph or sentence. A lengthy paragraph may mean that more than one topic has been covered in the paragraph; a short paragraph may mean that one topic has not been sufficiently developed in relation to the rest of the paragraphs. A lengthy sentence may mean that more than one idea has been included in a sentence or, if only one is in the sentence, its points may need to be treated in separate sentences. A short sentence may mean that an idea has not been sufficiently developed. The readability check asks the writer for the reading level of the intended audience, analyzes the readability level of the essay, and informs the reader of the discrepancy and ways to close the gap if the discrepancy is more than two levels. Reed (1987) has determined that the words-per-paragraph information is a reliable predictor of essay quality; words-per-sentence information is a reliable predictor of essay quality and words per T-unit; and, that the readability information is a reliable predictor of words per T-unit, words per clause, and clauses per T-unit.

The revision component will also check for homonyms, gender-related language, to-be verbs, and usage errors. There is also the option for teachers to insert comments in the text, if the teacher-reading of the essay is via the computer; the student can retrieve the comments.

THE POTENTIAL OF COMPOSING-PROCESS SOFTWARE FOR DEVELOPING WRITING-RELATED PROBLEM-SOLVING SKILLS

Certainly a much-needed area of research involves determining the effect of composing-process software on writing performance. Without evidence, what might be said is reduced to speculation. However, the speculation may easily hold true if we discuss such software in the context of problem-solving theory. Table 1 gives a comparison on the elements of problem-solving theory, the elements of writing theory, and the components of *Writer's Helper*. Although the table presents information in a linear manner, it is critical that people understand that such elements may be used at any point, depending on the emerging rhetorical text and how the rhetorical problem solver decides to deal with that text.

The inherent structure of *Writer's Helper* and the numerous other composing-process programs available should force a top-down approach to solving the rhetorical problem. By segmenting the writing task into prewriting, writing, and rewriting activities, the software requires that the writer deal with a particular kind of activity at one time. The activities isolate subprocesses involved in solving problems. Such subprocesses center on those activities needed to pro-

Table 1

The Integration of Problem Solving Theory, Flower's Version of Writing Theory, and the Components of *Writer's Helper*

Problem-Solving Theory	Writing Theory (via Flower)	*Writer's Helper* Components
Task environment	Testing the writer's image of problem	Brainstorms, Lists, The Questioner
Problem space	Explaining problem to the writer Making a plan to do and say Operationalizing goals Turning off editor and brainstorm	Brainstorms, Lists, The Questioner
Means-ends analysis	Talking to reader Systematically exploring topic Resting and incubating Expanding code words Building an issue tree Analyzing audience Anticipating reader's response Organizing for reader Setting up shared goal between writer and reader Developing reader-based structure Giving the reader cues	Crazy Contrasts, Three Ways of Seeing, Teacher's Questions Trees, Debating an Issue, Comparing and Contrasting, Five-paragraph Theme Exiting to a word-processing program
Means-ends analysis/ Pattern recognition	Comparing paper to plan Simulating reader's response to paper Editing for economy and style Transforming listlike sentences Revealing inner logic of paragarphs	Outline, Listing by Sentences Words per Paragraph, Words per Sentence, Readability Index, Homonyms, To-Be Verbs, Usage Errors

Note. Processes are recursive and are activated when there is a need.

duce content and to analyze the final-written product. As Table 1 indicates, there is a strong parallel between the strategies suggested by Flower and those in *Writer's Helper*.

Perhaps one of the most emphatic qualifiers is that how well people solve rhetorical problems is based on the knowledge and strategies they have at their disposal. Even though *Writer's Helper* and other composing-process software may make such strategies more available, there is not a guarantee that there will be immediate success, since optimal success comes about when the strategies are inherent to the writer, not merely external tools. However, such segmentation of specific rhetorical concerns and related strategies for dealing with those concerns should heighten an awareness of the task environment, the problem space, a means-end analysis, and pattern recognition. Much of the success will be due to the inherent abilities of a given writer. Better writers may be impeded by imposed strategies simply because they should already have effective prewriting and revising strategies. However, poorer writers should, *in the long run*, benefit. Acquisition, restructuring, and fine-tuning of such strategies should take much time. Although Norman (1978) claims that expertise at a particular skill takes anywhere from 5,000 to 10,000 hours of practice, such software should begin the process of acquiring skills needed for successfully solving rhetorical problems and sensitizing students to view writing as a problem-solving task. Certainly, empirical investigations are needed to determine if the promise of composing-process software is merely speculative.

REFERENCES

Daiute, C. A. (1984). Performance limitations on writers. In R. Beach & L. Bridwell (Eds.), *New directions in composition research* (pp. 205-224). New York: Guilford Press.

Emig, J. (1971). *The composing process of twelfth graders*. Urbana, IL: National Council of Teachers of English.

Flower, L. (1979). Writer-based prose: A cognitive basis for problems in writing. *College English, 44*, 19-37.

Flower, L. (1980). *Problem-solving strategies for writing* (1st ed.). New York: Harcourt Brace Jovanovich.

Flower, L. (1985). *Problem-solving strategies for writing* (2nd ed.). New York: Harcourt Brace Jovanovich.

Frederiksen, N. (1984). Implications of cognitive theory for instruction in problem solving. *Review of Educational Research, 54*, 363-407.

Lockard, J. (1985/1986). Computer programming in the schools: What should be taught? *Computers in the Schools, 2*(4), 105-114.

Norman, D. A. (1978). Notes toward a theory of complex learning. In A. M. Lesgold, J. W. Pellegrino, S. D. Fokkema, & R. Glaser (Eds.), *Cognitive psychology and instruction* (pp. 39-48). New York: Plenum Press.

Perl, S. (1979). The composing process of unskilled writers. *Research in the Teaching of English, 13*, 317-337.

Perl, S. (1980). Understanding composing. *College Composition and Communication, 31*, 363-369.

Reed, W. M. (1987). The speculated effectiveness of composing process software: An analysis of *Writer's Helper*. Paper presented at the annual conference of the Eastern Educational Research Conference, Boston.

Reed, W. M., Burton, J. K., & Kelly, P. P. (1985). The effects of writing ability and mode of discourse on cognitive capacity engagement. *Research in the Teaching of English, 19*, 283-297.

Reed, W. M., & Sherman, T. M. (in press). Using memory during prewriting: The effects of external storage, idea organization, and writing ability on syntactic complexity and quality. *Written Communication*.

Rohman, D. G. (1965). The stage of discovery in the writing process. *College Composition and Communication, 16*, 106-112.

Sommers, N. (1979). The need for theory in composition research. *College Composition and Communication, 30*, 46-49.

Sommers, N. (1980). Revision strategies of student writers and experienced adult writers. *College Composition and Communication, 31*, 378-388.

Stallard, C. (1974). An analysis of the writing behavior of student writers. *Research in the Teaching of English, 8*, 206-218.

Vinsonhaler, J. F., & Bass, R. K. (1972). A summary of ten major studies on drill and practice. *Educational Technology, 12*, 29-32.

Wresch, W. (1984a). Questions, answers, and automated writing. In W. Wresch (Ed.), *The computer in composition instruction: A writer's tool* (pp. 143-153). Urbana, IL: National Council of Teachers of English.

Wresch, W. (1984b). (Ed.), *The computer in composition instruction: A writer's tool*. Urbana, IL: National Council of Teachers of English.

Donovan W. Cook
Thomas G. Teates

School Science Problem Solving: A Dilemma

INTRODUCTION

Science educators have long advocated problem solving as an essential component of science instruction. Champagne and Klopfer (1981) reported that science educators almost unanimously recommend emphasis on problem solving in school science programs. In fact, it is one of the few things about which science educators agree! However, an examination of elementary and secondary school science instruction indicates that science educators do not practice what they preach. In spite of statements concerning the merits of problem solving in science classes, the fact is that science students get far too few opportunities to solve problems. Instead, the science taught in schools remains basically a collection of facts with students expected to display their knowledge-level command of these facts on school tests and standardized national exams. Raising the standards for expected student problem-solving performance on examinations is one way to encourage development of better problem-solving ability. One possible approach to better preparation of science students in school programs may be the use of computer software that addresses problem-solving goals.

The teaching of problem-solving skills is receiving unprecedented emphasis in public schools. Social studies, math, and English, as well as science, are calling for a focus on critical thinking. National reports, such as *A Nation at Risk* (1983), have stressed the

DONOVAN W. COOK is Assistant Professor of Education, Washburn University, Topeka, KS 66621.
THOMAS G. TEATES is Associate Professor, Science Education, Virginia Tech, Blacksburg, VA 24061.

importance of developing problem-solving skills to the future of our children and the well-being of our nation. Specifically, this report calls for the teaching of science to provide an introduction to the "processes of the physical and biological sciences . . . [and] the methods of scientific inquiry and reasoning" (p. 25). The 1983 National Science Board Commission Report, *Educating Americans for the 21st Century*, indicates that "elementary and secondary students in our nation's schools are learning less mathematics, science, and technology, particularly in the areas of abstract thinking and problem solving" (p. 1). Their recommended outcomes of science instruction for grades K-5 include the "ability to recognize problems, develop procedures for addressing the problem, recognizing, evaluating, and applying solutions to the problem" (p. 97). For secondary education the commission advocates a "continued development of students' skills in making careful observations, collecting and analyzing data, thinking logically and critically, and in making quantitative and qualitative interpretations" (p. 98). Finally, the 1986 College Entrance Examination Board's *Academic Preparation in Science* suggests that the focus of teachers should be to help students grasp what is distinctive about science content—especially the careful processes of investigation and verification in science.

Developers of educational software are beginning to respond to this need with the preparation of science-related problem-solving packages. This article examines some of what is commercially available in the field.

PROBLEM-SOLVING SCIENCE INSTRUCTION

Problem solving is perceived by most educators in the field as being the essence of science. On this point almost all science educators agree. In one early account, John Dewey (1916) spoke of the importance of the pupil understanding the "process" approach in science instruction and referred to it as "the heart of the scientific attitude" (p. 7). He republished the article (1945) almost 30 years later with the comments that "the course of events has reinforced what is basic in the article" (p. 119). However, the precise nature of problem solving is so complex that few science educators can agree as to how problem solving may be specifically defined, and a wide range of definitions has been used to describe this important aspect of the discipline. Champagne and Klopfer (1981), in their review of the history of problem solving in science teaching, indicated that it has undergone a continuous process of redefinition. The lack of a definitive conceptualization of problem solving has been a major difficulty in the school's attempts to implement and measure it. Downing (1928) established a list of essential components of thinking for science educators. Included were such elements as observation, analysis-synthesis, selective recall, hypothesis, verification, reasoning, and judgment. His inclusion of safeguards of scientific thinking, according to Keesler (1945), confused attitude with process and prevented subsequent researchers from developing a clear-cut definition of the scientific method.

Polya (1957) described problem solving as a four-stage process that involves (a) understanding the problem, (b) devising a plan, (c) carrying out the plan, and (d) looking back. He later defined problem solving as "finding a way out of a difficulty, a way around an obstacle, attaining an aim which was not immediately attainable" (p. ix). Novak (1961) added to the clarification of science problem solving by attempting to define and measure the process. Mettes, Pilot, Roossin and Kramers-Pals (1980) noted the importance of developing a systematic approach to solving problems and developing instruction where students learn to use this approach for a technical course such as thermodynamics. The "Program of Action and Methods" developed by Mettes and his colleagues is designed for use with advanced problems in science that require the determination of specific quantities such as work, force, or an equilibrium constant.

A Definition of Problem Solving

Various synonyms that are currently being used by science educators to denote problem-solving instruction are critical thinking, inquiry-oriented activities, process-approach, and use of the scientific method. For our purposes, we will define problem solving as a process within an instructional environment. This process requires (a) the recognition of a problem (motivation and challenge), (b) the organization and manipulation of a variety of variables that affect the outcomes of experiments or questions (decision making and choice among alternative solutions), (c) reflection on the process used to arrive at the solution, and (d) reflection on the nature and significance of the solution itself. Good problem-solving, science-related software should provide the student with an opportunity to engage in all aspects of this process. This problem-solving environment should have the following characteristics: It should (a) represent a real-world situation, (b) permit an easy user entry, (c) permit the user to manipulate a number of variables, (d) include the opportunity to seek information relevant to the task at hand, and (e) allow for user creativity.

CATEGORIES OF SOFTWARE

Science problem-solving software can be categorized as follows:

1. Science simulations
2. Microcomputer-based labs
3. General problem solving
4. Multimedia combinations

Science Simulations

Science simulation software comprises those programs that provide problem-solving experiences and at the same time create real experimental situations. Perhaps the premier example of this type of software is *Botanical Gardens* by Sunburst Communications, Inc. In this program, the user experiments with plant growth by controlling variables, or varying the amounts of the plant growth requirements. Interpretation of graphs which depict how much water for what level of temperature produces optimum growing conditions for the plants must be determined by the student.

The teacher maintains a degree of control with this program (if he or she chooses) by having access to the genetics laboratory. It is in this part of the problem-solving environment that seeds may be designed by the teacher to supplement the provided examples, test for ability in controlling variables, test for general problem-solving ability, etc. Written materials are provided for the teachers to use to facilitate problem solving and help students record data as they work through plant growth problems. This program receives high marks on all the criteria for a good problem-solving environment.

Oh, Deer! from the Minnesota Educational Computing Consortium (MECC) fits this category because it involves students in a realistic environmental problem. The residents of a community are confronted with a burgeoning deer population that threatens their quality of life. The user assumes the position of project director to alleviate this situation. Pertinent ecological and sociological factors are brought forward as the student develops a five-year plan. Annual feedback in terms of community support, cost, and population results is given to assist the project director. An opportunity to secure additional information that may assist in dealing with the problem is provided throughout the program.

The Halley Project: A Mission in Our Solar System by Mindscape, Inc., is a simulation that puts students in charge of a series of increasingly difficult interplanetary missions. Completion of the tenth mission allows them to qualify for admission to the Halley Project. As members, they may send in to the software company for the eleventh assignment. To be successful, the user must do off-line research of his mission objectives. This is an excellent requirement because it promotes scholarship. This problem-solving program presents astronomy in an interesting and exciting context.

Microcomputer-Based Labs

Botanical Gardens has been praised for its ability to simulate real scientific experimental situations. When the microcomputer is used as a tool to obtain, manipulate, and analyze actual data, the experience is enhanced. The microcomputer-based laboratory (MBL) allows the student to do just that. The full MBL package contains sensors and a connecting board, or interface box, which may be used to obtain external data. These data—such as temperature, light, and sound—may be interpreted as digital readouts on the monitor.

Biofeedback Microlab by HRM Software is an example of an MBL software tool that contains elements of problem solving. This package includes sensors to measure pulse rate, electrodermal activity, muscle tension, and skin temperature. Applications for problem solving are abundant with this program and are enhanced by the user's creativity. Students may, for example, study the physiological effects of stress by controlling muscle tension or study heart rate as a function of exercise. Data may be saved and printed out as a bar graph. In addition, data may be plotted against time or another data set and printed. This package comes with seven examples of experiments to help the student get started.

Science Toolkit by Broderbund Software, Inc., is a scaled-down version of the *Biofeedback Microlab* which offers a variety of experimental opportunities using heat and light. In this program, data are presented in two formats, a graph and a log table. *Experiments in Science* by HRM Software is an MBL that has experimental opportunities in a variety of science disciplines. Basic sciences, such as chemistry, biology, physics, earth and planetary science are represented in this package. It comes with a demonstration disk containing examples of experiments.

General Problem Solving

An example of a general problem-solving program with a science-like theme is *Incredible Laboratory* by Sunburst Communications, Inc. "Chemicals" with such names as *alien oil* and *goose grease* are combined by the students to create strange monsters. The various combinations of chemicals produce different features of the monsters. The program involves students in some aspects of scientific problem solving. The students use the process of trial and error and develop skills in record-keeping to learn the effect of each chemical. In so doing, students gain expertise in predicting which combinations produce what monsters. Although this is not real science, it has value in that it uses a problem-solving process that is used in scientific research.

Tribbles by Conduit is an interesting and challenging introduction to the scientific method. Students use information gathered by a satellite probe in orbit around a distant planet to identify the nature of the birth, growth, and death processes of a life form (the tribble). To solve the problem, the user must vary conditions in a systematic manner while a hypothesis that predicts behavior is developed and tested.

Discovery Lab, by MECC, is an excellent program in this category. The user selects nonspecific organisms and exposes them to a variety of variables. The opportunity to analyze the needs of the organisms by controlling one or more factors is provided at several levels of complexity: Training Lab, Explorer Lab, and Challenge Lab.

Discovery: Experiences in Scientific Reasoning, by Millikan Publishing Company, is another example of largely science-like problem-solving software. This package contains 10 programs that require the user to employ different strategies to solve problems in a variety of settings. The games, mazes, code problems, and simulations are varied and challenging. Each activity has an entrance level and two successively more difficult levels. The arena for solving each problem consists of a workspace, a practice area, a blackboard for viewing results, and finally what is referred to as the *Challenge*—a problem for students who have successfully completed problems in the three levels of difficulty.

Multimedia Combinations

Presented as a math and science unit, *The Voyage of the Mimi* is actually a multidisciplinary as well as multimedia integrated collection of learning materials. Emphasis is on scientific investigation and problem solving. The program involves students in a cast of characters who are on a scientific whale-study expedition. The unit uses a variety of materials such as videotapes, computer software, books, maps, and Bank Street Laboratory (BSL) equipment. The investigations unfold in a story format as they show scientists as real people dealing with realistic problems. Opportunities exist for the students to engage in individual or group problem-solving investigations in the areas of navigation, physical science, weather, and population study.

In doing the experiments, the students recreate some of what they have seen or read about. The inclusion of these hands-on experiences with the other activities creates a powerful overall experience for the participants. *Mimi* is an engaging work and has much to offer educationally. It is, however, somewhat restrictive financially, with a price tag of $987.16 for a full set of classroom materials. It is also restrictive in breadth relative to the extent of science concepts that may be covered within the unit. With available time and the curriculum requirements imposed by most state or local school systems, this program would need to be supplemented. An inventive, knowledgeable teacher would be required to sufficiently involve the children in the content and cover typical system curricular expectations.

A SCIENCE PROBLEM-SOLVING PERSPECTIVE

Several categories of science-related problem-solving computer materials are currently available. Pure science simulations with a heavy problem-solving orientation represent an exciting new type of material and include programs such as *Botanical Gardens*.

The MBL allows the computer to function as a tool for obtaining real data that allow students to do real science. To become good problem solvers, students need to experience the process often and the problems must be challenging. They may be led in the direction of the solution, but should not be provided with too much information. With knowledgeable teachers using proper discovery techniques and effective support materials, use of the MBL in problem-solving experimental settings should result in excellent learning opportunities in science.

General problem-solving software materials may be effective as preparatory experiences in science in lieu of quality pure science software. For example, *Discovery Lab* creates a laboratory environment in which fictitious "organisms" are analyzed.

The multimedia program *The Voyage of the Mimi* shows immense promise in the area of interdisciplinary problem-solving activities. It is one of the best examples of software that totally involves the students over an extended period of time and motivates them to accept the problem-solving challenge.

At this juncture of our trip through the problem-solving odessy, it seems clear that there are few good software programs currently available. These examples of "what could be" clearly signal the potential for much future development of the needed kind. Science teachers must demand and then use good problem-solving software. Developers must create products that offer real-world and intriguing experiences that permit teachers and students to easily enter the problem-solving environment of manipulation of multiple variables, information retrieval for use with the task at hand, and creative use of the information and imagination the student brings to the problem. It is suggested that a program similar to *Discovery Lab* be created that has characteristics of real organisms (such as bacteria) in the data banks. The program should challenge the user to identify real bacterial unknowns. Students should be able to use real data about real unknowns such as those encountered in solving an unknown for a qualitative analysis problem in chemistry or identifying the real growth conditions as well as the classification of a new plant or animal species. Access to real data bases coupled with establishment of motivating problem-solving situations may provide the type of new direction that teachers will value for their students.

It seems clear that appropriate development and use of computers in schools will not occur unless the public misconceptions about computers being electronic workbooks are replaced by recognition of and support for the types of unique problem-solving capabilities and challenges computers enable a teacher to present (Bitter &

Gore, 1985). Most current science educational software does not take advantage of the features of the computer that make it a unique tool for the sharpening of problem-solving skills. It is very clear that computer learning environments are unique, challenging, and effective for holding students' attention. What is unclear is whether educators will choose to use this capability to its fullest – or relegate it to the media graveyard with TV, film, and radio.

The current situation in the arena of problem-solving software for science in the elementary and secondary schools appears to be like a new child born with some serious but curable disease. There is a definite need for tender loving care and some expensive treatment, but there is hope for exciting development and growth. Whether teachers and others responsible for school science programs will demand the quality and quantity of software that can be prepared – or whether the developers will continue to provide such materials with or without the demands of the consumers – are critical issues. It seems clear that the capability of the developers and the needs of the educational community are ripe for the harvest of some exciting, attractive, and effective software such as the best described in this paper. There is a great need for good quality software and much to be gained by the students who might use it to sharpen their problem-solving skills in science.

REFERENCES

Bitter, G., & Gore, K. (1985). Trends in hardware/software. *Computers in the Schools, 2*, 15-22.

Champagne, A., & Klopfer, L. (1981). Problem-solving as outcome and method in science teaching: Insights from 60 years of experience. *School Science and Mathematics, 81*, 3-8.

College Entrance Examination Board. (1986). *Academic Preparation in Science*. New York: College Board Publications.

Dewey, J. (1916). Method in science teaching. *Science Education, 1*, 3-9.

Dewey, J. (1945). Method in science teaching. *Science Education, 29*, 119-123.

Downing, E. (1928). Elements and safeguards of scientific thinking. *The Scientific Monthly, 26*, 231-243.

Keesler, O. (1945). A survey of research studies dealing with the elements of scientific method as objectives of instruction in science. *Science Education, 29*, 212-216.

Mettes, C., Pilot, A., Roossin, H., & Kramers-Pals, H. (1980). Teaching and learning problem-solving in science (Part 1). *Journal of Chemical Education, 57*, 882-885.

National Commission on Excellence in Education. (1983). *A Nation at risk*. Washington, D.C.: U.S. Government Printing Office.

National Science Board Commission on Precollege Education in Mathematics, Science, and Technology. (1983). *Educating Americans for the 21st century*. Washington, D.C.: National Science Foundation.

Novak, J. (1961). An approach to the interpretation and measurement of scientific thinking. *Science Education, 45*, 122-131.

Polya, G. (1957). *How to solve it*. Garden City, NY: Doubleday Anchor.

Polya, G. (1981). *Mathematics discovery: On understanding, learning, and problem solving*. New York: Wiley.

Suzanne Bazak
Ben Bazak

Software in the Mathematics Classroom: Must We Digress?

It is the day before Easter break, and an Algebra I teacher comes up and asks for the *Moptown* (The Learning Company; Menlo Park, CA; $39.95) disk. She wants to take her class to the computer room for a pre-vacation activity. As a strong proponent of using software in the math classroom, I felt obligated to honor the request. The students went into the computer lab and had a nice experience. However, I cannot help but feel frustrated knowing that, for the most part, this is the extent of software usage in the math classroom. Don't get me wrong, *Moptown* is an excellent piece of software for teaching deductive reasoning and sequential logic. But this scenario typifies the current situation in mathematics. Software is used as an "add on" to the curriculum rather than serving as an integral part in the teaching of mathematics.

Software is now available that can dramatically alter the mathematics curriculum in several ways. The microcomputer, if used properly, is now capable of:

1. making the learning of mathematics the investigative journey that it was meant to be,
2. making the mathematics learned more relevant,
3. providing a new approach to teaching problem-solving skills,
4. freeing the math student from the burden of mastery of manipulative skills and providing more time for students to develop higher order thinking skills.

SUZANNE BAZAK is the Math and Computer Specialist, Janus Learning Center, Roanoke, VA.
BEN BAZAK is Chairman, Mathematics Department, William Fleming High School, Roanoke, VA.

In each of these ways, the computer serves not as an attachment to the mathematics learning environment but plays a major role in creating the environment. It is in this light that we can now see the tremendous potential impact of the microcomputer on mathematics learning.

Probably the most impressive and exciting software, in terms of its potential for changing the way we teach mathematics, is the *Geometric Supposer Series* (Sunburst; Pleasantville, NY; $99.00 each) developed by Judah Schwartz and Michal Yerushalmy. The series consists of four separate programs: *The Geometric preSupposer, Triangles, Circles*, and *Quadrilaterals*. These programs provide the student with an electronic drawing board for constructing and investigating geometric figures. The student, with a simple series of commands, can add auxiliary lines to the construction, subdivide segments, erase parts of the figure – essentially anything that can be done with a straight edge, compass, pencil, and eraser. Having been freed from the laborious task of making these constructions on their own, students can spend more time inspecting their properties. In addition, the *Supposer* allows students to make measurements (data appear on the screen) of line segments, angles, perimeters, and area. A most exciting feature found in the *Triangles* and *Quadrilateral* packages is the program's ability to take a student's construction on a particular figure and define it as a procedure that can be easily replicated on other figures. Picture this: A student draws a triangle, then constructs a line segment connecting the midpoints of two of the sides. Making measurements, the student finds that the length of the constructed segment is one-half the length of the third side. The student instinctively asks, "Is this always true?" With the use of the REPEAT command, the construction can be carried out on any number of different triangles. This does not constitute proof and is not intended to take formal proof out of the process. However, the student, through the conjecturing process, is actively participating in the development of geometry. The traditional approach to teaching geometry, whereby teachers impart time-honored axioms and theorems to a passive learner, can be turned on its head. The student and subject can now freely interact with the teacher playing a guide-on-the-side role.

Sunburst Software Corporation has informed us that they are looking into revising this package so that students will be able to obtain a hard copy of their constructions, making this exciting learning tool that much more powerful. Perhaps all that remains as an improvement for the *Geometric Supposer* (Sunburst) is the ability not only to repeat constructions (a feature that needs to be added to *Circles*) but also to repeat measurements as well (thereby cutting down on the repetitive nature of the measurement process as the student moves from example to example).

The authors will soon be coming out with a new series of software that will create a similar learning environment for algebra students. Students will see symbolic manipulation, such as transformations of equations in the solving or graphing process, acted out in visual terms. We do not know much more about this series at this time. However, if *Geometric Supposer* (Sunburst) is any indication, this new algebra-oriented software should be well worth the wait.

Computer software can also provide a powerful tool for teaching and investigating graphing concepts. There are several software packages that facilitate a deep understanding of the analysis of functions and their graphs. *Graphing Equations* (Sunburst; Pleasantville, NY; $59.00), *Interpreting Graphs* (Sunburst; Pleasantville, NY; $54.00), *Interactive Experiments in Calculus* (Prentice-Hall; Englewood Cliffs, NJ; $29.56) and *The Calculus Student's Toolkit* (Addison-Wesley, Menlo Park, CA; $19.75) are a few of many examples of software with graphing capabilities. These programs range in sophistication from the graphing of linear and polynomial equations in the "f(x)=" form to those that can graph equations stated implicitly (e.g., conics), trigonometric functions, polar and parametric equations. By being able to quickly inspect the graph of a given function, the student is able to generate several examples involving a particular concept in a limited amount of time. Teachers using large-screen presentations will reap the same benefit. This capability is crucial for students in the teaching and learning of graphing from a transformational approach.

The graphing package one picks truly depends on how it is to be used. For classroom demonstrations a teacher would want to select software with simple input and fast graphing capabilities. *Algebra I* and *Algebra II* (True Basic; Hanover, NH; $49.95) are excellent examples of this type. On the other hand, The *Super*Grapher (2-D)*, found on *The Calculus Student's Toolkit* (Addison-Wesley), has tremendous graphing capabilities but a more complex input process. While you are able to save your graphs using the *Toolkit*, you are not able to obtain a hard copy as with the *Interactive Experiments In Calculus* (Prentice-Hall).

For an intensive study of graphing functions, Addison-Wesley has a series of four software packages entitled *Computer Graphing Experiments* (Addison-Wesley; Menlo Park, CA; $60.00 each). Covering the topics Algebra I and Algebra II, Trigonometric Functions, Conic Sections, and Calculus, each volume comes complete with investigative worksheets aimed at allowing students to first collect data and then through analysis, draw preliminary conclusions. These lab activities, while far from being comprehensive, are ideal for students working in small groups and fit nicely into existing curricula.

Graphing Equations (Sunburst), at first glance, is not as powerful as many other graphing packages available. However, it contains a game that best exemplifies how computer gaming and graphing instruction can be integrated. We are, of course, referring to *Green Globs*. Students are challenged to write a function that, when graphed, will "explode" as many globs (located on the Cartesian Coordinate System) as possible. So often we teach graphing in a one-directional form: The student is given the function; the student graphs the function. Such innovative software urges us to teach graphing in both directions, producing a greater conceptual understanding.

Existing software compels us to take a strong look at how we teach mathematics. For example, take the solving of word problems involving units or rates. Current methodology teaches students to take the verbal expressions found in a problem, translate them into equations and then solve. Once the problem is translated into an equation (if the student can get that far), operations are performed on "isolated" expressions with little regard to the units or rates involved. Often this yields an answer which, whether correct or incorrect, holds little or no meaning to the student. An innovative software package called *SemCalc* (Sunburst; Pleasantville, NY; $95.00) suggests that we should try to solve these problems by keeping in mind the language in which the problems are written. It encourages the student to consider the units and rates they are given and in which they expect the answer to be. This gives students a sense of where they are and where they need to go. *SemCalc*, which stands for *semantic calculator*, is similar to a simplified electronic spreadsheet. However, students cannot enter a value without also entering the unit associated with that value. The program is designed to help students focus on the problem to be solved, while avoiding inappropriate calculations. When trying to add or subtract, students are forced to convert "unlike" units to "similar" units.

When performing any operation, students are first given the results in terms of units. For example, suppose the problem asks students to determine miles per hour. If students instruct the computer to divide hours by miles, they will be told that their answer will be in the form hours per mile. Students will be asked if that is the correct unit and then given the opportunity to rethink the problem. Students must think about numbers and operations as they relate to specific units.

So far we have discussed software for high school students in academic classes. But there is some fine software for the many students currently languishing in courses with titles such as "Math Applications" or "Consumer Math." Still laboring under the burden of achieving mastery of basic skills, these students are rarely able to get to, or appreciate, the application of the elementary mathematics they are learning. For them there is an excellent cadre of software that simulates real-life problem-solving environments. Four that I (and my students) particularly like are *The Budget Simulation* (EMC Publishing; St. Paul, MN; $29.95), *Applying Mathematics* (Laidlaw; River Forest, IL; $42.00 each), *The Whatsit Corporation* (Sunburst; Pleasantville, NY; $59.00), and *Survival Math* (Sunburst; Pleasantville, NY; $54.00). The first two are better than adequate simulations of the budgeting process. *The Budget Simulation* provides students with in-depth information about the consumer choices they have to make. The color graphics and surprise expenses at the end of each month make this program highly motivating. An interesting feature in the *Applying Mathematics* package is the presence of an on-screen calculator that the student may access as needed. The lower level student really appreciates the freedom from the tedious computation process and has more time for developing good problem-solving strategies.

The Whatsit Corporation (Sunburst) is perhaps too sophisticated for lower level students. But as a project for highly talented and motivated junior high students, it is first rate. It is an in-depth simulation of setting up and running all aspects of a manufacturing corporation. Perhaps more appropriate for lower level students is the small business simulation experience with *The Hot Dog Stand*; one of four simulations found in *Survival Math* (Sunburst). Students are asked to run a hot dog stand for eight high school football games. Before purchasing food and drinks for each game, students must take into consideration the size of the crowd, date and time of game, weather conditions, special occasions (e.g., homecoming), and quality of products. Though simplistic in theme, the more I watch students "play," the more I appreciate the subtleties of the simulation. Given the competitive spirit of high school students, *The Hot Dog Stand*, along with the other three simulations on the *Survival Math* disk, is an excellent motivator.

Microcomputer usage in the math classroom is ready to go beyond the divergent "activity" stage and can truly affect how we teach the traditional content areas. And, contrary to what we see in many new mathematics textbooks, integrating the microcomputer into the mathematics curriculum can be so much more than writing a computer program that will, for example, find the roots of a quadratic equation.

All of the software mentioned in this article is available for the Apple II series computers (with the exception of *True Basic*, which requires an IBM or a Macintosh), and none of them require any knowledge of programming languages. As a rule, any educational software worth purchasing is available for a 30-day review. We encourage you to take advantage of this. Software can be expensive; and, in the final analysis, you are the most important evaluator.

Wayne A. Nelson

Problem Solving and Software Design

Beginning students of computer programming are often given problems such as the following:

> Design a program which will input a list of numbers from the user, print out the numbers and their squares, and compute and print the sum of the numbers and the sum of the squares of the numbers.

Even in this simple example, the solution to the problem is not merely a collection of algorithms that perform the specified tasks. It is not surprising, however, that the algorithms occupy the majority of the students' attention. Dalbey and Linn (1986) have shown that much of the instruction in introductory programming courses involves the syntax of the language being studied. But other research has focused on the ultimate problem to be solved in this example, that is, design.

Definitions of design range from "finding the right physical components of a physical structure" (Jones, 1966, p. 3) to "bringing into being something new and useful that has not existed previously" (Jones, 1966, p. 3), or "the performing of a very complicated act of faith" (Jones, 1966, p. 3). Malhotra, Thomas, Carroll, and Miller (1980) have categorized theories derived from these and other definitions as: (a) algorithmic lists; (b) application specific models; (c) formal automation methods; and (d) verbal models of creativity. Much of the software design methodology literature emphasizes algorithmic lists or application specific models, while minimizing other approaches to design. Functional program specification (Ross & Schoman, 1977; Stay, 1976; Wirth, 1971), structured programming (Stevens, Meyers, & Constantine, 1974), top-down

WAYNE A. NELSON is a doctoral student, Division of Curriculum and Instruction, Virginia Tech, Blacksburg, VA 24061.

decomposition (Van Leer, 1976), and flowcharting are the major methods discussed. The effectiveness of flowcharting has been questioned, however (Schneiderman, Mayer, McKay, & Heller, 1977).

These methods tend to view software design as a set of activities to be followed, but design is more precisely a holistic process concerned with the requirements and constraints of the problem, the development of tentative or partial solutions, and the testing of these solutions within the parameters of the original problem. In other words, software design is a type of problem-solving activity requiring sophisticated strategies, extensive knowledge of the problem domain, and the ability to think creatively. Understanding the cognitive processes involved in problem solving and design in general provides a basis for an analysis of software design. With this preliminary orientation, software design methodologies can be examined from the perspective of a problem-solving interpretation.

COGNITIVE PROCESSES INVOLVED IN DESIGN

The difficulty usually encountered in solving problems is related to the amount of information that must be considered, as well as the complexity of organizing that information in order to generate a solution. Memory and the serial nature of the information processing system have been identified as critical components in the problem-solving process.

HUMAN INFORMATION PROCESSING

Psychologists have long used models as an aid in understanding the complexity of human thinking; and, for the past twenty-five years, the computer has served as an analogy when explaining the human information-processing system. Although a comprehensive discussion of the subject is beyond the scope of this article, a brief summary of the system will help to identify the components that are critical for problem solving and, therefore, software design. Interested readers are referred to Klatzky (1980), Zechmeister and Nyberg (1982), or Ellis and Hunt (1983) for more comprehensive explanations of human information processing.

The analogy between a computer and the human brain is reasonably clear. The computer must take information from the environment, store it in buffers until the central processing unit can work with it, and then process it with respect to previously received information. The information is then discarded or stored in some permanent format for future use. When the information is needed again, it can be retrieved relatively quickly, and usually with little loss of its original meaning.

Although the human brain certainly does not work like a computer, those who use the computer as a model for understanding human information processing, believe that many of the processes of input, storage, and output are similar. The brain, it is hypothesized, inputs information from the environment through the sensory receptors (primarily visual and auditory, but also including taste, touch, and smell), where it is stored in the sensory registers which are like the input buffers of the computer system. The information is veridically retained in the sensory registers for a very short time and is lost if perception and attention processes are not invoked to retain the information. Perception involves translation of the input into a recognizable form that is determined by the characteristics of the input stimulus and the context in which the information is presented. Information that passes through the sensory registers may also be lost if it is not attended to. We have all experienced this problem when trying to listen to two people talk at the same time. Because of the limits of the system, we can only attend to one input at a time, but attention may alternate between several competing inputs.

The activities of perception and attention are two of the more important functions of short-term memory (STM), which is usually considered to be analogous to the central processing unit of the computer. STM can hold a limited amount of information, usually in the range from five to nine "chunks" (Miller, 1956). Again, this information will simply be lost if further processing does not occur. Rehearsal refreshes the contents of STM and serves to retain the information for longer periods of time, as well as organizing the information for transfer into long-term memory (LTM). Chunking, which refers to the organization and labeling of information in compact units that can be stored more efficiently in LTM, is also a major activity of STM. Because the size of chunks increases with experience (Simon, 1973), the brain is able to compensate for the limited amount of information that can be managed at one time.

After it has been organized by STM, the new information is stored permanently in LTM by integrating it with previous knowledge. The efficiency of this process may be affected by the relationship and organization of both the new and old information. Sometimes the presentation of new information requires further processing by STM of both old and new information in order to store it for efficient retrieval. Several theories of long-term memory organization have been proposed (Klatzky, 1980).

The structure of memory and the problems of retrieval can impact on the ability to integrate and retain information at the elemental level. In addition, there are higher order structures such as schemata (sometimes referred to as scripts) which represent knowledge about more general topics. Schemata are general frameworks of everyday events that are stored as stereotypical descriptions. Schemata are instantiated, that is, the blanks are filled in, when a situation is encountered. The typical example given is the restaurant script, where general representations stored in LTM of the characters, items, or events of eating at a restaurant are filled with details each time a person goes out to eat (Schank & Abelson, 1977).

PROBLEM SOLVING

Newell and Simon (1972) have identified characteristics of human problem solving based on the information-processing model. These characteristics include the task environment, the mental representation of the problem, and selection of appropriate operations. The task environment involves the problem description, including the context of the problem as well as any information, requirements, or constraints that might be applicable to the problem. The mental representation, or problem space, developed by the problem solver contains ideas or hypotheses regarding possible solutions along with the representation of the problem. The problem space will change during the course of problem solution through interaction with operators which are applied by the problem solver in order to progress from the initial problem state to the goal state.

The various stages of problem-solving activities described by psychologists can be reduced to: (a) understanding the problem; (b) generating solution hypotheses and then selecting among the alternatives; and (c) testing and evaluating the solutions (Ellis & Hunt, 1983). Although these stages are logically ordered, many problems require a cyclical solution process where the problem solver returns to any previous stage if a tentative solution is found to be incorrect.

The key to successful understanding is the development of a clear picture, or problem representation, which is derived from the individual's interpretation of the problem. Identification of critical factors from the information given, criteria for solution, and constraints must be considered at this stage. The generation of solutions progresses in various ways, some systematically and others haphazardly. Typically, some type of strategy is adopted to provide an orderly solution process. Algorithms and heuristics are one class of strategies that provide either a set of rules or procedures to follow in the case of algorithms, or a strategy or approximate template for solution in the case of heuristics. The generate-test method (Newell & Simon, 1972), where a possible solution is developed and then tested for its effectiveness, is an example of one type of heuristic. Many other strategies have been identified, such as means-ends analysis, working backward, and problem decomposition (Mayer, 1983). The final stage, evaluating possible solutions, involves decisions regarding the effectiveness of the proposed solution. When solution criteria and goals are relatively clear, this can be a simple process. But when the problem is more complex, with vague goals and criteria, evaluation can be more difficult. In such cases, clearly identifying important aspects of the solution can be helpful (Ellis & Hunt, 1983). If the evaluation of the solution finds some inadequacies, the problem solver typically returns to an earlier stage, and the process is repeated.

DESIGN PROBLEM SOLVING

In *The Sciences of the Artificial* (Simon, 1969), considerations for the development of design methods based on the problem-solving process are identified. Design problems of all types are usually described as belonging to a set of problems which are termed ill-structured (Reitman, 1964). Though there may be an ultimate goal for the problem, the intermediate goals are often unclear, and the exact configuration of the final state is not known. In fact, there often are no readily available procedures for solution, and the transformations which the problem may be subjected to are nearly unlimited.

When ill-structured problems of design are encountered, the processes of problem solving must be adjusted to accommodate the "fuzzy" characteristics of the problem. Simon (1974) identifies two major processes, evaluation of specifications and coordination of the design effort, as being essential to successful design problem solving. The design task is said to evoke from long-term memory "a list of other attributes that will have to be specified at an early stage of the design" (p. 189). In other words, the designer is instantiating a schemata with the details of the problem at hand. As the design process continues, other schemata are evoked from memory as they are needed. The whole process of design, then, involves breaking an ill-structured problem apart to the point where each subproblem has well-defined characteristics. Simon (1974) uses the example of designing a house to illustrate this process. The word *house* elicits ideas of floor plan and structure. Structure is decomposed into supports, roofing, and utilities. Utilities evoke ideas about plumbing, heating, etc. Eventually, each subproblem reaches a point where it can be solved as a well-structured problem.

The other important component of design problem solving is the coordination of the process. Solutions to some subproblems could impose new constraints on other components. The designer must control the process to avoid this interaction between subproblems by managing problem decomposition so that design units are nearly self-contained (Simon, 1974). The emphasis placed on the solution of each subproblem, as well as the order in which the subproblems are solved, can influence the final product. Decisions made with respect to solution order and emphasis determine the "style" which the final solution will exhibit (Eastman, 1968). These decisions are often subjective, based on the personal characteristics of the designer, and also reflect the creativity that is an essential part of design problem solving.

SOFTWARE DESIGN

The relationship of software design to other types of design problem solving should be readily apparent. The task of software design involves generating requirements, or functional specifications, which are detailed enough to be translated into structural descriptions of a computer program that will solve the problem. Based on protocols of designer-client interactions and empirical studies of various aspects of software design, Malhotra et al. (1980) have developed a theoretical model which incorporates the processes of goal elaboration, design generation, and design evaluation. Their model is similar to those previously discussed, corresponding to the stages of understanding the problem, generating tentative solutions, and evaluating the solutions.

Goal elaboration is undertaken in commercial software development when a client and a designer discuss the problem and develop the goals of the system. These goals are often poorly defined at first, but eventually are elaborated and redefined as subgoals. In the other situation, where the designer *is* the client, this process still occurs, but is not as overtly apparent. In both cases, the designer "must possess detailed knowledge of the discipline in which the design is going to be realized" (Malhotra et al., 1980, p. 132) in order to elaborate the goals to the point where functional requirements can be specified. These functional requirements are typically in the form of module descriptions which specify the content, relationships, and interactions between modules.

During the design generation phase, the various modules are elaborated and reorganized to the point that their combination will satisfy the functional requirements. Design strategies such as Hierarchical Input Process Output (HIPOs), stepwise refinement techniques, flowcharts, and program specification languages can be the most beneficial at this stage. These strategies provide a heuristic to aid the designer in further problem decomposition and refinement. This can relieve some of the mental load on the designer, allowing the focus of thinking to be the details of the problem rather than the processes needed to control the design effort.

After a design has been generated, evaluation is undertaken to assess the properties of the design with respect to the achievement of the goals. New requirements might be uncovered, resulting in a repetition of the process in light of these new requirements. In fact, the whole process is highly iterative and interlaced in the sense that goal elaboration and design generation commonly interact throughout the process, and design evaluation may occur within the generation phase.

Jeffries, Turner, Polson, and Atwood (1981) suggest that the activity of problem decomposition is controlled by a design schema which helps to break the problem into a set of subproblems. Other schemata are then evoked when considering the individual subproblems. Finally, a design schema is retrieved to tie together each subproblem in order to form the final design. Soloway (1985) refers to these schemata as plan abstractions, or templates. He advocates the teaching of LISP and other programming languages through the gradual development and integration of these plan abstractions.

Design schemata are also important in the coordination of the software design process. The metacognitive function of these schemata aids in the choice of the current subproblem to be considered, and after the choice is made, the instantiation of new schemata can control the solution process. Ideally, this will occur in a top-down rather than bottom-up fashion because the refinement of a subproblem can often affect other subproblems yet to be considered (Jeffries et al., 1981). The coordination supplied by the design schemata may help to avoid potential interactions of this type. Deviations from this top-down process can determine the style of the final design. For example, designers who emphasize the human-computer interface during the design process often focus the bulk of their problem-solving effort on this aspect of the design. The software which results from this emphasis will be markedly different in function and appearance from that produced when the design emphasis is on some other system component.

SOFTWARE DESIGN CONSIDERATIONS

Many current software design methodologies emphasize the decomposition process but often fail to address the thinking that is necessary for coordination of the total design process. This often forces many software designers into an overly analytical and restricted design process where inspiration and creativity are lacking (Simpson, 1986). Often during the problem definition stage, the designer may need some kind of memory cue to trigger the retrieval of relevant information that may have been stored in a different context. Some designers use visual material, or a design handbook, to assist in this process (J. Maruska, personal communication, January 27, 1987). It has been suggested that some type of information-sharing network might be useful in software design (Malhotra et al., 1980). A design aid such as this can help the designer to better access information about similar problems, rather than relying solely on memory. This would help to integrate the information with the stimulus of the current design problem. Collaboration is also mentioned as a possibility for improving software design practice at the commercial level (Malhotra et al., 1980).

Carroll, Thomas, and Malhotra (1980) found that the availability of a graphic representation can also aid the process of design. Their study presented subjects with design problems in two isomorphic representations, either temporal or spatial, The solutions were examined on the basis of solution time, comprehensiveness, and compactness. It was suggested that certain presentations of problems "encourage graphic representation and are (thereby) rendered easier to solve" (p. 151).

Lobell (1975) suggests that design is a typical example of a creative activity. He contends that design is essentially an unconscious process, where "we bring a lot of data into the mind, much of it unquantifiable, and allow that data to dip in and out of the deeper structures of the mind, each time coming up with new integration forced by the powerful logics of the deep mind" (p. 127). Methodologies should be considered only as "tools" which help to integrate the information about the problem into useful forms. The real work of design, then, is involved with the creative process. Although beyond the scope of this article, the creative act is given a very detailed examination by Koestler (1976).

Extensive practice can develop and improve design skills. As expertise in programming develops, the chunking of information is more efficient, resulting in better problem representation and overall task performance (McKeithen, Reitman, Rueter, & Hirtle, 1981). It has been shown that exposure to the design process can develop the schemata necessary for successful design problem solving (Jeffries et al., 1981). This research indicates that novice and expert software designers differ not only in the amount and organization of knowledge about programming but also in their ability to recognize and control the design process. This expertise often develops in stages over a long period of time, and it cannot be expected that design problem-solving skills will readily transfer to other domains after only minimum experience (see the Burton & Magliaro article in this issue for further discussion of this idea).

SUMMARY

Closer examination of the software design process can provide a better understanding of the difficulty in learning computer programming. By characterizing software design as an intellectual activity rather than a product-oriented process, software design can be understood in terms of the way individuals develop schema and utilize their knowledge of design. This makes possible the analysis of the types and levels of thinking required for effective software design, as well as the development of more appropriate design theories and methods.

Students are often overwhelmed with the syntactic aspects of the language, and cannot focus on the broader issues of program design. When programming instruction emphasizes this aspect, the ultimate potential of computers may be better approached. The area of software design can provide the most effective experiences in problem solving for students. Although the development of expertise in this area may take a long time, the potential benefit of improved problem-solving skills is desirable.

REFERENCES

Carroll, J. M., Thomas, J. C., & Malhotra, A. (1980). Presentation and representation in design problem-solving. *British Journal of Psychology, 71*, 143-153.

Dalbey, J., & Linn, M. C. (1986). Cognitive consequences of programming: augmentations to BASIC instruction. *Journal of Educational Computing Research, 2*(1), 75-93.

Eastman, C. (1968). Explorations of the cognitive processes in design. Pittsburgh: Carnegie-Mellon University.

Ellis, H. C., & Hunt, R. R. (1983). *Fundamentals of human memory and cognition* (3rd Ed.). Dubuque, IA: W. C. Brown.

Jeffries, R., Turner, A., Polson, P., & Atwood, M. (1981). The processes involved in designing software. In J. R. Anderson (Ed.). *Cognitive skills and their acquisition* (pp. 255-258). Hillsdale, NJ: Lawrence Erlbaum Associates.

Jones, J. C. (1966). *Design methods*. London: Wiley.

Klatzky, R. L. (1980). *Human memory* (2nd Ed.). New York: W.H. Freeman.

Koestler, A. (1976). *The act of creation* (2nd Ed.). London: Hutchinson of London.

Lobell, J. (1975). Design and the powerful logics of the mind's deep structures. *Design Research and Methods Journal, 9*(2), 122-129.

Malhotra, A., Thomas, J. C., Carroll, J. M., & Miller, L. A. (1980). Cognitive processes in design. *International Journal of Man-Machine Studies, 12*, 119-140.

Mayer, R. (1983). *Thinking, problem solving, cognition*. New York: W. H. Freeman.

Miller, G. A. (1956). The magical number seven, plus or minus two: Some limits on our capacity for processing information. *Psychological Review, 63*, 81-97.

McKeithen, K. B., Reitman, J. S., Rueter, H. H., & Hirtle, S. C. (1981). Knowledge organization and skill differences in computer programmers. *Cognitive Psychology, 13*, 307-325.

Newell, A., & Simon, H. (1972). *Human problem solving*. Englewood Cliffs, NJ: Prentice-Hall.

Reitman, W. R. (1964). Heuristic decision procedures, open constraints, and the structure of ill-defined problems. In M. W. Shelley & G. L. Bryan (Eds.). *Human judgements and optimality* (pp. 282-315). New York: Wiley.

Ross, D., & Schoman, K. (1977). Structured analysis for requirements definition. *IEEE Transactions on Software Engineering, 3*(1), 69-84.

Schank, R. C., & Abelson, R. P. (1977). *Scripts, plans, goals, and understanding*. Hillsdale, NJ: Lawrence Erlbaum Associates.

Schneiderman, B., Mayer, R., McKay, D., & Heller, P. (1977). Experimental investigations of the utility of detailed flowcharts in programming. *Communications of the ACM, 20*(6), 373-381.

Simon, H. A. (1969). *The sciences of the artificial*. Cambridge, MA: MIT Press.

Simon, H. A. (1973). How big is a chunk. *Science, 183*, 482-488.

Simon, H. A. (1974). The structure of ill-structured problems. *Artificial Intelligence, 4*, 181-201.

Simpson, H. (1986). *Programming the Macintosh user interface*. New York: McGraw-Hill.

Soloway, E. (1985). From problems to programs via plans. *Journal of Educational Computing Research, 1*(2), 157-172.

Stay, J. F. (1976). HIPO and integrated program design. *IBM Systems Journal, 15*(2), 143-154.

Stevens, W. P., Meyers, G. J., & Constantine, L. L. (1974). Structured design. *IBM Systems Journal, 13*(2), 115-139.

Van Leer, P. (1976). Top-down development using a program design language. *IBM Systems Journal, 15*(2), 121-134.

Wirth, N. (1971). Program development by stepwise refinement. *Communications of the ACM, 14*(4), 221-227.

Zechmeister, E. B., & Nyberg, S. E. (1982). *Human memory*. Monterey, CA: Brooks/Cole.